The Nordic Nexus

The Nordic Nexus

A Lesson in Peaceful Security

Bruce Olav Solheim

Westport, Connecticut
London

Library of Congress Cataloging-in-Publication Data

Solheim, Bruce Olav.
    The Nordic Nexus : a lesson in peaceful security / Bruce Olav
Solheim.
      p. cm.
    Includes bibliographical references and index.
    ISBN 0-275-94743-2 (alk. paper)
    1. Scandinavia—Foreign relations. 2. Scandinavia—Politics and
government—1945- I. Title.
DL87.S65 1994
327.48—dc20   93-23479

British Library Cataloguing in Publication Data is available.

Library of Congress Catalog Card Number: 93-23479
ISBN: 0-275-94743-2

First published in 1994

Praeger Publishers, 88 Post Road West, Westport, CT 06881
An imprint of Greenwood Publishing Group, Inc.

Printed in the United States of America

The paper used in this book complies with the
Permanent Paper Standard issued by the National
Information Standards Organization (Z39.48-1984).

10 9 8 7 6 5 4 3 2 1

This work is dedicated to my mother, Olaug Solheim, who passed away on 4 May 1990, and my father, Asbjørn Solheim. I am eternally grateful for their love and guidance. They taught me the value of education, hard work, and family. They were immigrants in a land founded by immigrants and instilled in me a pride both in the land of my ancestors and in my country of birth. It is my wish that this legacy continue with my two sons: Bjørn and Byron.

Contents

Figures and Tables

FIGURES

TABLES

Preface

A great challenge in the post-Cold War age is to balance the forces of integration and fragmentation in the search for security and prosperity. During the Cold War, Norway—together with the other countries comprising Norden—remained cooperative, peaceful, and prosperous although they were of vital strategic concern to both superpowers. How this was accomplished and its implications for other regions are important questions for scholars and policymakers. This study will address the dilemma of balancing security with prosperity, and integration with fragmentation through a detailed, binational, interdisciplinary analysis of the Nordic region and the United States in the 1950s. Research in both Norwegian and U.S. archives provide the binational perspective. The way in which the Nordic countries survived and prospered during the Cold War—cooperating through diversity— may provide some lessons for the post-Cold War world. The framework of analysis will emphasize the Nordic region's system of integration and security known as the "Nordic Nexus" and the "Nordic Balance" and will also rely on the U.S. security policy of containment. The underlying purpose of this study is the construction of a model of "peaceful security" taken from the Nordic examples of integration and security. This model should stimulate further research and should be of interest to policymakers in both the industrialized and the developing worlds. Peaceful security, as originally conceived by this author, is a system of security that emphasizes nonviolent and less strident methods of foreign and security policy, and cooperation through diversity. This allows for regional prosperity to grow. It is a model that encompasses the regional integration model of the Nordic Nexus and the regional security model of the Nordic Balance. Its objectives are peace, security, prosperity, and freedom.

By looking to the Nordic Nexus, the Nordic Balance, and—by comparison—the Association of Southeast Asian Nations (ASEAN) as design prototypes that have tested successfully, and using them as guidelines or patterns for further exploration, other regions of the world may be able to develop their own approaches to integration and cooperation in the quest for world peace and prosperity.

I wish to acknowledge all those people who lent their support, guidance, and effort toward the successful completion of this study. My greatest appreciation goes to my mentor, Gary R. Hess, and to Kendall W. Stiles, Helge Ø. Pharo, Wayne S. Cole, and Bernard Sternsher for their patient, thoughtful, consistent, and intuitive advice. Special thanks are also extended to Don K. Rowney and Allen Emery for their suggestions and critiques. During my research trip to Oslo, I was fortunate enough to talk with Olav Riste, Rolf Tamnes, Nils Petter Gleditsch, Geir Lundestad, and Trond Bergh, who were all most helpful. Thanks also to my aunt, Walborg Westbye, and to my first mentor, Sidney T. Mathews. The staffs at the Eisenhower Library, the National Archives, the Seeley Mudd Manuscript Library, the Bowling Green State University Library, the Oslo University Library, the Norwegian Foreign Ministry, the Norwegian State Archives, and the Norwegian Labor Party Archives should be commended for their diligent work. This study could not have been completed without generous funding support from the Norwegian Ministry of Foreign Affairs, the Eisenhower World Affairs Institute, the Bowling Green State University Graduate College, and the History Department at Bowling Green. My gratitude is also expressed to Susanne and the rest of my family.

1

Overview: Containment, Norden, and Regional Integration

Every gun that is made, every warship launched, every rocket fired signifies—in the final sense—a theft from those who hunger and are not fed, those who are cold and are not clothed. This world in arms is not spending money alone. It is spending the sweat of its laborers, the genius of its scientists, the hopes of its children. This is not a way of life at all, in any true sense.
—Dwight D. Eisenhower, 1953

OVERVIEW

There exists a dilemma of balancing security with prosperity. How can a country have security without draining its national resources or being perceived as a threat to bordering lands? On the other hand, without security, how can a country concentrate on economic development and improve the daily lives of its citizenry? A great challenge in the post-Cold War era is to balance the forces of integration and fragmentation in the search for security and prosperity. These forces appear to be dominating the international system.[1] Integration can be seen in the efforts of the European nations to forge a strong regional organization, the European Community (EC), in order to meet the problems inherent in the modern political economy. Fragmentation is all too evident in the nationalist-driven ethnic conflict in the former Yugoslavia. The Nordic region has offered a unique way of balancing the forces of integration and fragmentation by building cooperation through diversity. The Nordic countries successfully cooperated using diverse methods to achieve the overarching goals of peace and prosperity. They used diversity to their advantage. During the Cold War, Norden remained cooperative, peaceful, and prosperous although, as a region, it was of vital strategic concern to both superpowers. How this was accomplished and its implications for other regions are important questions for citizens, scholars, and policymakers.

This study will address the dilemma of balancing security with prosperity—and integration with fragmentation—through a detailed, binational, interdisciplinary analysis of the Nordic region (hereafter referred to as "Norden")[2] and the United States in the 1950s. The framework of analysis will emphasize the Nordic region's system of integration and security known as the "Nordic Nexus"[3] and the "Nordic Balance"[4] and will also rely on the U.S. security policy of containment.[5] Norden and the United States developed these policies in response to the bipolarization of the international system during the Cold War.[6] A design prototype will be constructed from the Nordic regional integration and security systems and another regional security system, the Association of Southeast Asian Nations (ASEAN). These systems that have tested successfully can possibly be used as guidelines or patterns for further exploration. From this, other regions of the world may be able to develop their own approaches to integration and cooperation in their quest for world peace and prosperity.

This study will cover the period 1947-61. If it were mainly from a U.S. perspective, the year 1950 could have been chosen as a departure point because it was then that the United States became most interested in Norden, mainly as a result of the Korean War and the subsequent militarization of containment policy, including North Atlantic Treaty Organization (NATO) policy.[7] However, since the perspective is binational, in that it incorporates the views of the United States and Norway (representing the Nordic perspective),[8] the year 1947 was chosen instead because it was then that the Marshall Plan took effect and forced Norway to make a decision that would, in large part, determine its future course of policy throughout the Cold War. The Marshall Plan was a part of what has been called "Roosevelt's dialogue,"[9] or special détente with the Soviet Union, and the start of containment policy, which was in response to the fears of Soviet-led exploitation of economic, social, and political turmoil in Europe. At the outset, containment was primarily ideological and political in character. The Marshall Plan became a perfect extension of this approach because it stressed moral and economic recovery. It was also shortly thereafter, in 1948, that the United States formed its first comprehensive policy in Northern Europe (NSC 28/1). The cut-off point of 1961 chosen for this study marked the end of Dwight D. Eisenhower's "New Look" policy and the dawn of a new era and return to militarized containment under John F. Kennedy's "Flexible Response" strategy.[10]

So, one may ask, why is such a historical/theoretical study significant? Norden was known as the "quiet corner" of Europe. What can be learned from a lack of trouble? Well, one might have noticed that historians are, ordinarily, quite a grim lot. They tend to focus on the negative aspects of history: this terrible war, that bloody revolution, and so on. Only rarely does a historian focus on the issues of peace and stability. When a historian attempts to classify a certain period of history as being relatively peaceful, there are inevitably cries and moans from those who know of an especially bloody situation in country *X* or region *Y*. Consequently, history (particularly diplomatic history) is primarily concerned with war—probably because times of global peace are infrequent, war causes major changes, and, frankly, war is dangerous and therefore (in a morbid sense) more interesting. Equally valuable, however, is an examination of international stability by exploring a peaceful region of the world and discovering the reasons for its relative tranquillity. During the Cold War, Norway, together with the other countries comprising Norden, remained peaceful although they were of vital strategic concern to both superpowers.

To understand how the Nordic regional systems worked, one needs to comprehend the nature of the international system in the 1950s and of the United States' hegemonic power. Therefore, the study will begin by looking at U.S. containment policy in general, and U.S. Cold War interests in Norden in particular, from 1947-61. To accomplish this, U.S. security interests in Norden will be assessed based on the strategic calculus of the region. The first chapter will also lay out the framework of regional integration theory used in this study.

Chapter 2 examines Nordic policy in response to the Cold War. This will include looking at the Nordic countries' potential for cooperation, actual policy, and realization of that potential.

Chapter 3 looks at Norway and its relations with the United States, the Soviet Union, and the rest of Norden. This Norwegian perspective will be offset by a companion examination of U.S. policy toward Norden, including U.S. reaction to Norden's response to the Cold War. By integrating U.S. and Norwegian policy considerations, this study will gain a comprehensive view of the Nordic impact on international politics. Norway's situation was especially precarious due to the pressures exerted against it by the superpowers because of its strategic value and its degree of influence within Norden. Norway may have been the linchpin for both Soviet and U.S. security concerns in Norden. The relevant questions are as follows: (1) How did Norway view U.S. policy? (2) How did Norway view its role in Norden and in the conflict between East and West? (3) What strategies worked for Norway/Norden, and why? (4) How did the Nordic policies of Truman and Eisenhower differ? (5) Did the United States accept the Nordic Balance, and does this indicate a regional approach to understanding U.S. foreign policy? (6) Were U.S. and Nordic policy objectives similar, and were these objectives realized?

Finally, Chapter 4 will consider the questions whether the historical findings in this study confirm international relations theory regarding regional integration and whether they suggest a model for regional peaceful security.

The model suggested in this study should stimulate further research and should be of interest to policymakers both in the industrialized and developing worlds. "Peaceful security," as originally conceived by this author, is a system of security that emphasizes nonviolent and less strident methods of foreign and security policy, and cooperation through diversity. This allows for regional prosperity to grow. It is a model that encompasses the regional integration model of the Nordic Nexus and the regional security model of the Nordic Balance. Its objectives are peace, security, prosperity, and freedom. The success of Norden during the 1950s in staving off superpower strong-arming and intervention through utilizing diverse foreign policy orientations (despite the strategic temptations present in the High North) is one example of what can be accomplished through peaceful security. The model should stimulate further research to test its viability for application elsewhere in the world.[11] Additionally, this work will serve as a bridge between two societies, U.S. and Nordic, and will also increase the awareness of growing interdependency in the world. The study further elaborates on the special significance of small states and their reliance on regionally integrated systems (compared to superpower unilateralism) and their contributions to the international fabric of peace. This work is a binational, interdisciplinary analysis of a previously inadequately studied aspect of the Cold War period.[12]

THE UNITED STATES' VIEW OF NORDEN

Most Americans do not know how the United States defined its national security interests in the Nordic region during the Cold War. With the possible exception of a subplot in Tom Clancy's popular 1986 novel *Red Storm Rising*, the High North has been largely ignored—despite its great strategic significance. However, the U.S. role as the hegemonic power influencing Norden during the Cold War cannot be ignored. Therefore, this section will begin with a broad focused look at the development of containment policy from George F. Kennan through Dwight D. Eisenhower. The focus will then narrow to examine the implementation of containment in Norden, the U.S. perspective on the Soviet threat, and the problem of neutralism in that region. Narrowing even further, each Nordic country's profile, including its strategic importance to the United States, will be analyzed. These profiles will lead to a determination of what the United States held to be most vital in terms of its own security in each Nordic country. This will be accomplished through assessing each country's historical background, alliance status (vis-à-vis the West), strategic-geographic importance, and influence, control, or protection of other countries in Norden. After that has been accomplished, a specially designed value system will determine the most important country in Norden in terms of U.S. strategic interests from 1947 to 1961.

In sum, the following general objectives will be kept in mind in looking at U.S. policies for Scandinavia in general, and for each individual country in Norden: (1) How did the United States define its national interests in each of the countries in Norden and in the region as a whole? (2) What were the objectives and factors influencing any differences in approaches to the individual Nordic countries? (3) Which Nordic country was most important to the United States, and why?

Unlike the even-tempered, low-voltage style of politics in Norden, foreign policy in America has been seen as both driven by realist and idealist considerations, fueled by powerful gusts of popular emotion.[13] U.S. diplomat and historian George F. Kennan criticized U.S. foreign policy for its excessive moralism and legalism. His key contribution to U.S. foreign policy was his articulation of the policy of containment at the dawn of the Cold War. Known as the "father of containment," Kennan clearly made his most important point on containment in the famous 1947 "X" article: "the main element of any United States policy toward the Soviet Union must be that of a long-term, patient but firm vigilant containment of Russian expansionist tendencies."[14] In other words, hang on long enough and a more reasonable generation of leaders will appear in the Soviet Union. Earlier in his 1946 "Long Telegram," Kennan warned that "the greatest danger that can befall us in coping with this problem of Soviet communism, is that we shall allow ourselves to become like those with whom we are coping."[15] Most importantly, the containment doctrine stressed economic and political means, rather than military force.

An overlooked yet integral part of containment is what Kennan meant to be containment of extremist (i.e., anti-Soviet hysteria) tendencies in U.S. policy—what this author calls "restrained containment." His containment ideas were meant to contain the United States as much as the Soviet Union. In his Long Telegram, Kennan concludes by saying that the United States must not become "emotionally provoked or unseated by" Soviet communism.[16] He noted that Soviet leaders were very conscious that loss of temper and of self-control showed weakness in political affairs, and they were quick to exploit such weaknesses. For these reasons, it was a "*sine qua non* of successful dealing with Russia that the foreign government in question should remain at all times cool and collected."[17]

Kennan criticized the U.S. tendency toward an unrestrained legally and morally driven foreign policy, believing that it made "violence more enduring, more terrible, and more destructive to political stability than did the older motives of national interest."[18] It was this form of "restrained containment" that the United States continued to employ in Norden long after it had resorted to more militarized containment elsewhere in the world.

Containment took different forms under presidents Harry S Truman and Dwight D. Eisenhower. Like Kennan, Truman also saw a fatal flaw in the Soviet communist society. He noted that their system—a slave society—could not prevail over a free society: "I have a deep and abiding faith in the destiny of free men. With patience and courage, we shall some day move on into a new era." Truman's administration faced four threats to cooperative multilateral international order: (1) Soviet armies in Eastern Europe and Northeast Asia; (2) the rise of leftist movements in Greece, Italy, France, China, Korea, and other countries; (3) the demoralization of Germany and Japan where democratic traditions were not evident; and (4) the rise of Third World nations and the appeal of Marxist ideology. Faced with these threats, Truman and his advisors set out to contain the spread of Soviet communism.[19]

Truman came to realize that his administration's principal task was not to deal with Soviet military might, but to fill the postwar power vacuums, instill hope, stimulate economic reconstruction, and strive for self-determination without compromising vital interests. But the Truman administration could not do all of these things simultaneously, because of a lack of resources. Truman shrewdly realized that self-help mutual aid and flexibility would win over the Europeans and help them resist communism and accept U.S. hegemony in the international economy. This would serve as a magnet to attract the Iron Curtain satellites westward. The Marshall Plan was the principal expression of this policy, coupled with the Mutual Defense Assistance Program

(MDAP) that supplied weapons to the Western European allies. The Truman administration understood the nature of the Soviet threat and was able to tie economic strength to geopolitical success.[20]

Retrospectively, Truman did not realize that Western Europe needed security guarantees, not massive armaments. Turning away from Kennan's original call for calmness in facing Cold War threats, Americans distorted the implications of China's turn to communism in 1949, and of the Soviet Union's atomic bomb development. This was aggravated by the slowness of European integration and the rise of McCarthyism. Truman was pushed to formulate an overarching policy. This policy emerged in 1950 as National Security Council document 68 (NSC 68). Anticipating Soviet aggressiveness, the response to the North Korean decision to cross the 38th parallel seemed, in turn, threatening to the Soviets and may have circumvented efforts to reduce Cold War tensions.[21]

Although there were some similarities between Kennan's strategy of containment and NSC 68, the main difference was that Kennan advocated a strongpoint defense whereas NSC 68 called for a perimeter defense. NSC 68 was also alarmist and rhetorical in tone, stressing Soviet military capabilities and aggressiveness. NSC 68 concentrated on mainly military means instead of Kennan's combination of psychological, economic, and military means of containment. The experience in Korea appeared to prove the NSC 68 authors correct, as a peripheral nation was being overrun by communist forces ostensibly led by Moscow, and the United States was unprepared militarily. The United States responded by defining a set of global interests so vast as to be beyond the nation's will and capabilities. Something new was needed to balance these interests with the nation's economic capabilities.

Dwight D. Eisenhower, upon assuming the office of president in 1953, redefined "containment" as a "policy of boldness," or the New Look.[22] Eisenhower was determined to keep isolationism from spreading in the Republican party and forming a "Fortress America." John Foster Dulles as secretary of state brought with him a policy of boldness that, coupled with Eisenhower's wanting great military effectiveness at low cost, formed the basis of the New Look foreign policy. Together they espoused asymmetrical deterrence and liberation of the Soviet satellites. Just as Eisenhower was misunderstood, Dulles too was misunderstood. The latest view on the relationship between Eisenhower and Dulles is that sometimes Eisenhower took the lead in foreign policy and other times Dulles did; that is, they were truly a team.[23]

The New Look (as formulated in NSC 162/2 in 1953) was based on the fact that the United States had overwhelming nuclear superiority. Relying on nuclear weapons and cost effectiveness as no previous policy had done, the New Look came to be known as a "more bang for the buck" policy. The nuclear threat was made even more believable when smaller atomic weapons were developed in order to be used tactically on the battlefield. The New Look departed from NSC 68 in that it concentrated more heavily on developing more effective means to achieve the "end" of containment. Security at any cost was objectionable to Eisenhower.[24]

Dulles applied Christian morality to his conduct of international relations and he was preoccupied with threats. Contrary to Kennan's thinking, Dulles believed that communist ideology, as practiced by the Soviets, had the objective of extending throughout the world in order to establish a one-world state of socialism.[25] The New Look was not just a "massive retaliation" concept. Rather, the central idea to the New Look was asymmetrical response—using one's strength against an opponent's weakness.[26] Eisenhower and Dulles believed that substituting nuclear forces for conventional ones was economically prudent, but the New Look also put emphasis on alliances, covert operations, and negotiations as being wise security investments. "Brinksmanship" was another element of the New Look. It essentially entailed a willingness, or apparent willingness, to go to the brink of nuclear conflict in order to achieve objectives.[27] The morose Dulles gave the impression that he personally could go to the brink, thereby making the strategy more believable.

Eisenhower was the first postwar president to produce and implement a systematic strategy on war, peace, and security in the nuclear age.[28] He disagreed with those (e.g., nuclear weapons scientist Edward Teller) who conventionalized nuclear war by thinking in terms of winning or losing. He told the National Security Council in July 1953 that "the only thing worse than losing a global war was winning one." He never really considered the nuclear option a viable one, "except in the sense that one considers suicide viable."[29]

Unlike many of his contemporaries, Eisenhower defined national security broadly as the nation's core values and institutions as well as its physical safety.[30] Most importantly, to Eisenhower, security was the product of a "Great Equation." He explained that "spiritual force, multiplied by economic force, multiplied by military force, is roughly equal to security." Correspondingly, if one of these factors was to fall to zero, or near zero, the resulting product would do likewise.[31] Eisenhower defined external threats by their challenge to America's internal dynamics: its values, institutions, social cohesion—its way of life. Therefore, defense against military attack was no more important than defense against unbalanced budgets that could destroy America's economy, defense against irrational fear that could compromise America's democratic principles, or defense against international instability that could jeopardize America's globally tied political economy. These were the variables in Eisenhower's security equation.[32]

Eisenhower had a horrific vision of war and was keenly aware of the implications of the nuclear revolution on U.S. and NATO strategy. Critics have underscored Eisenhower's deemphasis on conventional forces but for the wrong reason. It was not simply the cost factor (i.e., nuclear weapons are cheaper than conventional forces), although that was a factor; for he also believed that—beyond sending appropriate signals to allies, clients, and enemies—the conventional forces did not matter very much. He believed that a conventional confrontation with the Soviets would not stop at that level. Since it could not be contained below the nuclear threshold, Eisenhower felt it ridiculous not to consider using nuclear weapons. Eisenhower therefore confronted a dilemma. The Cold War's logic required that he prepare for a nuclear response to Soviet military aggression, but that response could only result in the annihilation of both the United States and the Soviet Union.[33] Eisenhower, as an avid student of the classic war theorist Karl von Clausewitz, felt that survival was not enough. Why overcommit resources, why restructure the economy, why run the risk of undermining America's way of life, in order to defend against an indefensible threat? Key to understanding Eisenhower is his feeling that if the United States could endure long enough, be strong enough, communism would fail. Kennan and Truman had said much the same. Eisenhower's New Look strategy reflected these beliefs, perceptions, and objectives.

In the 1950s the High North became valuable with the increasing importance of strategic nuclear weapons planning and became the Northern Flank (AFNORTH) of NATO.[34] Prior to 1950 the United States was not overly concerned with the High North. After the beginning of the Korean War in 1950, and in line with NSC 68 thinking,[35] the United States wanted to maintain its bases in Iceland and Greenland as part of a growing "hemisphere defense" plan. Iceland and Greenland served as "stepping-stones" between the United States and Europe. Survival of the United States in the air age depended on early warning; the shortest air attack route was the Arctic path. Consequently, there was a heightened interest in the Nordic region, with the United States being primarily concerned with denying Iceland and Greenland to the Soviets.[36]

Norden acted strategically as both a bridge and a buffer—a bridge for air operations, and a buffer against swift operations because of its inhospitable geography. The superpowers valued the Baltic exits in between Denmark and Sweden that formed an important strategic chokepoint in Europe. Soviet naval operations depended on ready access through the Baltic exits. Another particularly strategic area in Norden was Norway's northern coastline. It bordered the natural maritime route leading from the Soviet naval base at Murmansk, through the Barents and Norwegian seas, and into the northeast Atlantic. U.S. strategists felt that if the Soviet Union could secure the Norwegian coastline, it would be able to interdict NATO sea lanes of communications.[37]

The Soviet threat from 1947 to 1961 in Norden could be expressed in direct geographic terms, with Soviet borders on Finland and Norway, and in terms of assets, that is, the Soviet nuclear submarine base on the Kola Peninsula (which was their largest), and the Soviet Baltic Fleet. The Soviet Union turned the Kola Peninsula into one of the most militarized regions in the world. This buildup not only enhanced Soviet strategic capabilities, but also became an inviting target for the West. The Soviet treaty with Finland and internal communist subversion within Norden also posed threats to U.S. interests.[38]

Neutralism was also seen as a threat to U.S. policy in Europe in the 1950s, and in Norden in particular. A 1955 U.S. government report addressed this problem. "Neutralism" was defined as an attitude or psychological tendency—as opposed to "neutrality," which is an actual status of government policy. Neutralism was a tendency to avoid taking sides or making ideological choices between competing international forces (i.e., democracy versus communism). More specifically, the report dealt with a brand of neutralism that comprised any attitude resulting in a "disinclination to cooperate" with the United States in its objectives in the Cold War, or a hesitation in not cooperating with the Soviets.[39]

The report listed Sweden and Finland as among those states that derived security from NATO programs without being forced to share the obligations thereof. The value of neutralist "freeridership" made neutralism even more attractive to Europeans. Finnish neutralism rested on the fear of Soviet retribution and also served to buttress Sweden's security. Swedish neutralism, in turn, influenced policies in Norway, Denmark, and Iceland partly for reasons of tradition and partly because of the continuing community of interest among the Scandinavian states.[40] Neutralist sentiments were prevalent throughout Norden, but seemed strongest in Iceland. The report held that neutralism caused these nations to maintain low levels of national defense spending and reluctance to grant base rights to the United States.[41] With the threat of neutralism in the background, the United States still saw each Nordic country as playing a different yet valuable role in preserving Nordic and U.S. security interests. To more clearly comprehend Nordic-American relations from 1947 to 1961, one must look at specific U.S. interests in each Nordic country—beginning with Norway, and followed by Sweden, Denmark, Finland, and Iceland.

Norway, as an original member of NATO, was considered a steadfast U.S. ally in the 1950s. As part of NATO, the United States sought effective Norwegian cooperation in the building of a strong and stable Atlantic community. The United States promoted the development of Norway's ability and willingness to participate effectively with other Western European countries in opposing communist threats.[42] Norway held strategic importance for the United States because of its protected ice-free harbors and its airfields, which lay close to the Soviet Union. Norway was also part of the early warning system, being able to warn the United States of any unusual or threatening Soviet actions.[43] According to the State Department, "the political and military value of Norway as an ally lies not only in the moral and material weight of an additional democratic country lining up with us against further Soviet expansion, but is due also to its strategic location." Norway also commanded the exits from the Baltic and Barents seas and possessed the third-largest merchant marine fleet in the world, which in the event of an emergency would be vital to an allied defense effort. Norway was also in a key position to influence Denmark and Iceland. Norway's westward orientation was a great advantage for U.S. policy in Norden from a diplomatic standpoint. Norway was important in the decision of both Denmark and Iceland to join NATO, and was considered a "helpful instrument in implementing . . . [U.S.] policies in northern Europe."[44] In fact, a U.S. government report in 1959 concluded that Norway's views carried influence in European Social Democratic circles far out of proportion to the country's size. Additionally, Norway's support of U.S. initiatives, such as in the United Nations, served as a valuable example to other Nordic nations. The U.S. government felt that any actions tending to weaken Norway and its support of NATO would have extended adverse effects throughout Norden, and in Denmark and Iceland in particular.[45]

Despite its neutrality or nonaligned status, Sweden's role was vital in U.S. strategic planning in Norden and interconnected to the defense of other Nordic countries. In fact, in considering certain Soviet attack scenarios in Norden, the State Department's director of Northern European affairs stated that there were "no legal commitments to Sweden, but if overrun, Norway and Denmark would be gravely threatened." The appropriate U.S. response, he felt, would have to depend on the circumstances at the time and what other moves the Soviets made.[46] U.S. policymakers saw Sweden holding a position of influence in Norden. For instance, in a 16 July 1958 memo to Eisenhower, Dulles advised that the new Swedish ambassador might ask about the U.S. landing of Marines in Lebanon. It was reported that there was widespread adverse reaction in Scandinavia. Worried about the impact on U.S. policy, Dulles concluded by writing that Sweden was most influential in Norden, implying that some accord would have to be reached with Sweden on this issue, in order to ameliorate tensions throughout Norden.[47]

Denmark was of great importance to U.S. national security because of its control over Greenland, which, by its geographic position, was a major outpost for the defense of North America.[48] Denmark was also important because of its location on the Baltic Straits, which could deny the Soviets use of their Baltic submarine fleet.[49] Greenland's strategic value based on its geographic position was abundantly clear, and the prevailing attitude of the Eisenhower administration was that the United States needed defense facilities in Greenland because it was vital for defense of North America.[50] A November 1957 "Nash Report" on overseas U.S. bases discussed U.S. forces occupying airbases in Greenland, and future plans for radar sites, as part of the DEW (Distant Early Warning) line. U.S. airbases in Greenland provided forward-strike facilities for strategic air operations and convoy coverage for shipping in the area. DEW line operations connected Greenland to other facilities in the Faeroes, the United Kingdom, and the Azores; and U.S. navigational facilities supported the air and sea lanes in the area. The Defense of Greenland Agreement of 1951 (UNCL) provided the legal basis for the presence of U.S. forces and facilities in Greenland as a function of collective defense under NATO.[51] Not by coincidence, the Greenland agreement was signed the same year as the Iceland defense agreement. This provides evidence of the serious impact the Korean War had on U.S. defense and foreign policies.[52]

U.S. interests in Finland tended to be more diluted than in the other Nordic nations. Finland shared a 700-mile border with the Soviet Union and was the only Nordic country to have been at one time a part of Russia—Finland having been a Russian grand duchy until 1917. That Finland was a separate nation at all was really quite remarkable. Although the United States was initially displeased with Finland's official neutrality and friendship treaty with the Soviets, it later came to appreciate the balance that resulted from that arrangement.

A special relationship with the Soviets held certain dangers for the Finnish government. The Finns were economically vulnerable to the Soviets and were careful politically so as to avoid absorption into the U.S.S.R. However, if the Soviets had attempted to capture Finland, there would have been adverse effects. Sweden would have moved closer to the West and probably into NATO. A propaganda setback would also have been felt, as Finland was the Soviet's primary example of "peaceful coexistence." The American foreign policy establishment realized that Finland's independence contributed to the security of Scandinavia in particular and Western Europe in general.[53] This idea of Finland as a buffer was also integral to the concept of the Nordic Balance. In an oral interview, former U.S. Ambassador to Finland John Hickerson may have summed up U.S. interest in Finland: "Not a major post from the standpoint of U.S. policy . . . it [was] a very good listening post for obvious reasons."[54]

Borrowing a line from Winston Churchill's famous observation about the Soviet Union, Iceland was an "enigma wrapped in a riddle." Outside of the relatively unknown Nordic community, even less was known of Iceland. Its climate is dominated by the intemperate weather of the North Atlantic, and its landscape is rather harsh and barren. Roughly 82 percent of the land is uninhabitable: made up of glaciers, lakes, lava fields, sand, and marshes. The nation is both psychologically and physically isolated. However, Iceland's strategic position in the North Atlantic played a major role in Cold War strategy. A 1957 U.S. government report held that Iceland's principal value as a base to the United States was due to its geographic position and its being part of a link in the North Atlantic defensive screen. U.S. forces operated Strategic Air Command (SAC) facilities, antisubmarine operations, the Atlantic extension of the DEW line, and airline communications to Western Europe.[55]

Iceland was of particular strategic importance to the United States because of its position along the sea lanes between North America and Western Europe and the great-circle air routes between North America and Eastern Europe. These considerations made it imperative that Iceland be kept available as a base for operations by the United States and NATO in case of war.[56] U.S. policy was to keep American forces in Iceland and to retain the availability of bases. To do this, the United States encouraged Iceland to remain an active NATO partner and to reduce Soviet economic and political influence in the country.[57] The importance of Iceland to the United States was made clear by the State Department's director of Northern European affairs in 1950: "for strategic reasons brought about by geography, it is clear that we would have to repel immediately any attack on Greenland or Iceland."[58] U.S.

officials were concerned that Iceland would develop an economic dependence on the U.S.S.R. because the Soviets were one of the biggest customers for Iceland's only export, fish. The United States sought to increase non-Soviet consumption, particularly by the United Kingdom, to lessen that interdependence.[58]

Having looked at U.S. security interests in the Nordic region both by individual country and overall, one should be able to determine which country held the greatest strategic value to the United States. Table 1 condenses U.S. security interests in Norden and places an assigned numerical value (on a scale from 0 to 3) to each of three categories: (1) alliance value; (2) strategic-geographic value; and (3) influence, control, and protection value. The first numerical value is based on the nature of each country's alliance relationship with the United States. It reflects whether or not the country was a member of NATO, and if that membership was conditional. The higher the number, the greater the security interest value. Iceland scored highest not only because of its NATO membership, but also because of its U.S. base. Finland ranked lowest because of its neutrality and special relationship to the Soviet Union.

Table 1
U.S. Security Interest Values in Norden, 1947-1961

	Alliance Status	Alliance Value	Strategic-Geographic Value	Influence, Control, and Protection Value	Total Value
Denmark	NATO[a]	2	3	1	6
Iceland	NATO[b]	3	3	0	6
Finland	Neutral[c]	0	1	2	3
Norway	NATO[a]	2	2	3	7
Sweden	Neutral	1	2	3	6

Key: 3=Greatest Value, 2=Great Value, 1=Some Value, 0=No Value

[a]Denmark and Norway both forbade foreign bases and stationing of foreign troops.

[b]Iceland maintained no standing military force, but allowed U.S. military personnel and basing on its soil.

[c]Finland has maintained a Treaty of Friendship, Cooperation, and Mutual Assistance (FCA) with the Soviet Union since 1948.

The second category is a strategic value for each country based on geography. The third category is the amount of influence, control, or protection a particular country afforded the rest of the region. The total of all three categories reflects each Nordic nation's overall strategic value to the United States. The data in Table 1 indicate that Norway had the greatest strategic value to the United States, and Finland the least.[60] This was not only because of the geographic-strategic value of Norway's coastline and airbases, but also from its influence over Iceland and Denmark. Denmark, Iceland, and Sweden tie for the second most important Nordic country to the United States—Denmark primarily due to its control of Greenland; Iceland because of its strategic location; and Sweden because its geography, neutral influence, and defensive military capability that helped protect the rest of Norden.

The importance of Finland, however, cannot be ignored. Despite its having a low strategic value score, Finland's role in the defense of Norden was vital. Finland acted as a buffer and provided the West with an opportunity to listen in on the Soviets. Because of their buffer role, the Finns took criticism from both sides—East and West. The Soviets would criticize them for being too capitalist, and the West would call Finland's policies a product of "Finlandization."

It can safely be said that Finland sacrificed the most to ensure Nordic security. Yet, the five countries of Norden together upheld U.S. interests. In spite of Norway's slightly greater strategic value, no single Nordic country could be left out of any security calculations. The closely grouped values shown in Table 1 indicate that U.S. security interests were interconnected in the Nordic region.

DEVELOPMENT OF REGIONAL INTEGRATION THEORY

In looking at security cooperation among nations, one must be able to comprehend the structure of the international system. However, conceptualization of the international/global system in which international relations take place is not an easy task. It is quite tempting for one to venture off into some uncharted realm filled with fascinating theoretical landscapes. One way to begin is by looking at units of analysis in international relations. Nation-states have been the basic unit of comparison in international relations theory. However, we now live in an era of interdependence. The modern international system is like a "tapestry of diverse relationships," and in such a world one must look beyond state-level analysis and be cautious of simplified models that seemingly explain all situations.[61] The competing forces of integration and fragmentation in the current international system can be seen in the struggle between the power of regionalism and nationalism. The complexity of international cooperation and the technology required to solve today's problems have contributed to the increasing interdependency among nations and regionalism. Yet, at the same time, the breaking down of the Cold War system has unleashed a fury of nationalist sentiments that is literally tearing apart formerly sovereign nation-states. To more clearly comprehend the international system one needs to step up one level of analysis—from the nation-state to the regional level.[62]

In the 1950s, bipolarity (a system dominated by the United States and the Soviet Union) largely described the nature of the international system. However, the countries of Norden were wary of envisioning the world in such simple terms. Instead, they chose to move ahead and remain on the leading edge of the transforming international system—toward regionalism and transnationalism. The regional system is the intermediate unit of analysis between the nation-state on the one hand and the global system on the other.[63] As a regional system, Norden had the ability to self-regulate and coordinate the interests of its members. The system of security in Norden—a region that combined North Atlantic Treaty Organization (NATO) membership, neutrality, and Finland's special agreement with the Soviet Union (inappropriately called "Finlandization"[64])—was evidence of how actors with seemingly discordant interests could unite achieving one overarching goal, that of regional peace and security.[65] Yet, this was not simply self-defense writ large; Norden was also actively engaged in world affairs.

Regionalism constitutes a middle way. Regionalism is "a half-way house between the nation-state and a world not ready to become one."[66] Regionalism is a term that covers diverse functional as well as geographical phenomena including European integration, NATO, the British Commonwealth, and voting blocs in the United Nations.[67] Defining "regionalism" has traditionally been problematic. In the absence of a widely accepted definition, almost any type of nonglobal international association has come to be known as a regional organization.[68] The term region lies at the base of this ambiguity. An "international region" has been defined "as a limited number of states linked by a geographical relationship and by a degree of mutual interdependence." A geographical relationship is constituted by a common border or general location. International regionalism in the descriptive sense is the formation of interstate associations or groups.[69] Functionality is also a major determinant in defining regions.[70]

The concept of integration has developed from studies in economics and regionalism. Whereas regionalism is somewhat ambiguous, integration—as a process—is comparatively more clear. Generally speaking, to integrate means to make a whole out of parts, and to turn previously separate units into components of a coherent system. Integration, then, is a relationship among mutually interdependent units that jointly produce system properties that they would separately lack. Political integration, as a subcomponent of the general concept, is the integration of political actors or units (i.e., individuals, groups, municipalities, regions, or countries) in terms of their political behavior.[71]

Two questions have arisen that are fundamental to the study of integration theory. Why do citizens defer to the political unit within which they live? And how are procedural and substantive consensus achieved and sustained within political systems? Two incentives for political integration emerge from these questions:

1. Political systems gain and retain cohesiveness because of widely shared values among members and the general framework of the system. The system is based on procedural consensus; the greater the procedural and substantive consensus, the greater the integration.
2. Political systems become or remain cohesive because of the presence or the threat of force.[72]

There have been numerous theories concerning the possibilities, stages, and dynamics of integration among nation-states. There have also been various attempts to bring these together under general categories or schools of thought. It seems easiest to divide the theories of integration into four general groups: pluralist, functionalist, neofunctionalist, and federalist.[73] These theories are not mutually exclusive, nor are they necessarily at odds with one another. The four general theories each have capabilities that seem to explain certain aspects of integration better than the others. This study contends that certain aspects of each, if combined, could help explain real-world examples of regional integration.

Pluralist theories, for example, seem to explain, quite adequately, the initial stages of regional integration, but fall short in explaining how it is maintained and to what end the process is intended. Traditionally, functionalist and neofunctionalist theories are not overly concerned with initial or final stages of integration; rather, they deal with the dynamics of expansion and operation. As a general rule, federalists are primarily concerned with the final stages and the end product of integration. In looking at an example such as Norden, one can see that the Nordic countries integrated using various aspects of the different theories of integration. This is not unlike the building of successful coalitions in domestic politics where no one is elected by gathering the support of only one interest group; the successful politician must skillfully draw various, sometimes opposing, groups together. Likewise, in successful regional integration, various aspects of different integration theories are applied as they prove useful.

The pluralist approach to integration envisions a community of states engaged in a "continuous process of sensitive adjustment to each other's actions, supported usually (although not necessarily) by the socio-political behavior and attitudes of their populations." This approach can best be represented by a "security community"—a group of people, nations, and other organized units that has become integrated. Under this model, integration is the attainment, within a territory, of a sense of community and institutions and practices that assure dependable expectations of peaceful change among its population. Sense of community ensures that the individual units in the group are willing to resolve common social problems through a process of peaceful change. Peaceful change assumes the resolution of problems without resorting to physical force. There are two types of security communities: amalgamated (a merger of two or more previously independent units into one), and pluralistic (a community wherein the units retain their separate governments and decision-making centers). Pluralistic communities are more readily developed and preserved more easily. Three elements are essential for preservation of the security community: (1) compatibility of major values relevant to political decision-making; (2) capacity of participating political units or governments to respond to each others needs and actions quickly and adequately, without resorting to violence; and (3) mutual predictability of behavior.[74] Figure 1 represents pluralist integration. The three triangles represent independent nations within a regional system. The dashed lines between them indicate that there is a sense of community or connection between them, but it is not formal and binding.

Figure 1
Pluralist Integration

The concept of the security community centers on the linkage between transactions and conflict. According to the pluralists, this linkage process involves certain characteristics: communication must be taking place; there must be a mutual interest; the relationship among cooperating nations must be different from that with noncooperating ones; and it is unlikely that a high degree of international interaction would be accompanied by high tension and conflict.

As communication increases, the level of complexity rises and so too does the formalization of the nations' interactions to handle these complexities—which furthers cooperation. Sometimes integration can commence without formalization of integrative procedures. A region may have advanced to a stage of integration where formalized institutions are no longer or never required (e.g., Canada and the United States, and, in some respects, Norden).[75]

Functionalists hold that form follows function and that structures exist to satisfy functional needs. Modern functionalists have focused on the world system and tended to argue for an economic determinism—the idea being that political integration comes about automatically as a result of economic integration. Economic cooperation between states results in working relationships; these relationships can be attained through international organizations. The transfer of functions to the international organization ultimately draws loyalty and support from the national to the supranational organization and eventually leads to the formation of a political community. However, it seems logical that before nations could achieve economic integration they need to cooperate at lower levels first.[76] Figure 2 represents functionalist integration. Here, members of the regional community are connected by solid lines indicating deeper levels of commitment and cooperation than in pluralist regions.

In Figure 3, neofunctionalist integration is depicted by the three nations, connected by heavy lines (indicating strong levels of cooperation), within a dashed-line circle.

Figure 2
Functionalist Integration

Figure 3
Neofunctionalist Integration

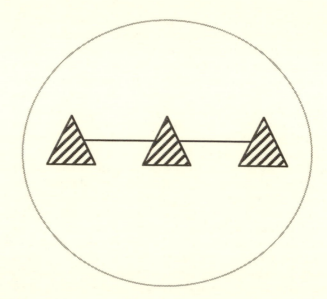

The circle in Figure 3 represents the limited growth of central institutions that would begin supplanting some national authority. Neofunctionalists tend not to believe that economic integration automatically leads to political integration. Instead, political actors, technocrats, and bureaucrats manipulate the process and give it a political push resulting in a "cultivated spillover." This spillover becomes the central analytical concept for the neofunctionalists. They believe in the "expansive logic of sector integration." In other words, by meshing the smaller gears of the society and getting them to turn, eventually one could hope to turn the larger wheels. They see integration as an ad hoc, step-by-step process characterized by gradual continuous movement toward regional integration.[77]

Figure 4 illustrates federalist integration. Federalists stress that the nation-state must be accommodated in any attempts to reorganize world politics. They believe that autonomous states can be influenced by diplomacy and communications, but they can be controlled only by giving up some of their power to a recognized supranational authority.

Figure 4
Federalist Integration

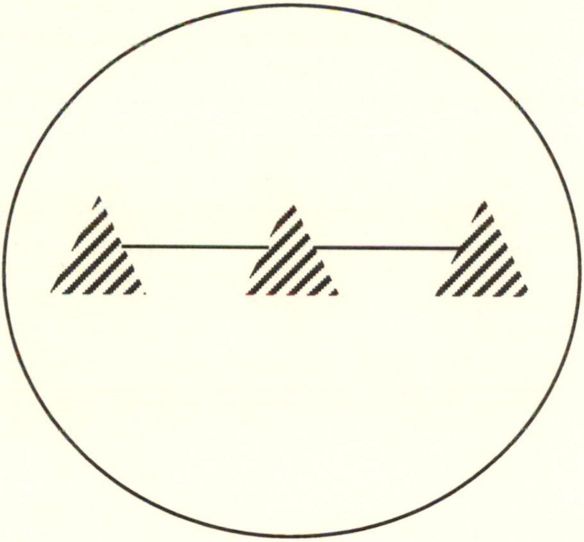

The federalist emphasizes the need for an overarching worldwide institution because the world is so diverse and variegated that only a global organization can prevent war and promote cooperation for the good of all humankind.[78] Federalism has been criticized in that by its nature and tendency a political union must be nationalistic, and therefore it will naturally impede any general system of peace and development. Under the pressures of a planned and radical social transformation such as federalism requires, it is bound to become a centralized system—closed, exclusive, competitive.

Accordingly, federalism will not be suited for mediation of ideological disputes or be able to temper the raw nationalism of new states and guide them through mutual cooperation into an international community.[79] The heavy-line circle in Figure 4 indicates that the once independent nations are now integrated within one supranational institution. The former national triangles are now without borders, indicating their loss of sovereignty.

Having reviewed the four general types of integration theory, one could then compare their structures and systems. The structure refers to the type of organizational shape the integrated regional group would have—a static concept. For example, in a region that is pluralist, the structure would be a community of states. The system describes the dynamic concept of that regional group's integration strategy. In the case of a pluralist type region, the system could be described as informal, and self-sustainingly interdependent. Table 2 compares the four general theories of integration discussed thus far.

The operational levels of integration lie at the base of the four general theories of integration. The three levels are economic, social, and political. These levels determine the dynamic functioning of the integration system. In other words, a formal structure such as a regional council with limited jurisdiction over certain issue areas can be considered a form of integration. This, however, is a static concept. The dynamics are inherent in the system under which the formal structure operates. The levels of integration determine the sweep and breadth of integrative action.

The economic operational level of integration is complex. In order to achieve successful economic integration, some regional communities use protection in their trade practices (common protective measures).

Table 2
General Integration Theories

Theory	Structure	System
Pluralism	Community of states	Informal, self-sustaining interdependence
Functionalism	Responsive administrative community network	Technical self-determination, functional needs and technological change
Neofunctionalism	Supranational decision-making organization	Growth of central institutions through forward linkage
Federalism	Supranational state	Redistribution of power and authority

Source: Charles Pentland, *Integration Theory and European Integration* (New York: Free Press, 1973), p. 190; and Gerhard Mally, *The European Community in Perspective* (Lexington, MA: Lexington Books, 1973), pp. 25-39.

This serves to increase each other's interdependence, yet a net loss can occur if the interdependent and protected trade is less than the unprotected international trade potential.

The lowest level of economic integration is a free trade area with no tariffs or quotas. The next highest is a customs union with the added feature of common external tariffs. The common market is next with the addition of a free flow of factors, followed by an economic union that adds a harmonization of economic policies. The final step is total economic integration that includes a unification of policies and institutions.[80]

The social level of integration can best be described as the sharing of common national core values within a region. Core values are those values that are basic to a given society's ideological make-up. For example, in the United States, rugged individualism is a basic core value. In Norden, cooperation and deference are shared core values. From this basic tenet, rules, laws, and even foreign policy can emerge. The social level can also be measured by transactions[81] among actors. The more transactions, the greater the level of social integration. One must be able to distinguish, however, between transactions among the societies in general and their ruling elite classes. Political-level integration is the most ambiguous of the three operational levels because theorists are not always clear about whether political interaction and a sense of community are both necessary elements in an adequate definition of "political integration."[82]

Integration is not so much a matter of time as of fact. Nation-states are interdependent and already have informal functional ties. This irresistible force, along with nationalist fragmentation, seem to be shaping the future world order.[83] Thus far, "regionalism" and "integration" have been defined, but what is "regional integration"? Combining both elements of regionalism and integration theory, regional integration may be said to be made up of five necessary but not sufficient elements:

1. high levels of social and cultural homogeneity;
2. similar political attitudes and behavior;
3. some political interdependence;
4. some economic interdependence; and
5. geographical proximity.[84]

The depth of regional integration is also a key subject. Combining these elements or characteristics, a region can attain different levels of regional integration: (1) *token integration;* (2) *security community;* (3) *limited functional cooperation;* (4) *international economic integration;*

and (5) *direct political unification.* The lowest level—token integration—simply implies a sense of community with no restructuring of interests. A security community adds an institution for protecting members from violent conflict, but is too weak to achieve economic benefits. If a regional organization shares the costs of limited services within the community (e.g., regional airlines), they are said to be at the level of limited functional cooperation. A more complex level of integration is international economic integration. In this case, a given community of nations has expanded its market size by abolishing discrimination of economic factors among the member states. This ranges from merely a free trade area to total economic union. The highest level of regional integration is direct political integration.[85]

Certain forms of cooperation lie beneath the surface of integration theory. Although integration theory mainly deals with nation-states, cooperation can also be carried out by nonnational actors who can, in turn, influence the state. One example of this kind of cooperation is the international regime. International regimes are defined as sets of norms, principles, rules, and decisionmaking procedures used by actors (states or nonnational entities) to cooperate on certain issue areas. These regimes are often decentralized, informal, and appear to lay the groundwork for more formal integration. There are also entities known as epistemic communities that consist of groups of transnational technical experts who develop a consensus over certain issue areas. These communities gain influence because the increasingly technical nature of society and the complexity of issues and problems faced by nation-states cause policymakers to depend more on technical expertise. Through use of these two types of cooperation at an informal or nonnational level, nation-states grow closer and form ties that can later be translated into more formal integration patterns.[86]

Using these theories of regional integration, the next step is to put them into an operational framework. One could do this in analyzing Norden's particular regional integration system. A hybrid theory of integration could then be constructed from the Nordic example. The two basic incentives for political integration outlined earlier have been generally thought of as mutually exclusive; however, in the case of Norden, they were not. In Norden there was a procedural and substantive consensus and a threat or presence of force by outside powers, contributing to the integration process. By combining the two integration incentives, one can obtain a clearer picture of Nordic regional integration after World War II.

A general model of regional integration patterned after the Nordic Nexus can now be constructed. It constitutes a synthesis of integration theory (pluralist, functionalist, neofunctionalist, and federalist), including the nature of integration, its components, and transformation.[87]

Regional integration in Norden can be seen conceptually as both static and dynamic. The forms of integration discussed thus far can be thought of as successive stages (pluralist being the least amount of integration and federalism being the greatest). The structure (static concept) of regional integration in Norden can be seen as formal and informal (formal being the surface appearance; informal being the true nature of the regional system). The formal structure was pluralist in nature in that it comprised a community of states. The informal structure was functionalist in that Norden also comprised a responsive administrative network. Figure 5 represents the structure and system of Nordic regional integration.

The system of regional integration in Norden provided the dynamic characteristics—that is to say, how the integration actually operated, at what levels, with what actors, and in what capacity. Norden's unique form of regional integration did not fit under any one particular type, but systematized elements of three types of integration.

Figure 5
Nordic Regional Integration

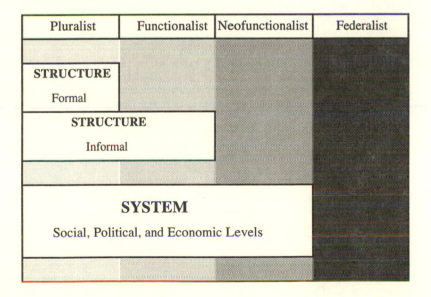

Pluralist	Functionalist	Neofunctionalist	Federalist
STRUCTURE Formal			
STRUCTURE Informal			
SYSTEM Social, Political, and Economic Levels			

Norden's system of regional integration was pluralist in that it was informal and interdependent. It was functionalist in that functional needs were determined by technological change. And it was neofunctionalist in that there was limited growth of central institutions. Under the system dynamics of Nordic integration, one can also find the three basic operational levels of regional integration—economic, social, and political—and identify the Nordic application.

The economic level of the Nordic Nexus was best represented by the Nordic Council and the European Free Trade Association (EFTA). The social level was best represented by the shared core values among Nordic peoples expressed also in the Nordic Council; and the political level was also embodied in the Nordic Council, the regional security arrangements (the Nordic Balance), and the pervasive Nordic Social Democratic party. This Nordic Nexus, then, can be represented graphically in Figure 5. What all of this reveals is that Norden after World War II was integrated at informal levels and was apparently independent at formal levels. This is especially important in applying these ideas to other areas in the world. This might be a way of balancing the forces of fragmentation and integration. Given this sense of community and functional regional integration (the Nordic Nexus), Norden responded to the rising tensions of the Cold War in the 1950s by forming a regional security system: the Nordic Balance.[88] The framework presented in this chapter will now be used to support the historical findings that follow. These findings should confirm the theory and suggest a model for regional peaceful security.

NOTES

1. Ninety-five percent of the world's nation-states are multinational. There are approximately 168 states and anywhere from 3,000 to 5,000 nations. Charles W. Kegley, and Eugene R. Wittkopf, *World Politics: Trend and Transformation* (New York: St. Martin's Press, 1993), p. 449.

2. *Norden* is a commonly agreed on term developed by the nations of Sweden, Denmark, Norway, Finland, and Iceland to replace the term *Scandinavia*.

3. The *Nordic Nexus* refers to the regional aspects of integration among Norden countries, regardless of superpower penetration. Credit for the term *nexus* goes to political scientist Martin O. Heisler in his "Introduction" to *Annals of the American Academy of Political and Social Science* 512 (November 1990): 17.

4. The *Nordic Balance* is a term that refers not to an inter-Nordic balance but, rather, to an effect achieved in terms of the Nordic region's strategically stable and balanced position between the United States and the Soviet Union. Combining various methods of security arrangements, the

Nordic countries maintained peace in their region.

5. *Containment* refers to containing the spread of Soviet communism.

6. Integration in Norden has a historical basis that will be discussed in later chapters.

7. Rolf Tamnes, *The United States and the Cold War in the High North* (Brookfield, VT: Dartmouth Publishing, 1991), p. 61.

8. There are three reasons why Norway was chosen to represent the Nordic perspective in this study. First, Norway was the most influential and strategically important Nordic nation in the bipolarized international system. Second, Norwegians have been the most prolific writers on Nordic security issues. Third, and perhaps most important, Norway has relatively open archives compared to the mostly closed archives in the other Nordic states.

9. Tamnes, *United States and Cold War*, p. 20. The advent of the Marshall Plan (1947) and the formation of NATO (1949) could both be good choices. If one looks at U.S. policy documents on Scandinavia, and their release dates, it can be determined approximately when major developments dictated major changes in direction of policy: NSC 28/1 (1948), NSC 121 (1952), and NSC 6006/1 (1960). The short amount of time between the first two policies indicate that something major had occurred and called for serious reformulation of policy: this, of course, was the Korean War. It appears, then, that 1947 is the most appropriate starting point when taking both the Nordic and American perspectives into account.

10. Hence, we can learn from the period 1947-61 that there were three distinctive strategies of containment. A preeminent U.S. diplomatic historian, John L. Gaddis, divided the history of postwar U.S. foreign policy into what he called "geo-political codes." The first such code he considered as containment as envisioned by U.S. diplomat, historian, and strategist George F. Kennan, from 1947 to 1949. The next period was from 1950 to 1953, which was dominated by the influence of the first comprehensive Cold War policy; NSC 68. This policy document militarized containment. The third period was from 1953 to 1961—the era of Eisenhower, John Foster Dulles, and the New Look policy. John L. Gaddis, *Strategies of Containment: A Critical Appraisal of Postwar American National Security Policy* (New York: Oxford University Press, 1982).

11. Heisler, "Introduction," p. 17. Heisler notes that Norden developed a "Nordic nexus." However, he points out, the "Nordic nexus and the development of a complex, multidimensional region have been almost entirely ignored." Moreover, he concludes that Norden "is a nexus for unique security arrangements that may be apposite models for other parts of the world."

12. Little attention has been given to Norden in major works on U.S. national security policy during the Cold War (e.g., recent works by John L. Gaddis and Melvyn Leffler). The approach used for this study is not a standard one. In recent articles, John L. Gaddis and Michael H. Hunt pointed out the need to do non-English language archive research and to borrow international relations theory to enrich historical analysis. As for the

Nordic perspective, leading Norwegian historians Helge Ø. Pharo, Knut E. Eriksen, and Geir Lundestad have called for more comprehensive and comparative studies; this has been called *international history*. This study takes advantage of foreign archives, and has been greatly enriched by both government documents and secondary works in the Norwegian language. The interdisciplinary aspect of this study is evident in the theoretical framework that is drawn from current international relations theory. The historical analysis adds the dimension of time, and the tracing of forces of change over time, to the theoretical framework. The theoretical framework adds a dimension of abstraction that stimulates a wider acceptance of ideas and further expands the frontiers of academic exploration through identifying major elements that can be used for comparative analysis. A study that is based on binational historical analysis supported by international relations theory should, in effect, reach a larger community of scholars and policymakers and hopefully break down some artificial barriers not only between academic disciplines, but also between societies. John L. Gaddis, "New Conceptual Approaches to the Study of American Foreign Relations: Interdisciplinary Perspectives," *Diplomatic History* 14 (Summer 1990): 406; Michael H. Hunt, "Internationalizing U.S. Diplomatic History: A Practical Agenda," *Diplomatic History* 15 (Winter 1991): 1, 7; Knut E. Eriksen and Helge Ø. Pharo, *Norsk Sikkerhetspolitikk som Etterkrigshistorisk Forskningsfelt*, LOS-senter notat 92/13 (Bergen, Norway: LOS-senter, 1992), p. 52; and see *Diplomatic History* 14 (Fall 1990).

13.   Adam B. Ulam, *Dangerous Relations: The Soviet Union in World Politics, 1970-1982* (New York: Oxford University Press, 1983).

14.   George F. Kennan (Mr. X), "The Sources of Soviet Conduct," *Foreign Affairs* 25 (1947): 572-576, 580-582.

15.   George F. Kennan, "Long Telegram," 22 February 1946, in Thomas H. Etzold and John Lewis Gaddis, ed., *Containment: Documents on American Policy and Strategy, 1945-1950* (New York: Columbia University Press, 1978), pp. 62-63.

16.   Ibid.

17.   Kennan, "Sources of Soviet Conduct," pp. 572-576, 580-582.

18.   George F. Kennan, *American Diplomacy, 1900-1950* (New York: Mentor Books, 1951), p. 87. He also made an interesting analogy when he said that the United States "must be gardeners and not mechanics in our approach to world affairs." George F. Kennan, *Realities of American Foreign Policy* (Princeton, NJ: Princeton University Press, 1954), pp. 93-94; and George F. Kennan, *The Nuclear Delusion: Soviet-American Relations in the Atomic Age* (New York: Pantheon Books, 1976), pp. xx, 67-68, 229-230.

19.   Melvyn Leffler, *A Preponderance of Power: National Security, the Truman Administration, and the Cold War* (Stanford, CA: Stanford University Press, 1992), pp. 495-498.

20.   Ibid., pp. 499-516.

21.   Ibid., pp. 516-518.

22. Gaddis, *Strategies of Containment*, pp. 89-126,

23. Richard H. Immerman, ed., *John Foster Dulles and the Diplomacy of the Cold War* (Princeton, NJ: Princeton University Press, 1990), p. 9.

24. Gaddis, *Strategies of Containment*, pp. 132-133.

25. Ibid., p. 137.

26. Ibid., p. 147; and Richard H. Immerman, "Confessions of an Eisenhower Revisionist: An Agonizing Reappraisal," *Diplomatic History* 14 (Summer 1990): 324; and Stephen E. Ambrose, *Rise to Globalism: American Foreign Policy, 1938-1970* (Baltimore: Penguin Books, 1971), pp. 224-225. This description of asymmetrical response sounds almost like a martial arts strategy.

27. Ambrose, *Rise to Globalism*, p. 225; and Thomas G. Paterson, ed., *Major Problems in American Foreign Policy.* vol. 2: *Since 1914,* 2nd ed. (Lexington, MA: D.C. Heath, 1984), p. 490.

28. Immerman, "Confessions of an Eisenhower Revisionist," p. 325.

29. Ibid., p. 326.

30. Eisenhower was fixated with the mutual dependency between security and solvency. Most notably his conceptualization of the "military-industrial complex."

31. Immerman, "Confessions of an Eisenhower revisionist," p. 328.

32. Ibid., pp. 329-330.

33. Ibid., p. 331.

34. Immerman, *John Foster Dulles*, pp. 63-64; and Committee for Economic Development, *Economic Aspects of North Atlantic Security* (New York: Research and Policy Committee of the Committee for Economic Development, 1951), p. 4. AFNORTH can mean Allied Forces Northern Europe or the Northern Flank of NATO.

35. Tamnes, *United States and Cold War*, p. 61.

36. Gerard Aalders, "The Failure of the Scandinavian Defence Union, 1948-1949," *Scandinavian Journal of History* 15, no. 2 (1990): 135; and Tamnes, *United States and Cold War*, pp. 33-35.

37. Paul M. Cole and Douglas M. Hart, eds., *Northern Europe: Security Issues for the 1990s* (Boulder, CO: Westview Press, 1986), pp. 7-11; and John R. Lund, "Don't Rock the Boat: Reinforcing Norway in Crisis and War," Ph.D. dissertation, Rand Corporation, 1987, p. 1.

38. Cole and Hart, *Northern Europe*, pp. 2-6.

39. Report to Nelson A. Rockefeller from Robert Murphy, Deputy Under Secretary of State, "Neutralism in Europe," 19 August 1955, White House Office, NSC Staff Papers, 1948-61, Planning Coordination Group Series, Box 2, Folders 1-4 Bandung, pp. 1-3, Eisenhower Library.

40. This idea seems to provide evidence that the administration was beginning to see a Nordic Nexus, a connection between all five states.

41. Report to Nelson A. Rockefeller from Robert Murphy, Deputy Under Secretary of State, "Neutralism in Europe," 19 August 1955, White House Office, NSC Staff Papers, 1948-61, Planning Coordination Group Series, Box 2, Folders 1-4 Bandung, pp. 7-9, Eisenhower Library.

42. Policy Statement Prepared in the Department of State, 15 September 1950, in *Foreign Relations of the United States [hereafter FRUS] 1950*, vol. 3: *Western Europe* (Washington, DC: Government Printing Office, 1977), p. 1530.

43. "Northern European Chiefs of Mission Conference, London, 19-21 September 1957: Conclusions and Recommendations," in *Foreign Relations of the United States [hereafter FRUS] 1955-1957*, vol. 4: *Western European Security Integration*, (Washigton, DC: Government Printing Office, 1986), pp. 621-623; and folder 101 Forskningsprogram (rapporter) 1957-58, "A Study of Guided Weapons for Air Defence of the Netherlands and Norway, revised edition, vol. 1," main text report from Anker Committee, August 1957, Forsvarsdepartement H-Arkiv, 1946-52, pakke 71, Norwegian National Archives, Oslo. This report was misfiled in the archive. More than likely it was not supposed to be released to the general public.

44. Policy Statement Prepared in the Department of State, 15 September 1950, in *FRUS 1950*, vol. 3, p. 1531.

45. Telegram from the Ambassador in the United Kingdom (Aldrich) to the Secretary of State (Dulles), 27 September 1955, in *FRUS 1955-1957*, vol. 4, pp. 571-572; Presidential Committee to Study the U.S. Military Assistance Program [hereafter Draper Committee Reports], 1958-59, Category V, May-June 1959, U.S. European Command Report Book 3, Box 18, White House Central Files, Eisenhower Library.

46. Memorandum by the Deputy Director of the Office of the British Commonwealth and Northern European Affairs ([Joseph C.] Satterthwaite) to the Deputy Assistant Secretary of State for European Affairs ([Llewellyn] Thompson), 8 February 1950, in *FRUS 1950*, vol. 1, p. 144.

47. Memo, [John Foster] Dulles to [Dwight D.] Eisenhower, 16 July 1958, "Suggested Comments by the President to the Swedish Ambassador Regarding U. S. Action in Lebanon," Whitman File, Dulles-Herter Series, Box 8, Eisenhower Library.

48. JCS1769/1, United States Assistance to Other Countries from the Standpoint of National Security, 29 April 1947, in Etzold and Gaddis, *Containment*, p. 75.

49. Draper Committee Reports.

50. "Northern European Chiefs of Mission Conference, London, 19-21 September 1957: Conclusions and Recommendations," in *FRUS 1955-1957*, vol. 4, pp. 610-611.

51. Appendix, "U.S. Overseas Military Bases," Report to the President [hereafter Nash Report], November 1957, Whitman File, Administration Series, Box 27, p. 34, Eisenhower Library.

52. In fact, in a 1950 speech by Norwegian Foreign Minister Halvard Lange, he noted that the Korean affair had hastened defense planning by NATO members under American leadership. Telegram, from Oslo Embassy to State Department, Excerpts from Foreign Minister Lange's Speech to the Storting, 22 September 1950, 26 September 1950, Record Group 84,

Foreign Service Posts of the Department of State, Norway, Oslo Embassy, 1950-52, Box 47, Washington National Records Center.

53. NSC 5914/1, U.S. Policy toward Finland, 14 October 1959, pp. 1-5, White House Office, Office of the Special Assistant for National Security Affairs, NSC Series, Policy Papers Subseries, Box 27, Eisenhower Library. NSC 5914/1 was later replaced by NSC 6024 on 30 December 1960. NSC 6024, however, reflected only editorial changes from NSC 5914/1—no policy changes.

54. Oral interview, John D. Hickerson, ambassador to Finland, John Foster Dulles Oral History Project, Transcript p. 21, Seeley G. Mudd Library, Princeton University.

55. Nash Report, pp. 69-70.

56. Policy Statement Prepared in the Department of State, 15 May 1950, in *FRUS 1950*, vol. 3, pp. 1457-1467.

57. "Northern European Chiefs of Mission Conference, London, 19-21 September 1957, Conclusions and Recommendations," in *FRUS 1955-1957*, vol. 4, pp. 610-611.

58. Memorandum by the Deputy Director of the Office of the British Commonwealth and Northern European Affairs (Satterthwaite) to the Deputy Assistant Secretary of State for European Affairs (Thompson), 8 February 1950, in *FRUS 1950*, vol. 1, p. 144.

59. NSC 5426, Operations Coordinating Board, Progress Report, 12 July 1954, p. 7, White House Office, Office of Special Assistant for National Security Affairs, NSC Series, Policy Papers Subseries, Box 12, Eisenhower Library.

60. This importance for Norway is also reflected in the Draper Committee Report that listed Norway's U.S. military aid at $61 million per year from 1959 to 1963 and Denmark's at $31 million for the same timeframe.

61. Robert O. Keohane and Joseph S. Nye, *Power and Interdependence: World Politics in Transition* (Boston: Little, Brown, 1977), pp. 3-4.

62. James N. Rosenau, "Global Changes and Theoretical Challenges: Toward a Postinternational Politics for the 1990s," in Ernst-Otto Czempiel and James N. Rosenau, eds., *Global Changes and Theoretical Challenges: Approaches to World Politics for the 1990s* (Lexington, MA: D.C. Heath, 1989), p. 8; James E. Dougherty and Robert L. Pfaltzgraff, Jr., *Contending Theories of International Relations: A Comprehensive Survey*, 2nd ed. (New York: Harper & Row, 1981), pp. 13-16; Andrew M. Scott, *The Functioning of the International Political System* (New York: Macmillan, 1967), pp. 106-125; and Ole R. Holsti, "Models of International Relations and Foreign Policy," *Diplomatic History* 13 (Fall 1989): 23, 26-27, 42.

63. See Talcott Parsons, "Social Systems," in *International Encyclopedia of Social Sciences*, vol. 15 (New York: Macmillan, 1968), pp. 458-472; and Anatol Rapoport, "General Systems Theory," in ibid., vol. 15, pp. 452-458.

64. *Finlandization* is, in reality, a derogatory and inappropriate term. Further discussion of this term appears in Chapter 2.

65. Another interesting question is, what significance does size and numbers of regional members have on the level of cooperation and success of regional groups? Peace researcher Johan Galtung, in studying small group theory and international relations, found that something is lost and something is gained with high numbers of units (nations) in a system. With a system that increases beyond five to seven units there is more formality and structure, a tendency toward subgroup formation, and more disagreement. A group of five (incidentally there are five in Norden) combines the virtues of cohesion, self-expression by members, and no possibility of subgroup formation since they cannot break into subgroups of equal size. Based on his findings, he concludes with a definition of the direction of further peace research—defined as a discipline concerned with group and international conflicts focusing directly on what is relevant for peaceful settlement of disputes and the development of cooperative patterns of interaction. By researching lower-level social systems as "reservoirs of hypotheses" for international relations theorization, Galtung contends that these peaceful and egalitarian cooperative systems will provide fertile ground for further research. Johan Galtung, "Small Group Theory and the Theory of International Relations: A Study in Isomorphism," in Morton A. Kaplan, ed., *New Approaches to International Relations* (New York: St. Martin's Press, 1968), pp. 292-295.

66. Joseph S. Nye, Jr., ed., *International Regionalism* (Boston: Little, Brown, 1968), p. 5.

67. Karl Kaiser, "The Interaction of Regional Subsystems: Some Preliminary Notes on Recurrent Patterns and the Role of Superpowers," *World Politics* 21 (October 1968): 85. The general concept of regionalism can be traced back to ancient times (i.e., the Lacedaemonian League of ancient Sparta). But for practical purposes regionalism did not truly develop until the emergence of the modern nation-state.

68. J. P. Garg, *Regionalism in International Politics* (Delhi: P. Jain, 1970), p. 7.

69. Nye, *International Regionalism*, pp. vi-vii.

70. Peter Smithers, "Towards Greater Coherence among Intergovernmental Organizations through Government Control," in Berhanykun Andemicael, ed., *Regionalism and the United Nations* (New York: Oceana Publications, 1979), pp. 26-27.

71. Karl W. Deutsch, *The Analysis of International Relations*, 3rd ed. (Englewood Cliffs, NJ: Prentice Hall, 1988), pp. 212-213; and Joseph S. Nye, Jr., *Peace in Parts: Integration and Conflict in Regional Organization* (Boston: Little, Brown, 1971), p. 24.

72. Dougherty and Pfaltzgraff, *Contending Theories*, pp. 417-418.

73. Phillip Taylor, *Nonstate Actors in International Politics: From Transnational to Substate Organizations* (Boulder, CO: Westview Press, 1984), p. 31.

74. Karl W. Deutsch, Sidney A. Burrell, Robert A. Kann, Maurice Lee, Jr., Martin Lindgren, Francis L. Loewenheim, and Richard W. Van Wagenen, *Political Community and the North Atlantic Area: International*

Organization in the Light of Historical Experience, publication of the Center for Research on World Political Institutions at Princeton University (Princeton, NJ: Princeton University Press, 1957), p. 5.

75. Taylor, *Nonstate Actors*, pp. 32-34.

76. Functionalist theories of integration are drawn from the social theories of Herbert Spencer and the structural functionalism of Talcott Parsons. Ibid., p. 34; Garg, *Regionalism*, p. 154.

77. Joseph Nye thinks of neofunctionalists as "federalists in functionalist clothing, pursuing federalist ends through what appeared to be functionalist means." Taylor, *Nonstate Actors*, pp. 34-35; and Nye, *Peace in Parts*, pp. 48-54.

78. Notable federalist theorists include C. J. Friedrich, Peter Hay, and Amitai Etzioni. Taylor, *Nonstate Actors*, pp. 37-38; and Bruce M. Russett, *International Regions and the International System: A Study in Political Ecology* (Westport, CT: Greenwood Press, 1975), p. 227.

79. David Mitrany, "The Prospect of Pntegration: Federal or Functional?" in Nye, *International Regionalism*, pp. 43-73.

80. Nye, *Peace in Parts*, pp. 24-32.

81. These transactions are trade, travel, mail, telephone, radio, and other technical communications.

82. Nye notes some of the implicit aspects of political-level integration: (1) at least some basic institutional structure; (2) interdependence in policy formation; and (3) a sense of mutual identity and obligation. Nye, *Peace in Parts*, pp. 27-48.

83. Dougherty and Pfaltzgraff, *Contending Theories*, pp. 433-434. Deutsch et al., *Political Community and North Atlantic Area*, pp. 5-6.

84. Russett, *International Regions and International System*, pp. 10-11.

85. Nye, *International Regionalism*, pp. 377-378.

86. Helen Milner, "International Theories of Cooperation Among Nations: Strengths and Weaknesses," *World Politics* 44 (April 1992): 466-96. Also see Peter M. Haas, "Introduction: Epistemic Communities and International Policy Coordination," *International Organization* 46 (Winter 1992): 1-35; and Janne Haaland Matláry, "Beyond Intergovernmentalism: The Quest for a Comprehensive Framework for the Study of Integration," *Cooperation and Conflict* 28, no. 2 (1993): 181-208.

87. Nye, *International Regionalism*, pp. 550-551.

88. Bengt Sundelius, ed., *Foreign Policies of Northern Europe* (Boulder, CO: Westview Press, 1982), p. 182.

2

Norden and the Superpowers: Policy and the Question of Nordic Cooperation

But there is yet far to go before we—as individuals and as nations—become world citizens in thought, word and deed. There is a dramatic contrast between the mastery science and technology have given us over natural forces and our mastery of the human mind, between the possibilities we know we have to ensure for all who live on the globe a decent life and our ability to live together as individuals, groups and nations so that we can exploit these possibilities in cooperation. This contrast is the biggest challenge to the people of our time.

—Halvard Lange, 1959

Peaceful cooperation may be an evolutionary process. In order to understand this process in the international system, it would be necessary to examine an example of successful cooperation. Norden has been known for its peacefulness. Was this luck? Or have the Nordic countries mastered the techniques of peaceful cooperation? This chapter will look at three critical questions in terms of Nordic cooperation. First, was there a historical basis for Nordic cooperation in policymaking? Second, what policies were made? And third, was cooperation evident in the making of policy?

THE POTENTIAL FOR NORDIC COOPERATION: HISTORICAL BACKGROUND, OR THE NORDIC NEXUS

The Nordic Nexus was Norden's regional integration system. To understand this system, it may be best to begin by examining what was unique about the political culture in Norden that enabled cooperation to take place. Norden could be seen as part of a larger framework of interstate relationships during the Cold War. The area performed important functions of delimitation and transition with respect to the East-West division in Europe. Nordic countries eased superpower insecurity and severely limited superpower opportunism in their region. However, in this role, Norden's high-level policy failed (i.e., the Scandinavian Defense Union, and the Nordic Customs Union); and its low-level integration, which capitalized partially on the cultural and social homogeneity and affinity of the people in Northern Europe, succeeded. Nordic countries successfully built on lower levels of cooperation and fit their integration strategy into the East-West tension. The region remained stable in spite of the different roads chosen by the Nordic countries with respect to high policy. They cooperated through diversity. However, one might ask, with such strong affinity why did joint arrangements seem so informal and weak among the Nordic countries?[1] The main reason was, that because of the high level of affinity among Nordic countries, strong arrangements were not necessary. Cooperation remained informal because of the countries' familiarity. The form of cooperation and relationships in Norden has been described as "a web of relationships"[2] where contacts were plentiful and commitments were few. In a 1934 speech, Swedish Prime Minister Per-Albin Hansson expressed the concept of Nordic cooperation through diversity.

We have never been subject to any illusions about a fusion (among the Scandinavian states) which eliminates all reasons for friction; we have not dreamed of new unions which would make Scandinavia into a Great Power in the usual sense; we do not speculate about defense pacts and such things. What we strove for and are striving for, is nothing other than a trusting and practical cooperation without any encroachment on the various countries' independence.[3]

Keeping the statement above in mind, one can see that to understand the Nordic Nexus one must first look at the common Nordic heritage and the roots of regional cooperation—the Scandinavianist movement of the nineteenth century.[4] However, Scandinavianism cannot be studied without considering Norden's relations with Russia—factors contributing to Scandinavianism being interwoven into Russo-Nordic relations. This is also important in understanding modern Cold War Soviet-Nordic relations.

Two thousand years ago Germanic tribes living along the coasts of the Baltic and North seas began to migrate to other areas, settling in what is now known as England, Germany, the Netherlands, and the Scandinavian countries. Later, during the Viking age in the ninth century, the Scandinavian people had a large impact on Europe and other parts of the world—even taking time to make a trip to North America more than 500 years before Columbus.[5]   Although long lasting positive effects of the Viking age are not so apparent today, it cannot be discounted that the role the Vikings played was significant at the time. Commonly heard in the churches and monasteries of northern France from the ninth through the eleventh century was the following prayer: "From the wrath of the Northmen, O Lord, deliver us."[6] It is odd to think that hanging in the historical closets of the peaceful and accommodating Nordic societies of today are the likes of Sweyn Forkbeard, Harald Bluetooth, Harald Wartooth, and Erik the Victorious. Despite their Viking past, the people of Norden have developed peaceful, socially democratic, modern welfare societies.

The roots of regionalism in Scandinavia go deep. They are closely tied to relations with Russia—a country that, in many respects, considered itself a Nordic country. Since this study deals not only with regional integration and cooperation, but also with Norden's precarious balance between the United States and the Soviet Union during the Cold War era of the 1950s, it would be worthwhile to gain a firm grasp on the Nordic region's relations with both superpowers.[7] What is Scandinavianism? And how did Russia figure in? It is especially important to look at these relations when Scandinavianism was at its apex—during the time after the Crimean War (1856) until the Danish-German War of 1864 when the failure of fellow Scandinavians to come to the aid of Denmark diminished its focus.[8]

It is easy to underestimate Russia's historic interest in Scandinavia. Geographically, Russia has been greatly concerned with Northern Europe—especially Finland. Whether one speaks of the former Soviet Union or tsarist Russia, traditional Russian interest in Scandinavia has remained the same; the geography has not changed. Peter the Great once remarked, "The women of St. Petersburg cannot sleep freely as long as the Finnish border is so close to our main city." And along the same lines, many years later Josef Stalin said of the Russo-Finnish border: "We can't move Leningrad, so therefore we must move the border!" The increase in Russian power and influence in Europe in the late nineteenth century was matched by its increasing insecurity. This led to the Russians' expanding area of concern in the North (e.g., in search of icefree ports, strategic strongholds, etc.).[9]

Policies toward Finland and Sweden demonstrated a powerful continuity in Russian attitudes. Changes in the eastern border of Finland have historically reflected shifts in the balance of power between Sweden and Russia. During the Crimean War (1853-56), despite bombardment by the French and British, Finland remained loyal to Russia and was rewarded with greater liberalization. Finnish fortunes often fluctuated depending upon the Russian autocrat who was in power.[10] It is important to note that the Russians have held historical ambitions toward establishing a toehold in the Atlantic. Russians tend not to forget history or geography; they do not forget what was once imperial land and territory. They like to think of themselves as being Nordic.[11]

By definition, "Scandinavianism" was "a union or confederation of Scandinavian countries, irrespective of the form in which it was expressed." Scandinavianism really began as a movement for development of closer cooperation and fraternal feelings in the 1830s on the part of well-known Swedish and Danish leaders. This culminated in 1844 with a great gathering in Copenhagen of students, professors, and others interested in Scandinavianism. Scandinavianism was often disparaged because of its being primarily a student movement. But what was forgotten was that these students were from the upper classes and would someday be the leaders of Scandinavia.

The Scandinavianist attitude was captured by the following quote: "A misconceived national pride has divided us and brought foreigners to consider our achievements of little significance. Let six million Scandinavians place their entire weight in one scale, and surely it shall not be found too light."[12] The Scandinavianists intertwined the ideas of a northern union, a defense community, and a dynastic confederation, among others. This movement both benefited and harmed the union between Sweden and Norway. Some supporters of Scandinavianism— Bjørnstierne Bjørnson and Henrik Ibsen, among many other prominent individuals—supported strong pro-union programs. Others, mixing somewhat a mystical idea of Scandinavian brotherhood with a solid belief in the liberal principles represented by Denmark, supported a freer union.[13]

In the aftermath of the Crimean War, Russia's Baltic policy was plagued by three problems: Scandinavianism; Dano-German conflict over the Elbe duchies; and Finland. The central problem, however, was Scandinavianism since the Russians were concerned with maintaining the status quo in the Baltic.[14] They were worried that, if Denmark lost the Elbe duchies, the Danes would fall into the Scandinavian union. Russia reacted very sharply to any signs of Scandinavianism, especially in its political form. This sensitivity to a Scandinavian union was based on military, strategic, and psychological considerations. Russia was afraid that a similar situation would develop in the Baltic as had happened in the Black Sea after 1856. It was also afraid to lose favorable provisions from the Treaty of London (1852), which stipulated that a Russophile would take the throne in Copenhagen upon the death of King Frederick VII.

The Russians believed that, if Scandinavia became united and allied with the Western powers, Russia's guaranteed passage through the Baltic Straits would be in jeopardy. Their passage and contacts with the West through the Baltic were literally a matter of life and death for the Russians. Peter the Great was the first Russian leader to realize this. It may have been because of this fear that the Russians came to overestimate the threat from Scandinavianism after the Crimean War.[15]

Russia's consistently negative attitude toward Scandinavianism merits explanation. It stemmed from Scandinavianism's representing, first, a liberal and a constitutional movement reminiscent of the national movements in Western Europe (with their anti-Russian sentiments) and, second, a threat to the predominance in the Baltic that Russia had gained in the eighteenth century. Fear that the united Scandinavian states would close the Baltic Straits lay beneath the tsar's (Nicholas I) severe negative reaction to rapprochement between Denmark and Sweden.[16] From 1830 to 1848 the Scandinavianist movement in Denmark was seen as seditious by the Russians. This feeling was also evident in the case of Sweden's movement, and it did not diminish after the Crimean War. There were open meetings of Scandinavianist students in 1856 in Uppsala, Stockholm, Copenhagen, and (more sensitive for the Russians) Helsinki. Scandinavian monarchs met together in the spirit of Scandinavianism, and political declarations were made by leaders who threatened to annul the Treaty of London. Russia was also concerned because of the international aspects of Scandinavianism, and Franco-Swedish rapprochement. The Russians received reports that Napoleon III approved of rapprochement with Scandinavia. Additionally, Polish emigrés openly declared how unification of Scandinavia would help Poland. Cooperation between German liberals and Scandinavians also caused Russians to be concerned.[17]

Russian diplomat Aleksandr M. Gorchakov overestimated international factors and underestimated internal resistance to Scandinavianism. In many ways, the union of Scandinavia rested in the "dreams of idealistic Scandinavianists." Russians did not factor in the tensions that emerged between Sweden and Denmark when Denmark lost Norway to Sweden in 1814. Denmark saw Germany as its main enemy, and Sweden saw Russia as its.[18] Despite inherent difficulties in such Scandinavianism, the tsar—encouraged by Gorchakov—took extreme measures. He used diplomatic means, as well as investigations of Scandinavianist organizers—especially those who targeted activities in Finland.[19] But with the failure of Norway-Sweden to aid Denmark in the war with Prussia (1863-64), Scandinavianism effectively died. Bitterness prevailed. One liberal leader in Norway exclaimed, "Enemies of our independence and nationality live not in Germany or Russia but in Sweden and Denmark."[20]

The Scandinavian countries were similar to Russia in that after the Crimean War they embarked on vigorous programs of industrialization and achieved remarkable progress in a relatively short time. The Scandinavians held silent on the international scene and quietly developed their national political economies. By the dawn of World War I, Scandinavian citizens were looked on as very fortunate in the eyes of most of their European contemporaries; the gap between the rich and poor was not a giant chasm as in many other states. This was due to their small-scale societies being permeated by popular movements such as cooperative organizations, trade unionism, and social democracy. Separatist nationalism became an increasingly powerful force, evidenced in Norway's independence in 1905 and Finland's struggles against Russian rule, which became well known throughout Europe.[21] Although Scandinavianism did not turn out to be the fearful entity envisioned by Gorchakov and Alexander II, the Northern Europeans have successfully navigated their way through the nineteenth and most of the twentieth century through integration at a functional level, and emerged as effective social democracies.

Keeping in mind the roots of Scandinavianism, one can then identify four elements in Nordic cooperation, or the Nordic Nexus: (1) some form of political consensus that stresses social justice in society; (2) an incremental approach to integration and negotiation (favoring a combination of low-level agreements to grand schemes); (3) low-voltage politics that stress less strident forms of political and economic behavior; and (4) overriding common objectives based on shared core values (e.g., regional peace and prosperity, democracy, and social equality).

In the twentieth century, the common glue that held the modern Nordic states together was a spirit of political consensus based on the heritage of Scandinavianism. In examining the political culture of Norden, one must take the impact of social democracy into consideration as part of this consensus. However, the social democrats have often been divided on issues. The real base of Nordic cohesiveness—and the first element in the Nordic Nexus—is the spirit of political consensus inherent in the character of Nordic societies.

Examinations of group behavior in twentieth-century Norden have found that the variety of organized groups is no greater than in other industrialized regions. However, what is distinctive to Norden has been the combination of the following characteristics: the legitimacy, density, and centralization of groups; and their systematic incorporation into the legislative and administrative process. Legitimacy means that the Nordic societies combine the supreme worth of the individual with the desirability of collectiveness. This has resulted in a very powerful social norm according to which everybody should belong to a group. Density of organizations means that many of the potential members do in fact join (e.g., 90 percent of wage earners are union represented, as are 70 percent of white collar workers). Centralization has more effectively utilized the scarce resources inherent to small countries.[22]

It is productive to compare the Nordic and U.S. political cultures because the differences may help point out the weaknesses and strengths of both societies and because it would be in keeping with the binational nature of this study. Nordic political culture is not individualistic as in the United States. Political thinking in Norden has been called "sociological thinking" in that intent and effect are not separated. Competence—not flamboyance—is the Nordic style; politics is not theater. Nordic societies believe that aid to one sector of the community will provide benefits to the whole. This sense of interconnectedness has led to the formulation of a labor policy of continuously retraining workers, thus realizing the relationship between social justice and economic development. In summary, politics in Norden are characterized by broad scope, political responsibility, competence, and continuous political education.[23]

The political culture and institutional structure in Norden has tended to exhibit deferent values and accommodationist institutions. This is in contrast to the United States, where self-assertive values and adversarial institutions are pervasive. Modern Nordic political culture evolved from a system of monarchy to the concept of a modern social democratic state in which individuals defer to the will of the government and leaders chart their own course with self-confidence. They are not overly burdened by the worries inherent in a legalistic adversarial society. With the dominance of the Social Democratic party since the 1930s, modern Nordic people have perpetuated the tradition of accommodation and deference, for it is easy to retain this type of system when the face of government does not change much.[24]

In the twentieth century, while the United States increased its reliance on adversarial institutions, the Nordic countries' accommodationist institutions pushed to the top of the power structure those individuals who adjusted their views to those of others. Negotiations produced mutual respect among representative parties, promoting broad-mindedness and altruism in a way that the adversarial American system has not. The overly legalistic American society does not nurture cooperation and tends to perpetuate bad feelings based on decisions imposed by an undemocratically appointed legal structure. Nordic-type deference is also directly opposed to the concept of rugged individualism that has been so pervasive in American culture.[25]

Social democracy emerged from this Nordic tradition of accommodation and deference. From their earliest origins, socialist parties throughout Northern Europe were closely related to working-class organizations, and together they constituted the labor movement. Through their ability to integrate and unite under common policy programs and objectives, the labor movements transformed their crucial role in the capitalist system into an effective political voice.[26] The middle course between acknowledgement of the principle of class struggle inherited from the German social democratic tradition upon which the Nordic movements based their programs and denial of its revolutionary implications was generally accepted by the parties at the turn of the century. By 1910 all of the Nordic Social Democratic parties were holding steady at about 25 percent of the vote. During World War I, the gains slowed for the Social Democrats. The effects of the Depression from the late 1920s and through the 1930s served to temper the Social Democrats' demands. They no longer sought to struggle only for the interests of the workers and to seize power. They felt they needed to change the structure of society in order to safeguard Norden from the effects of the Depression. Since the 1940s the new social democratic strategy has been to collaborate with nonsocialist forces and to build unity and integration of the labor movement with the aim of facilitating rapid expansion of economic resources in order to finance social reform.[27]

The Nordic countries' governmental control over their economies was in effect the social democratic answer to their traditional socialist detractors. The Nordic people increased social justice in their societies while harnessing all of the advantages—and suffering none of the disadvantages—of the capitalist mode of production.[28] Social democratic ideology has combined welfare, egalitarianism, and economic control with the continued dominance of individual ownership—giving rise to the paradox some extremists on either end of the political-economic spectrum apparently see. Socialists describe the Nordic region as "capitalist," and capitalists describe it as "socialist."[29]   One analyst once said of Denmark that the secret of governing in Denmark (among Europe's most stable societies) is not in creating a working majority, but in making sure no majority is working in opposition.[30]   Most importantly, Nordic societies have learned to live with change.

Corporatism in the small European states, and their experience in the international economy, illustrate a traditional paradox in international relations: the strength of the weak. The small states developed economic flexibility: they have a preference for "reactive and flexible" policies of industrial adjustment.   The corporatist arrangements that distinguish the small European states originated in the Depression and World War II when the unions, businesses, and both the conservative and progressive political parties agreed to put aside their arguments and come to grips with the crises that threatened their societies. The political-economic system of the Nordic states can be described as "democratic corporatism." Three traits distinguish democratic corporatism: (1) an ideology of social partnership; (2) a centralized concentrated system of interest groups; and (3) voluntary and informal coordination between interest groups, parties, and bureaucracies. The Nordic and other small European states differ from larger ones in how they have responded to economic change. They have combined international liberalization with domestic compensation—free trade with no protection, and protection for domestic industrial investment. In linking international liberalization of trade and domestic compensation, these states have responded to fluctuations in the world economy with flexible policies of adjustment that were ongoing and incremental steps, not large sweeping programs.   The heart of democratic corporatism is its openness, which has created vulnerability but has also bred closeness and a spirit of social partnership among the political, business, and labor interests.[31]

Three of the most distinctive features of Nordic politics have been the system of corporate pluralism, the functioning multiparty system, and the dominance of the Social Democratic party.   Throughout the postwar era in Norden, the Social Democrats were in control for the most part, making for stable cabinet governments.   The overall stability of the political systems in Norden was largely due to the progressive growth of the Social Democratic party and the spirit of political consensus, democracy, and social justice.[32]

Incrementalism was the type of decisionmaking used by Norden in the functional integration process. Disjointed incrementalism describes decision-making under conditions of uncertainty among participants with partly convergent and partly opposing interests. Fragmented issue linkage, as a companion concept, recognizes the tension among actors (nations) as they confront decisions through rationalization. Essentially, nations build cooperative frameworks piece by piece, finding smaller issues on which to agree before moving on to larger ones.[33] Although large cooperative efforts have failed in Norden, often ignored are the small pieces that were woven together to form less grand examples of cooperation. Through small steps, the substance of large comprehensive agreements passed through incremental development. The driving force in the region has been not to unite, but to keep the region intact. Regional relations have been interwoven in such a way that they resemble domestic policy. This process of political integration has been less dependent on centralization of regional authority than on finding collective and nationally acceptable solutions to pressing national problems.[34] This, then, appears to be an example of pluralist leaning toward functionalist integration. With the world's increasing complexity, the pluralist nature of the Nordic community became more functionalist.

The nations of Norden persuaded each other to pursue the goal of regional peace and prosperity through stabilization achieved by using low-voltage politics—the third element of the Nordic Nexus. Interestingly enough, the superpowers were also persuaded—at least in terms of their behavior within Norden. Just as the Nordic countries practiced cooperation at the international system level, their internal political systems allowed for the cooperation of multiple parties that at one time had discordant interests. The countries accomplished this through pursuing selective agreements on less controversial issues, thereby building a base on which to solve more difficult problems. This model of cooperation and flexibility extended outward as well as inward—into the regional security system and the international system through contacts with the superpowers in the region.

One key to the Nordic nations' successful regional integration is their ability to seek accommodation. There has been a noticeable absence of overly formal legal structure or compliance mechanisms. Deferring to governmental authority, people of the North trust their governments' ability to make decisions that will benefit everyone as equitably as possible. Yet these governments have stopped short of deferring to international bodies in any official way. The Nordic countries prefer informal international structures wherein they can take part but not submit to supranational authority. This spirit of accommodation and deference at the national level, and of cautious informal association at the regional level, was necessary for successful cooperation without total political integration. The Nordic community forms an example of how effective regional integration can be, especially for Third World nations. This type of regional integration exemplified in the Nordic Nexus could allow nations to retain their sovereignty while facilitating needed regional goals of mutual benefit to their member nations in the spirit of harmony and cooperation. In this way, diversity need not stand in the way of cooperation.

The overriding common objectives Norden held in the 1950s were peace, security, freedom, and prosperity (grounded on a political consensus over democracy and social justice). This forms the fourth element of the Nordic Nexus. To achieve these goals, the Nordic countries were able to develop an elasticity in their foreign, domestic, and economic policies that adapted well to changes. They were also able to weave together their key interests in economics, culture, and government. Underpinning common objectives are shared core values,[35] which derive from ideological, economic, and geopolitical considerations and interests that emerge after a process of trade-offs has occurred among key groups within a society. These interests are then pursued, often at great cost.[36] The national interests of the Nordic countries had substantial convergence. Dissimilarities in policy did not stand in the way of common goals, especially in terms of security.

In international relations, the countries of the Nordic region found a "middle way" between anarchic use of force and political amalgamation. Among themselves, they would neither fight nor unite. Instead they followed the way of cooperation, which required a persistent joint effort to increase mutual advantages. This was done with the clear realization that the world was becoming increasingly interdependent. These advantages were officially defined in the 1962 Helsinki Agreement to include the "fostering of similarities and the elimination of hampering differences in legal systems, social policy, transportation regulation, educational structure, and economic opportunity." This provides evidence that Norden was practicing "regionalism." Because the Nordic countries retained their individuality and avoided establishing a superstate, they were not totally integrated. These five nations remained separate and had structurally distinct foreign and domestic policies.[37] They were integrated along functional lines and at informal levels that were not apparent on the surface. They cooperated in the spirit of achieving their collective objectives.

Returning to the five generally recognized elements of regional integration presented in Chapter 1, how does the Nordic Nexus compare?

1. *High levels of social and cultural homogeneity.* With the exception of the Finnish language, Norden's people share similar languages and culture. No passports are required for Nordic citizens to travel in the five member states, jobs can

be found in other states, medical benefits are shared, and university education benefits are available for citizens in any of the five countries.

2. *Similar political attitudes and behavior.* The Social Democrats have, for the most part, dominated in all five countries. But, most importantly, a spirit of political consensus has effectively tied their political agendas together.

3. and 4. *Some political and economic interdependence.* The Nordic Council is an organization that tends to inter-Nordic domestic affairs. Also, the five countries also belong to the European Free Trade Association (EFTA).

5. *Geographical proximity.* With the exception of Iceland, Norden is geographically centralized on the northern periphery of Europe.

The seeming similarities shared by Nordic countries are also deceptive. These countries also take pride in their individuality. Owing to their past national arrangements—Norway having been part of Denmark and then Sweden; Iceland having been part of Norway and then Denmark; and Finland having been part of Sweden and then Russia— each Nordic country is happy being its own national entity. Each country establishes its own individual political and economic policy and its own individual security orientation.

NORDIC POLICY: FENDING OFF THE SUPERPOWERS, OR THE NORDIC BALANCE

How did each country in Norden contribute to the cooperative effort that has stabilized their region and allowed for development? This section looks at each Nordic country's policy (starting with Norway, followed by Sweden, Denmark, Finland, and Iceland), both to form a basis for comparison and to see how each Nordic country depends on the others in terms of security.

Norway's history as a state can be thought of in three different ways. As a nation and as a people, its history goes back to the age of the Vikings from the ninth to the eleventh century. As an autonomous state defined by its own constitution and political structures, its history can go back nearly 180 years; but as an independent country with its own foreign policy, it can only go back to the year 1905.[38] From the Viking period onward, Norway was periodically controlled by Denmark and Sweden.[39] Norway's break from Denmark was inspired in part by fears of entanglements with the continental powers (only eighteen years after George Washington's famous words to this effect in his Farewell Address). Norway's geographic remoteness from the main continent of Europe fed its isolationist sentiments, much as did America's remoteness. Norway's only real concern throughout the nineteenth century was its great neighbor to the East—Russia. But the general feeling at the time was that England would not sit idly by if Russia were to make advances upon Norwegian territory. This led to Norway's feeling that it should not directly meddle in foreign affairs, lest it spoil the arrangement. After its total independence from Sweden in 1905, Norway relied on these three cornerstones of national security: (1) geographic remoteness; (2) protection by Britain and its sea power; and (3) a determination not to become entangled in foreign affairs.[40]

Norway's foreign policy reflected its traditional relationship with Europe. Continental Europe had always represented a foreign culture, unacceptable forms of economics and social democracy, a threat to established ways of Norwegian life, and, concerning union endeavors, a threat to Norway's chosen path. This old distrust of European ways was combined with economic suspicion and skepticism of large powers.[41] Norway has adopted six different foreign and security policy arrangements since its independence in 1905:

1905-1914	No alliances (isolationism)
1914-1919	Neutrality
1919-1940	Collective security through the League of Nations
1940-1945	Atlantic alliance while government in exile
1945-1949	Bridgebuilding between East and West
1949-present	NATO alliance[42]

In 1948, faced with the ominous implications of a communist coup d'état in Czechoslovakia and with the Soviet-Finnish nonaggression pact, Norway decided that it could no longer remain on the fence of East-West confrontation. Norway felt threatened by the Soviet Union and saw no other alternative but to join NATO (1949) and cooperate with the West.[43]   Direct cooperation among the Nordic countries proved unproductive in establishing a unified defense pact against the Soviet threat.[44] There is even some evidence to indicate that Norway may have sabotaged the process of establishing a Scandinavian Defense Union (SDU). According to that view, Norway was suffering from the "9 April syndrome" (the Germans invaded Norway on 9 April 1940) amid increasing Cold War tensions, and wanted the security that only a superpower could provide.[45]

In terms of Norway's adaptation to the Cold War environment, the

Norwegian dualist policy of allowing no foreign bases yet retaining NATO membership—thereby making its membership conditional—was an effective tool in keeping both superpowers at a distance and ameliorating tensions in Norway and in Northern Europe.[46] Given that Norway was the only NATO country to share a border with the Soviet Union, the basing policy was reassuring to the Soviets. However, Norway was definitely Western in orientation.

During the Cold War Sweden, was neutral, as it had been since the Napoleonic era. The objective of Swedish foreign policy was de facto neutrality unsupported by international guarantees or by conventional international law such as in the cases of Switzerland or Austria. It was basically a policy of total defense. Sweden had a parliamentary democracy that blended socialist traditions with a largely capitalist, industrialized economy giving Swedes one of the world's highest standards of living. To achieve their policy of total defense, the Swedes required a strong (but not nuclear) defense to preserve their neutrality, and found no contradictions between a strong defense and international work for disarmament. Sweden's military position played a critical role in the Nordic Balance by preventing instability that could have invited a superpower confrontation in Norden.[47] The Swedes regarded their traditional policy of nonalignment as a key factor in the preservation of Finnish independence and hence in the interests of the West.[48] Sweden's nonalignment helped reassure the Soviets so that they would stay out of Finland and, correspondingly, saved Sweden the cost of the military preparedness that having Russians on the border would have entailed.

Sweden did not agree with the other Nordic countries in forming a Scandinavian Defense Union in 1948. It is known that Sweden did not want their defense arrangements to involve the United States; what is not well known is that Sweden probably did not want to give up its dominant position in Nordic affairs—which is what made the security arrangements with the United States unacceptable to the Swedes. The Swedish government wanted to stay out of bloc-building in the Cold War. The SDU was considered part of this bloc-building. Because neutrality had worked for more than 135 years, the Swedes were not eager to give up on that policy.[49]

Although Sweden officially proclaimed neutrality, American officials recognized that Sweden was tacitly tied to the West and NATO. There were the Swedish veiled threats of "reevaluating foreign policy" whenever Finland's security was breached by the Soviets. As an example of these Western ties, the Swedes held a military exercise concurrently with NATO operation MAINBRACE in 1952.[50] Another example was evident in a policy document from the Norwegian Defense

Department in 1954 that laid out wartime instructions for airline captains on Scandinavian Airlines System flights (SAS is jointly controlled by Sweden, Norway, and Denmark). These instructions were for Swedish pilots as well, of course. Another Norwegian Defense Department document discussed U.S. pilots training Scandinavian pilots. It stipulated that Swedish pilots could also be trained, but only on flight characteristics, not tactical combat techniques—obviously showing both the U.S. connection and the inherent sensitivity.[51]

Achieving Denmark's membership in NATO, although backed by a substantial majority in the Folketing (Parliament) and the ruling Social Democrats, was nonetheless a hard battle in 1949. Membership was viewed as a sharp break from Denmark's traditional neutrality—an attitude that was coupled with a pragmatic realization that Germany lay just to the south and constituted the largest military power in central Europe. Neutrality did not help Denmark when the Germans invaded on 9 April 1940, so the Danes swore never to be caught unprepared again. Before joining NATO, the Danes had hoped to establish a Nordic collective security arrangement (i.e., SDU), but this effort fell short due to disagreements between Norway and Sweden over Norway's Atlantic ties. Danish Foreign Minister Hans Rasmussen called the failure of the SDU "a black day in Nordic history," adding that the "Scandinavian alliance would have been better than the Atlantic Pact."[52] Since choosing NATO, Danish public opinion has fluctuated markedly on the issue of membership—from a low of 27 percent favoring a continued membership in 1955 to a high of 69 percent in 1983.[53]

Denmark's foreign policy and security policy has been described by some as "a walk in the wilderness." The Danes did not know whether to seek alignment with Germany to the south, England to the west, or the Soviet Union to the east, or to choose neutrality. Geography played a major role in Denmark's predicament. The nation lies on an indefensible peninsula, with predominantly flat terrain, and holds a strategic position at the entrance to the Baltic Sea. Fifty percent of all Soviet shipbuilding, and the maintenance capacity required to keep the Soviets at sea, were located in the Baltic. Left with few options, Denmark chose NATO membership and a path similar to that of Norway.[54]

Denmark had a long history of neutralism and pacifism that began after Denmark's disastrous defeat by Prussia in 1864 and continued through its noninvolvement in World War I and German occupation in World War II. The United States felt that Danish military participation in NATO was not as effective as it should be, but Denmark considered its Greenland contribution to be of great value. The Hungarian Revolt of 1956 and a threatening letter from Soviet Minister Nikolai Bulganin in March 1957 served to solidify public support of NATO. However, neutralist and pacifist strains remained. Because of the great distance that separated Denmark from its territory in Greenland, there was a tendency to think that U.S. forces there protected the continental United States more so than Denmark.[55]

Finland's position in the global system was somewhat of an anomaly. In World War II, Finland twice fought the Soviet Union and twice lost against overwhelming odds. After the war, Finland was compelled to sign an agreement with the Soviets—the Treaty of Friendship, Cooperation, and Mutual Assistance (FCA) in 1948—which limited Finland's sovereignty in foreign policy decision-making, military matters, and its defense establishment. However, through skillful diplomacy, especially by President Urho Kekkonen throughout the 1950s, Finland secured a position of national sovereignty and considerable autonomy in foreign affairs.[56] The Finns were defeated but not conquered; their social fabric was intact, and the continuity of their political institutions was unbroken.[57] This autonomy was evident in Finland's national political system, which remained pluralistic and democratic, and in its economic system, which encouraged private enterprise. Finnish culture was staunchly Western. For Finland, the Soviet relationship was a practical matter, given the long and bloody history of its vulnerable eastern border. Finland attached great importance to its relationships with other Nordic countries (i.e., through their active participation in the Nordic Council).

Finland's difficult position in Norden was evident in its deliberations over accepting Marshall Plan aid. The Finns chose to decline Marshall Plan help that they desperately needed. The Finnish leader at the time, Juho Paasikivi, said that the Marshall Plan was designed to save Europe; however, by declining it and avoiding the wrath of the Soviets, Finland was saved.[58]

Finland based its state sovereignty on an internal democracy balanced with a external policy of friendship with the Soviet Union, making its geostrategic position quite unique. As a result, Finland was worried about seeming to be too aligned with the West (what it truly wanted). This policy became known as the "Paasikivi Line." The Paasikivi Line hypothesis holds that Soviet interests in Finland were mainly based on military/security concerns and not economic or ideological ones. As long as Finland did not represent a military/security threat, it would be left alone. In 1949 the Soviets accused Finland of violating their FCA treaty and having a bad attitude toward the Soviet Union. The Soviets also charged that Finland was greatly influenced by Anglo-American reactionaries. Despite its necessary relationship with the Soviet Union, Finland cooperated closely with the other Nordic countries, whose policies always considered the implications for Finland.[59]

The U.S. view of Finland was positive until the mid-1950s. It was then that U.S. officials began to see Finland more as a willing tool of Soviet foreign policy. This was in reaction to the Soviet policy of "peaceful coexistence" (a doctrine that emphasized accommodation between different social systems) and Finnish neutrality. Neutrality was seen by the United States as playing into the hands of the Soviets. Unlike the countries of Eastern Europe, Finland was able to remain independent from the Soviets. In spite of this accomplishment, U.S. foreign policy elites in 1955 began to see Finland in a negative light.

Finlandization[60]—a term that became synonymous with the idea of limited sovereignty—may be an inaccurate term given Finland's difficult position as a peace buffer between East and West and its role in Nordic security. Finlandization was more an "exercise in skillful maneuvering to avoid the fate of Eastern Europe."[61] Acting with moderation, patience, and a long-term view, the succession of Finnish governments were able to live with the limitations imposed by the FCA. The Finns showed political prudence. They had shown the Soviets their ability and willingness to fight, which may have convinced the Soviets that swallowing Finland might not mean digesting it.

Iceland was one the founding members of NATO, even though Icelanders were pacifist by nature and had no standing army. Iceland did not attain full sovereignty until 1944. Thus, through eleven centuries of its history, Iceland was dominated by foreign incursion into its affairs. Iceland differed from the other Nordic nations in that the Icelandic government allowed the stationing of foreign troops. Icelanders tolerated the presence of U.S. troops during the Cold War, yet showed signs of reluctance as well.[62] The Eisenhower administration wanted to placate the Icelanders, even to the extent of removing U.S. Army security personnel (who provided the only defense force on the island). It was feared, however, that this would send a signal to the local communists that the United States was abandoning Iceland.[63]

After the formation of NATO and the start of the Korean War, NATO delegated the United States to protect Iceland. Pursuant to this, the United States and Iceland signed a defense agreement on 5 May 1951 wherein the United States built and manned bases on Iceland. This agreement was expanded in May 1954. The U.S. mission in Iceland was considered to be so vital and sensitive that Americans were compelled, on occasion, to accede to requests made by the host government, including the removal of senior U.S. officials.[64] The fear that the Korean War would escalate into a general war may have led

Icelanders to sign the stationing-of-foreign-troops agreement in 1951—a controversial step. In fact, those opposed to NATO staged demonstrations over the decision, and violence occurred for the first time in modern Icelandic history. After 1,000 years of isolation and neutrality, Icelanders were extremely worried about foreign troops disrupting and contaminating their culture and society. This fear of cultural contamination was overcome by the perceived international danger from the Korean War. Later the Icelanders were influenced more by neutralism and nationalism and felt that lessened military tensions in the world should obviate the need for U.S. troops.[65]

REALIZATION OF THE POTENTIAL FOR COOPERATION: THE NORDIC BALANCE IN THEORY AND ACTION

Faced with heightened superpower pressure at the end of the 1940s, Nordic countries found it necessary to cooperate in terms of regional security, and to do so without conflicting with the U.S. system of containment. To what degree did the Nordic countries cooperate, and at what levels? The Nordic Balance concept, as theorized in this study, best describes Norden's regional security system in the 1950s. The Nordic Balance largely depended on a spirit of regional cooperation—the Nordic Nexus. Under this Nordic Nexus, the line between external and domestic issues in Norden was often fuzzy. Nordic nations were sensitive to the effects that national decisions had on the other members of their region.[66]

The concept of the Nordic Balance has been somewhat controversial. There has been little direct evidence to indicate that Nordic governments clearly envisioned a comprehensive Nordic Balance while formulating their security policies. This, however, is indicative of Nordic politics; low-level agreements are favored over grand schemes. By its very sensitive political nature, the Nordic Balance could not be advertised by the Nordic governments. It is therefore difficult to find evidence of deliberate design. In any case, no one can argue with the success of the Nordic region in staving off superpower penetration during the Cold War.

Johan J. Holst, the current Norwegian Foreign Minister, is a prolific writer on Nordic security, and he contends that the term *Nordic Balance* is misleading because Nordic countries were not poised against each other. Instead, there existed a pattern of mutual restraint with respect to the national defense policies that the Nordic states pursued, most particularly in relation to the military penetration of the area by outside powers. Holst notes that there was no balance in relation to outside powers, either. According to Holst, Norden was not balanced; it was firmly Western in orientation.[67] Yet, in the 1950s—and this is something Holst passes over—Norden's Western orientation was not particularly clear to Americans. The influence of McCarthyism colored U.S. perceptions of social democratic societies; Americans tended to view socialist-leaning societies with suspicion. This created insecurity in the United States and made relations with the Nordic nations more problematic.   As a result, Nordic societies feared hysterical anticommunists as well as radical communists.

Political scientist Steve Lindberg does not refute the concept of the Nordic Balance, but holds that Iceland and Denmark were not included. In his formulations, Iceland was excluded because it had no defense of its own and had an American airbase on its territory. Lindberg excludes Denmark because it had strong bonds to the Common Market and defense arrangements with West Germany within NATO.[68] Yet, it was precisely these differences in security policy orientations that contributed to the success of the Nordic Balance. This combination of diverse security approaches stabilized the region as it stood between the two superpowers.

Part of the argument about the existence of the Nordic Balance has been a matter of semantics. The term *balance* does not only mean a weight or force that counteracts another weight or force. It can also be thought of more as a condition of stability—stability that dulled superpower penetration. It is this definition that most clearly represents this study's conception of the Nordic Balance.   In spite of the controversy, since the 1960s it has become common to refer to Nordic security policy in terms of a balance. The term was first used by Halvard Lange, the Norwegian foreign minister during the "Note Crisis" (described below) in 1961 when he was referring to Norden's regional security arrangements.[69] The Norwegian Institute of Foreign Affairs then began to research the unique security problems of the Nordic region; the result was a Nordic Balance theory. Arne Olav Brundtland emerged as the preeminent Nordic Balance theorist and has been the most prolific writer on this subject since the 1960s. He contends that the Nordic Balance model clearly explains the peace and stability of Norden since World War II.[70] The term *Nordic Balance* expressed a notion that the stability of the Northern European area reduced superpower insecurity and opportunism. Although both the United States and the Soviet Union had limited influence on the fringes of Norden (Iceland and Finland), the Nordic Balance effectively neutralized the superpowers, thereby decreasing tensions in the region.   This reduced potential for conflict made "restrained containment" possible for the United States. Both superpowers engaged in operations designed to deny the other a foothold in the region and based on a system of restraints—restraints that the Nordic countries wished to remain intact.[71]

Brundtland's central conceptions are contained in three policy dimensions, and three operational factors. The three policy dimensions are global (bipolar), regional (Nordic), and combined global-regional. The operational factors are these three: (1) Norway and Denmark's conditional NATO membership (policy of deterrence and reassurance), and Iceland's full membership; (2) Sweden's neutrality or no-alliances policy; and (3) Finland's neutrality and its FCA treaty with the Soviet Union.[72]

The bipolar dimension arises from superpower strategic interests in the Nordic countries as positioned between East and West. The Nordic dimension is the regional context. The combined global and regional dimension is more complex and involves the interplay of operational factors within the region. One must keep in mind that the Nordic Balance is not a military alliance. It is more of an "equilibrium between different kinds of 'political phenomena.' "[73]

Figure 6 illustrates these dimensions. The divided East-West circle represents the bipolar dimension in the 1950s. The box labeled Norden represents the Nordic dimension. Norden is placed near the middle of the East-West division, but it is oriented toward the West. The individual national boxes below Norden represent the interplay of regional (Nordic) and global (bipolar) dimensions. One can see that Norden's Western position is partly achieved through the effects of the combined positions of the five Nordic countries. Iceland is the furthest to the Western side because of its NATO alignment and U.S. base. Norway and Denmark are more toward the middle because of their conditional NATO membership (no basing and no nuclear weapons). Sweden is almost in the middle owing to its neutrality and its Western orientation. Finland is more on the Eastern side due to its treaty with the Soviet Union, but is not as far from the line as Iceland. This is not to say that Finland was solidly in the Soviet camp. This merely reveals the strategic placement of Finland within the bipolar world.

The Nordic Balance can be seen in two ways: as a static concept, and as a dynamic concept. The static concept simply articulates the three operational factors mentioned earlier. The dynamic concept is more compelling. In the dynamic approach, one asks the question of whether there is any dynamic linkage between the security policies of the Nordic countries. This dynamic linkage could then be examined and broken down into elements that can be identified.

Figure 6
The Nordic Balance

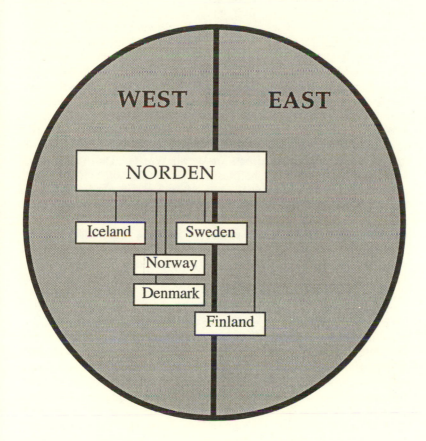

Figure 6 did not simply represent the sum total of all the individual states' security orientations. It was an integrated network. Adding to the controversial nature of the Nordic Balance was that, to work, the Nordic Balance had to be subdued and not officially pronounced. Finland and Sweden could not have played their roles if it were commonly known that they took part in such a balance. Therefore, the reason there has been little direct evidence of its existence was that it could not be openly discussed for fear of severe political repercussions (i.e., on Finland and Sweden's neutral status). If both superpowers had to admit officially that the Nordic Balance existed, it would not work.[74]

Any type of balance involving the West was antithetical to the Soviets since the Marxist-Leninist view would link a Western balance as part of the capitalist conspiracy. The concept of the Nordic Balance, then, was made up of three elements: first, common overriding objectives based on shared core values; second, balanced, regionally based, nationally articulated approaches to security; and third, low-voltage foreign policy.

The first element of the Nordic Balance is the set of common objectives derived from shared core values (peace, prosperity, democracy, and social equality). Despite differences in their societies, Nordic countries shared basic core values and the common objective of maintaining security in their region in the 1950s. And despite differences in policy orientation, and perhaps *because* of these differences, they were successful in keeping peace in their region. In part, this was due to the effects of World War II. During the war, Sweden and Denmark felt helpless. As a result, some of the most visionary ideas of Nordic unity emerged from the experiences of World War II; it was resolved among the Nordic countries that never again would the security of Norden be breached.[75]

The second element of the Nordic Balance was the balanced, regionally based, and nationally articulated approaches to security in Norden. National security policy involves protecting a nation's people, vital economic and political interests, and territory from the aggression of other nations. In the case of the Nordic region during the Cold War, its members saw threats from both the Soviet Union and the United States. A balance was necessary for the Nordic countries to remain peaceful. Each country used its own national security policy in concert with the others. Norway's base policy helped Finland keep the Soviets from establishing bases in Finland. Sweden's neutrality helped all the Nordic countries stabilize superpower interests. These diverse orientations gave strength to the Nordic security system and allowed for more political policy maneuverability.

The Nordic Balance refers to "a balance in the limitations of the applications of political or military power,"[76] which can be defined in either dynamic or static terms. The five Nordic nations developed a network of formal and informal relationships that successfully tempered superpower interests in their region. This network, which developed in the postwar years since 1945, helped regulate the regional security obligations that each Nordic nation accepted. In practice this meant that before a security issue was decided by any one Nordic nation, consideration was given to the other Nordic countries, and the issue examined for any potential impacts on them. The Nordic Balance was not a law or any formal type of structure. It was a blending of the unique elements found in the security policy of each Nordic nation.[77]

The Nordic community combined NATO membership (Norway, Denmark, and Iceland) with neutrality (Sweden and Finland) to effect this balance.

Despite formal differences in individual Nordic foreign and defense policies, there were important similarities in terms of politics, culture, and tradition that led to a high degree of cooperation. However, in regional integration, the level of affinity is not all that matters. What also matters is the incentive to nurture similarities and mutual trust. This method is most conducive to maintaining a high level of cooperation, and ensures that the region will remain both peaceful and stable.[78] In the 1950s the Nordic security system was balanced, in that stability was achieved (peace and security); it was regionally based, because each nation took the others into account when making security policy decisions; and it was nationally articulated, because each Nordic nation maintained its own sovereignty and unique security policy orientation.

The third element of the Nordic Balance was a low-voltage foreign policy (similar to the low-voltage politics of the Nordic Nexus). Smaller nations tend to employ techniques of statecraft that minimize the cost of conducting foreign policy. Consequently, small states rely on international government organizations (IGOs) more so than large states. Another foreign policy method employed by small states is to direct their influence toward groups of states and at IGOs rather than individual nations. This has been described as "low-voltage politics."[79] The foreign policy behavior of small states is characterized by less overall activity, due to limited resources, multilateral rather than bilateral diplomacy, and lower risk behavior coupled with a high degree of specificity (i.e., economic development).[80] Small states also tend to use regional arrangements to pool their resources, thereby amplifying their voice in international affairs.[81]

Contributing to the understanding of low-voltage foreign policy is the concept of functionalism. This can best be imagined as the meshing of small gears in order to turn larger ones. Nordic countries found cooperation and agreement on basic issues, and that led to cooperation at higher levels. Functionalist thinking in foreign policy integration in Norden contributed to the success of Nordic policy during the Cold War.[82] Taken together, these elements contributed to the functioning of the Nordic Balance concept. Separate, the Nordic nations were isolated and vulnerable; together, they were strong. When the orientations of all five Nordic nations were woven together, the effect was stability and strength (balance) without sacrificing national sovereignty.

The Nordic pattern of security (or Nordic Balance) was successful because everyone (in Norden) agreed it was a good system, and it was not disturbing to the major powers. It maintained a balance of power between East and West. NATO gave Norway's position great credibility, as did Sweden's neutrality, the stability of Norden internally, and mutual respect for Finland's integrity in its relations with the Soviets.[83] Norway's role in the Nordic Balance has been described as the "watchdog." Norway preserved traditional Nordic interests against NATO interests. This also allowed Sweden room to maneuver in its policy. The Nordic Balance was strong because of diversity and flexibility.[84]

The Finnish Note Crisis of 1961 provided evidence of the Nordic Balance in action. In 1961 NATO established a joint German-Danish command for the Baltic approaches. The Soviets demanded that Finland, under the provisions of the FCA, enter into consultations leading to the acceptance of Soviet bases on Finnish soil. This Note Crisis was avoided after Finnish President Urho Kekkonen personally reassured Soviet Premier Nikita Khrushchev, and Norway vowed to reverse its basing and nuclear weapons policies.[85] There was also some question of whether or not the Swedes would move toward NATO membership. The dynamic aspects of the Nordic Balance were evident in this averting of a major crisis.

Despite this example, the Nordic Balance remains controversial, partly because it involved several security policies from several countries. With the Note Crisis, the Norwegians became especially aware of the Nordic Balance. But that does not mean that it did not exist before 1961. No critiques have totally disproven the theory, but some have noted limitations in its explanatory power.[86] The "Nordic Balance" is a term that can be used descriptively in that it can explain the reality of security in Norden in the 1950s. It can also be used explanatively for theoretical formulations. And it can be used normatively to form a type of doctrine.[87] However, the most critical aspects of the Nordic Balance were the Finnish and Norwegian dimensions. They had the most possible room to move and to affect the others. Naturally, Finland could never claim the existence of a Nordic Balance because it would tie the Finns to Norway's and Denmark's membership in NATO.[88] The Nordic Balance was not simply a descriptive sum of Nordic security orientations. It allowed Nordic nations a substantial amount of political breathing space and maneuverability with their alliance partners. To do this, the Nordic Balance had to reduce superpower tension.[89]

Recent developments in Norden, as archives come increasingly under pressure to release closed documents, show that there is more evidence for a Nordic Balance. In the Norwegian prime minister's conference files from 1952, there was mention of organizing the Nordic form of cooperation in such a way as not to resemble an overparliament that duplicates or infringes on functions of other government organs in each country. By having committees carry out the work, this cooperation and joint venture was to be played down so as to protect the delicate positions of the neutral members of Norden.[90] In a speech by Finnish Prime Minister Esko Aho on 4 May 1992, he said that Finland had always counted on the Atlantic dimension in Norden (especially through Norway) to preserve Finnish security. Finland and Norway's security orientations complemented one another, Aho claimed, and NATO secured all of Norden (including Finland) during the Cold War. This news strongly supports the Nordic Balance theory.[91]

In examining security in Norden, there is a connection between the concepts of "integration and screening" and "deterrence and reassurance."[92] Nordic countries used deterrence and reassurance against the East (the Soviet Union), and integration and screening against the West (the United States). To understand this, one must keep in mind that the goal for Norden was to achieve both peace and prosperity. It wanted all of the benefits of peaceful relations with the superpowers, but not all of the entanglements. Figure 7 combines these two concepts and places them on a scale.[93] The scale has been valued from -2 to +2 based on the effect a particular policy had on the recipient. To the right is integration, which receives a +2 value; and to the left is deterrence, which receives a -2 value. In between are the screening (-1) and reassurance (+1) policies. Nordic countries maneuvered along this spectrum in forming their East-West policy. Certain situations called for integration; but when Western contact became too intimate and problematic, screening measures were used. Likewise, certain situations called for deterring the Soviets, but the reassurance policy could be used

Figure 7
Nordic Cold War Dynamic Policy Spectrum
(Positive and Negative Effects)

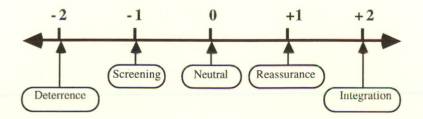

to avoid conflict. Next, using the policy spectrum in Figure 7, each Nordic country's individual policy range can be evaluated.

According to Table 3 and Figure 7, the best the Soviets could hope for was reassurance, whereas the West could flirt with integration. In other words, Norden favored the West. Nordic countries were willing to approach the West for security guarantees and economic assistance, but were much more reluctant to do so with the Soviets. The policies directed by Norden toward the West ranged from a high of +2 to a low of -1, whereas those directed at the Soviets range from a high of +1 to a low of -2. These ranges provide a snapshot of individual Nordic policies toward the superpowers in the 1950s, based on an arbitrarily chosen scale. The interesting point here is looking at the ranges for each Nordic country in relation to the others. For example, this table indicates that Finland's range of policy was more limited than that of Norway. Also interesting is the fact that the mean range for Norden reflects its Western orientation: in policies with the West, Norden as a whole ranges from -0.8 to +1.4, whereas the range for the East is from -1.6 to +0.8.

The next step in understanding Nordic security policies is to construct a value system wherein the orientations of the five Nordic countries can be evaluated according to both the Eastern and Western perspectives. The five security orientations of the Nordic countries are evaluated in Table 3 for both their Eastern and Western perspectives.

Table 3
Policy Spectrum Ranges for Individual Nordic Countries (Positive and Negative Effects)

		Low Range	High Range
Denmark	East	-2	+1
	West	-1	+2
Finland	East	0	+2
	West	-1	0
Iceland	East	-2	0
	West	0	+2
Norway	East	-2	+1
	West	-1	+2
Sweden	East	-2	0
	West	-1	+1
Norden (Mean)	East	-1.6	+0.8
	West	-0.8	+1.4

Table 4
The Nordic Balance Static System and the Strategic Values for East and West

	Security Orientation	East Value	West Value
Iceland	NATO with base	0	4
Norway	NATO without base	1	3
Denmark	NATO without base	1	3
Sweden	Neutral	2	2
Finland	Neutral with treaty	3	1
Total Value		7	13

Key: 4=Most Valuable, 3=Valuable, 2=Some Value, 1=Little Value, 0=No Value

Table 4 shows that Norden was very Western in orientation during the Cold War. The Nordic Balance, then, was not simply a balance between East and West; it was a system of stability wherein the Nordic countries could safely retain their Western sociopolitical, cultural and economic orientations without fear of Soviet military reprisal or loss of sovereignty to the United States. They successfully fended off the superpowers.

Returning to the five levels of regional integration mentioned in Chapter 1—token integration; security community; limited functional cooperation; international economic integration; and direct political integration—which one best describes the regional integration system in Norden? This chapter has shown that the Nordic Balance could not have existed were it not for the Nordic Nexus. They were connected concepts: the Nordic Nexus was the base while the Nordic Balance provided the security element of the system. Norden was at least at the second level of regional integration; it was a security community. It also had characteristics of limited functional cooperation, and political and economic integration. The key was that these higher levels of integration were not formal or restrictive.

Chapter 3 will examine in greater detail the period from 1947 to 1961 in the Nordic region. The examination will implement a Nordic perspective to afford a clearer understanding of the regional dynamics and the substantive issues discussed regarding European integration. This period was chosen because it was the critical time after the war when increasing Cold War pressures forced the Nordic nations to cooperate in such a way as to achieve regional and economic security.

Specifically, Chapter 3 will examine Norwegian relations with the superpowers and with the rest of Norden within the context of Washington's evolving containment strategy and the corresponding development of a Nordic Balance (in which the regions participants, including Norway, tried to balance security through NATO ties and a careful low-voltage diplomacy toward the Soviet Union). With U.S. strategic policy as outlined in NSC 28/1 (1948) and NSC 6006/1 (1960) serving as the backdrop, the chapter describes Norway's long-term effort to juggle NATO commitments with regional links to neutral Sweden and Finland without alienating Moscow.

NOTES

1. Bo Stråth, "The Illusory Nordic Alternative to Europe," *Cooperation and Conflict* 15 (1980): 104; Barbara G. Haskel, *The Scandinavian Option: Opportunities and Opportunity Costs in Postwar Scandinavian Foreign Policies* (Oslo: Universtitetsforlaget, 1977), pp. 5-6, 10.

2. Inter-Nordic relations were both official and unofficial. Contacts were distinguished by frequency, regularity, scope, and density. Foreign ministers met twice a year; social affairs ministers, every other year. These meetings were at several levels: administrative, parliamentary, private organizations, and intergovernmental. Examples of administrative level contacts were fisheries and social policy committees; at the parliamentary level, the Nordic Council; and at the private organization level, the Social Democratic party. Coordination at all of these levels was extremely important. Foreningen Norden (Norden Association), established in 1919 and having 500 branches and members in five countries, was also important because it encouraged closer cooperation among the Nordic countries through comprehensive contacts. In general, Nordic cooperation was organized in three different ways: (1) measures to make Norden one unit in legal and social matters (customs, passports, and harmonization of laws); (2) development of common projects (e.g., the Scandinavian Airlines System or SAS); and (3) coordination and cooperation in external Nordic affairs (Nordic Balance). Haskel, *Scandinavian Option*, pp. 17-19.

3. Ibid., p. 23.

4. In this section the terms *Scandinavia, Scandinavianist*, and *Scandinavianism* will be used meaning the combined Norway, Sweden, and Denmark. These three countries make up the core of Norden because of their relative power and influence within the region. Due to this regional influence, looking at primarily the three core countries is justified for this study.

5. The Native Americans, of course, were the first people to inhabit the North American continent.

6. Johannes Brøndsted, *The Vikings* (New York: Penguin Books, 1975), pp. 9, 30-31.

7. That is to say, Sweden-Norway (since they were united until 1905), Finland, and Denmark.

8. Stein Tønnesson, "History and National Identity in Scandinavia: The Contemporary Debate," mimeographed manuscript, University of Oslo, 1991, p. 23; and Emanuel Halicz, "The Scandinavian Countries and the January Insurrection," in Béla K. Király, ed., *War and Society in East Central Europe: The Crucial Decade: East Central European Society and National Defense, 1859-1870*, vol. 14 (New York: Columbia University Press, 1984), p. 203.

9. Jahn Otto Johansen, *Sovjetunionen og Norden: Konfrontasjon eller naboskap?* (Oslo: J.W. Cappelens Forlag, 1986), pp. 14-15.

10. Ørjan Berner, *Soviet Policies toward the Nordic Countries* (New York: University Press of America, 1986), pp. 7-8.

11. This was often expressed by Soviet statesman Alexei Kosygin in the twentieth century. Johansen, *Sovjetunionen og Norden*, pp. 16, 23, 44.

12. T. K. Derry, *A History of Scandinavia* (Minneapolis: University of Minnesota Press, 1979), pp. 238-239.

13. Raymond E. Lindgren, *Norway-Sweden: Union, Disunion, and Scandinavian Integration* (Princeton, NJ: Princeton University Press, 1959), pp. 48-49.

14. Emanuel Halicz, *Russian Policy towards the Scandinavian Countries in 1856-1864* (Copenhagen, Denmark: Copenhagen University, 1985), pp. 68-72.

15. Halicz, *Russian Policy towards Scandinavian Countries*, pp. 72-73.

16. Ibid., p. 74.

17. Ibid., pp. 74-75.

18. Ibid., pp. 75-76.

19. Ibid., p. 76.

20. Lindgren, *Norway-Sweden*, pp. 49-50.

21. Derry, *History of Scandinavia*, pp. 249-250.

22. Haskel, *Scandinavian Option*, pp. 14-15.

23. Ibid., pp. 16-17.

24. From this type of political culture, the Social Democratic party evolved. In 1920 the average percentage of Social Democratic vote in Norden was 31 percent. By 1929 all of the Social Democratic parties in the Nordic region were firmly established, except in Iceland. And by the 1950s the percentage of the Social Democratic vote had risen to over 40 percent. Francis G. Castles, *The Social Democratic Image of Society: A Study of the Achievements and Origins of Scandinavian Social Democracy in Comparative Perspective* (Boston: Routledge & Kegan Paul, 1978), p. 6.

25. Steven Kelman, *Regulating America, Regulating Sweden* (Cambridge, MA: MIT Press, 1981), pp. 119-120, 232-233.

26. Three aspects of the development of Nordic labor movements were influential in determining their strength, unity, and integration: (1) the relative absence of impediments to working-class industrial and political organization; (2) the timing and social context of organizational growth;

and (3) the nature of the strategic choices made by the movements. The response by authorities in the Nordic region to labor organization and protest were quite mild in comparison to the rest of Europe. Although there was substantial unrest—1848-51 in Norway, 1871-77 in Denmark, and 1876 in Sweden—by the 1890s freedom of industrial and political organization was the general rule throughout Norden. Ibid., pp. 13-14.

27. Ibid., pp. 22-38.

28. This is a pattern that should be applicable to other regions as well.

29. Francis G. Castles, "Scandinavia: The Politics of Stability," in Roy C. Macridis, ed., *Modern Political Systems: Europe*, 5th ed. (Englewood Cliffs, NJ: Prentice-Hall, 1983), pp. 421-422.

30. Ibid., pp. 421-422; and Peter J. Katzenstein, *Small States in World Markets: Industrial Policy in Europe* (Ithaca, NY: Cornell University Press, 1985), pp. 97, 101.

31. Katzenstein, pp. 18, 20-24, 32, 39, 47, 57, 80.

32. Castles, "Scandinavia," p. 419; and Stanley V. Anderson, *The Nordic Council: A Study of Scandinavian Regionalism* (Seattle: University of Washington Press, 1967), p. 5.

33. Ernst Haas, "Turbulent Fields and the Theory of Regional Integration," *International Organization* 30 (Spring 1976): 183-210; James E. Dougherty and Robert L. Pfaltzgraff, eds., *Contending Theories of International Relations: A Comparative Survey*, 2nd ed. (New York: Harper & Row, 1981), p. 437; and Bernt Schiller, "At Gunpoint: A Critical Perspective on the Attempts of the Nordic Governments to Achieve Unity after the Second World War," *Scandinavian Journal of History* 9 (1984): 221-238.

34. Bengt Sundelius, ed., *Foreign Policies of Northern Europe* (Boulder, CO: Westview Press, 1982), pp. 182-187.

35. Consisting of at least three elements: political consensus; social democratic institutions; and Nordic cultural affinity.

36. Melvyn Leffler, "National Security," *Journal of American History* 77 (June 1990): 143-145.

37. Anderson, *Nordic Council*, pp. viii, 143, 147-148.

38. Olav Riste, "The Historical Determinants of Norwegian Foreign Policy," in Johan J. Holst, ed., *Norwegian Foreign Policy in the 1980s* (Oslo: Universitetsforlaget, 1985), p. 12.

39. Norway was united with Denmark from 1381 to 1814, and with Sweden from 1814 to 1905.

40. Riste, "Historical Determinants," pp. 12-13.

41. Helge Ø. Pharo, "Norge og Europeisk Integrasjon som Etterskrigshistorisk Forskningsfelt," mimeograph, University of Oslo, 1990, pp. 25-26.

42. Geir Lundestad, "Nasjonalisme og internasjonalisme i norsk utenrikspolitikk: Et faglig-provoserende essay," *Internasjonal Politikk*, no. 1 (1985): 39.

43. Norwegian security concerns over the Soviet Union in 1948 figured prominently in triggering British and American initiatives leading

to the negotiation of the North Atlantic Treaty and to the creation of NATO. See Wayne S. Cole, *Norway and the United States, 1905-1955: Two Democracies in Peace and War* (Ames: Iowa State University Press, 1989), p. 132.

44. Norway preferred a regional Nordic defense pact that was in line with NATO; Sweden preferred a pact that was neutral; and Denmark was torn between the two, but leaned toward the Norwegian position.

45. Gerard Aalders, "The Failure of the Scandinavian Defence Union, 1948-1949," *Scandinavian Journal of History*, 15, no. 2 (1990): 153.

46. Paul M. Cole and Douglas M. Hart, eds., *Northern Europe: Security Issues for the 1990s* (Boulder, CO: Westview Press, 1986), p. 18.

47. William J. Taylor, Jr., and Paul M. Cole, eds., *Nordic Defense: Comparative Decision Making* (Lexington, MA: D.C. Heath, 1985), pp. xix, 127-129, 150-152, 179-180.

48. "Northern European Chiefs of Mission Conference, London, 19-21 September 1957: Conclusions and Recommendations," in *Foreign Relations of the United States [hereafter FRUS 1955-1957*, vol. 4: *Western European Security and Integration* (Washington, DC: Government Printing Office, 1986), pp. 637-638.

49. Kristen Wahlbåck, *Den svenska neutralitetens røtter*, series no. 3 (Stockholm, Sweden: UD informerar, 1984), pp. 51-53. The pressure of maintaining a western orientation and neutrality was tremendous for the Swedes. See also Wilhelm Agrell, *Alliansfrihet och Atombomber* (Stockholm, Sweden: Liber Förlag, 1985); and Agrell, "Farväl till Svensk Neutralitet," in *EG/EU: Till Vilket Pris?* (Stockholm, Sweden: LTs Förlag, 1992), pp. 12-20.

50. A.J. McWhinnie, "Sweden's Fear is Spies," *London Daily Herald*, 11 September 1952.

51. Memo from the Norwegian Defense Ministry to the Foreign Ministry, 29 January 1954, H917/53/I.3.(310), p. 29, Forsvarsdepartement H-Arkiv kopibok no. 30, Norwegian National Archives, Oslo. Currently, the Swedish press is uncovering more evidence of Sweden's secret ties to the United States and NATO.

52. Telegram, Ambassador [H. Freeman] Matthews to the U.S. State Department, 6 March 1950, Foreign Service Posts of the Department of State, Record Group 84, Norway, Oslo Embassy, 1950-52, box 47, Washington National Records Center.

53. Taylor and Cole, *Nordic Defense*, pp. xix, 2, 11.

54. Ibid., pp. xiv-xv.

55. Appendix, "U.S. Overseas Military Bases," Report to the President (Nash Report), November 1957, Whitman File, Administration Series, Box 27, pp. 35-36, Eisenhower Library.

56. George F. Kennan praised the Finns (in his book *The Cloud of Danger*) for their composure and firmness in the face of Soviet pressure and objected to use of the term *Finlandization*. This was, however, a reversal of his prior position on Finland. There has been some post-Cold War evidence that indicates Kekkonen may have been taking money from the Soviet

Communist party. Although this would affect the historical reputation of Kekkonen, it does not change the fact that peace was maintained, and Finland remained sovereign. See Walter Laquer, "A Postscript on Finlandization," *Commentary* 95 (June 1993): 53; also see George F. Kennan, *The Cloud of Danger: Current Realities of American Foreign Policy* (New York: Little, Brown, 1977).

57. John Lukacs, "Finland Vindicated," *Foreign Affairs* 71 (Summer 1992): 50.

58. Lukacs, pp. 50, 56, 57.

59. Arne Olav Brundtland, "Nordiske aspekkter ved norsk sikkerhets politikk," in Johan J. Holst and Daniel Heradstveit, eds., *Norsk Utenrikspolitikk* (Oslo: TANO, 1985), pp. 119-120; Letter from Norwegian Embassy in Washington to the Foreign Ministry, 24 March 1949, no. 298, "State Departments syn på sovjetisk presskampanje mot Finland," in Folder 25.4/47, De Forente Stater Politikk, bind 17, 1 February 1949 to 31 December 1949, Royal Norwegian Foreign Ministry, Oslo.

60. The term has been credited to conservative West German politician Franz-Josef Strauss. Lukacs, "Finland Vindicated," p. 60.

61. Taylor and Cole, *Nordic Defense*, pp. 37-41; Patricia Bliss McFate, "To See Everything in Another Light," *Dædalus* 113 (1984): 31; and Johan J. Holst, "The Pattern of Nordic Security," Daedalus 113 (1984): 197. For an extensive discussion of Finlandization from a Finnish perspective, see Jussi Hanhimäki, "Containment, Coexistence and Neutrality: The Return of the Porkkala Naval Base as an Issue in Soviet-American Relations, 1955-1956," *Scandinavian Journal of History* , 18, no. 3 (1993): 217-228; and D.G. Kirby, *Finland in the Twentieth Century* (Minneapolis: University of Minnesota Press, 1979).

62. Taylor, and Cole, *Nordic Defense*, pp. 63-65.

63. Nash Report, pp. 73-74. Could this be a lesson drawn from Dean Acheson's ill-fated nonmention of Korea in reference to U.S. security—that supposedly invited Soviet pressure for a North Korean invasion? This, once again, provides evidence that Korea was the real turning point in Cold War U.S. policy in the High North, as well as general U.S. policy. On the darker side, Korea might have been used by the United States as a way to militarize and tighten control over NATO. It stands to reason, under that scenario, that Iceland and Denmark were pressured into signing basing agreements.

64. In one case, General Robert Pritchard, the commander of the Icelandic Defense Force, was removed in September 1959 not for dereliction of his duty, but because he was blamed for incidents by his forces and was caught up in local political crossfire and preelection hysteria. Memo for General [Andrew J.] Goodpaster from John A. Calhoun, Director, Executive Secretariat, "General Pritchard's Transfer from Iceland," 19 September 1959, White House Office, Office of the Staff Secretary: Records of Paul T. Carroll, Andrew J. Goodpaster, L. Arthur Minnich, and Christopher H. Russell, 1952-61, International Series, Box 7, Eisenhower Library.

65. NSC 5426, Operations Coordinating Board, Progress Report, 12 July 1954, pp. 2-3, White House Office, Office of Special Assistant for

National Security Affairs, NSC Series, Policy Papers Subseries, Box 12, Eisenhower Library.

66. C. Robert Dickerman, "Transgovernmental Challenge and Response in Scandinavia and North America," *International Organization* 30 (1976): 213-240.

67. Johan J. Holst, "Norway's Role in the Search for International Peace and Security" in Johan J. Holst, ed., *Norwegian Foreign Policy in the 1980s*, Norwegian Foreign Policy Studies No. 51 (Oslo: Universitetsforlaget, 1985), pp. 150-151; and Holst, "Pattern of Nordic Security," pp. 200-201.

68. Steve Lindberg, "The Illusory Nordic Balance: Threat Scenarios in Nordic Security Planning," *Cooperation and Conflict* 26 (1981): 57.

69. Use of the term in 1961 does not necessarily mean that the "Nordic Balance" did not exist before. Common use of terms to describe periods in history often come late or after the fact.

70. Erik Noreen, "The Nordic Balance: A Security Policy Concept in Theory and Practice," *Cooperation and Conflict* 28 (1983): 43-44.

71. Arne Olav Brundtland, "The Nordic Balance," *Cooperation and Conflict*, no. 2 (1966): 30; and Brundtland, "Nordisk Balanse før og nå," *Internasjonal Politikk* (1966): 491-541.

72. Although Brundtland did not include Iceland's NATO membership here, I do; Noreen, *Nordic Balance*, p. 44.

73. Ibid., p. 46.

74. Arne Olav Brundtland, "The Nordic Balance and Its Possible Relevance for Europe," in Daniel Frei, ed., *Sicherheit durch Gleichgewicht?* (Zurich, Switzerland: Schulthess Polygraphischer Verlag, 1982), pp. 119-120. This mainly applies to the Soviets. There seems to be some evidence that the United States accepted and understood the value of a Nordic Balance.

75. Haskel, *Scandinavian Option*, p. 24.

76. Brundtland, "Nordic Balance and Its Possible Relevance for Europe," p. 119.

77. Taylor and Cole, *Nordic Defense*, pp. viii-ix.

78. Ibid., p. xix.

79. Maurice A. East, "Size and Foreign Policy Behavior: A Test of Two Models," *World Politics* 25 (1973): 565-566; and Katzenstein, *Small States in World Markets*.

80. East, "Size and Foreign Policy Behavior," pp. 559-562.

81. In a study by Nikolaj Petersen he concluded that small states tend to be either super loyal, loyal, or moderately independent in relation to their great power partners. Norway, Denmark, and Iceland chose to be moderately independent. Petersen noted the four pillars of foreign policy success in Norden were its UN focus, NATO security guarantees, work toward European integration and cooperation, and Nordic cooperation. An example of this type of policy was the concept of "deterrence and reassurance." The alliance status of Norway and Denmark served both to deter and to reassure the Soviet Union because their membership in NATO was conditional (i.e., no U.S. bases allowed). Holst feels that Norway was pivotal in the Nordic

pattern of security due primarily to its deterrence and reassurance policy, which he calls "a major vehicle for management of the security system in Northern Europe." Holst, "Pattern of Nordic Security," pp. 200-201; Nikolaj Petersen, "The Alliance Policies of the Smaller NATO Countries," in Lawrence S. Kaplan and Robert W. Colawson, eds., *NATO after Thirty Years* (Wilmington, DE: Scholarly Resources, 1981), pp. 95, 105.

82. Pertti Joenniemi, *Nordic Security*, Current Research on Peace and Violence No. 1-2 (Tampere, Finland: Tampere Peace Research Institute, 1986).

83. Nils Andrén, "Prospects for the Nordic Security Pattern," *Cooperation and Conflict* 13 (1978): 181-192.

84. Kristen Wahlbäck, *Sverige, Norden och stormakterna*, series no. 4 (Stockholm, Sweden: Kungele Krigsvetenskapsakademiens Handlingar och Tidskrift, 1978), p. 218.

85. Arne Olav Brundtland, "The Context of Security in Northern Europe," in Cole and Hart, *Northern Europe*, p. 17; Arne Olav Brundtland, "Nordisk Balanse på Nytt," *Internasjonal Politikk* (July-September 1976): 599-639; Richard A. Bitzinger, *Denmark, Norway, and NATO: Constraints and Challenges*, Rand Note N-3001-RC (Santa Monica, CA: Rand Corporation, 1989), p. 18; and Daniel D. Devlin, "Soviet-Norwegian Relations. Norwegian Reactions to Soviet Pressures," M.A. thesis, Naval Postgraduate School, 1979, p. 17.

86. Robert Dalsjø, "Tungt vågande kritik? En granskning av kritik mot teorin om Nordisk Balans," *Militærhistorisk Tidskrift* (Svensk 1987): 136.

87. Joenniemi, *Nordic Security*, p. 7.

88. Arne Olav Brundtland, "Den klassiske, de omsnudde og den fremtidige Nordiske Balanse," in Ole Nørrgaard and Per Carlsen, eds., *Sovjetunionen, Østeuropa og dansk sikkerhedspolitik* (Esbjerg, Denmark: Sydjysk Universitetsforlag, 1981), pp. 83-85.

89. Iver B. Neumann, "Russlands regionale rolle i Nord-Europa," *Internasjonal Politikk* 50 (1992): 123-136.

90. Conference Memo, Prime Minister's Office, "Det nordiske råd," 10 March 1952, Statsministerens kontor, referat fra regjeringskonferanser, 1947-61, Norwegian National Archives, Oslo.

91. Speech by Prime Minister Esko Aho, 4 May 1992, "Finlands säkerhet och närområdena: En granskning av förändringarna," transcript provided by Finnish Embassy in Oslo, Norway.

92. These concepts are not universally accepted. Some Nordic scholars feel that Norway and other Nordic countries were pawns of the United States. I will deal with Norway's base policy in the next chapter wherein this controversy will be explored further. For more on integration and screening see Rolf Tamnes, *The United States and the Cold War in the High North* (Brookfield, VT: Dartmouth Publishing, 1991). And for more on deterrence and reassurance see Johan J. Holst, "Norsk sikkerhetspolitikk i strategisk perspektive," *Internasjonal Politikk*, no. 5 (1966); and Knut E. Eriksen and Helge Ø. Pharo, *Norsk Sikkerhetspolitikk som*

Etterkrigshistorisk Forskningsfelt, LOS-senter notat 92/13 Bergen, Norway: LOS-senter, 1992, p. 35. Norwegian historian Geir Lundestad has written about "integration" and "defense" in relation to Norway's alliance with the West. He refers to integration with the West and defense against common Western enemies. He also wrote of "screening" and "conciliation," referring to screening of U.S. influence, and to conciliation in terms of opening a line of communication with the Soviets. Geir Lundestad, "The Evolution of Norwegian Security Policy: Alliance with the West and Reassurance in the East," *Scandinavian Journal of History* 17, no. 3 (1992): 227-228.

93. The numbers chosen for Figure 7 are for comparative purposes in this example and do not equate to any other known scale.

3

Norway, the Superpowers, and Norden, 1947-1961

They treat us like a vassal state.

—Einar Gerhardsen, 1960
(on U.S. treatment of Norway after the U-2 and RB-47 incidents)

This chapter looks at Norway and its relations with the United States, the Soviet Union, and the rest of Norden from 1947 to 1961. This Norwegian perspective will be combined with an examination of U.S. policy toward Norden. This is justified because of the United States' hegemonic status and influence in Norway and the rest of Norden. Norway was the linchpin for both U.S. and Soviet security interests in Norden in the 1950s. Moscow's awareness of Norway's strategic importance was an outgrowth of World War II, when Germany used the protected harbors on the Norwegian coast to operate U-boats and interdict allied shipping to Murmansk. After the war, the Soviets took a slice of northern Finland that left them with a 110-mile border with Norway. This bleak territory, Norwegians say, was land that God forgot but strategists remembered.[1] Norway's strategic position on the perimeter of Russia forced the Soviet government to keep a close watch on Norwegian foreign policy. After World War II, Soviet-Norwegian relations centered around three main issues: the status of Spitsbergen (Svalbard); Norway's participation in NATO; and overflight of Soviet territory by the Western allied powers.[2]

Figure 8
Norden

In examining the strategic calculus of the Nordic region (as shown in Figure 8) during the Cold War, it is important to understand the polar dimension. U.S. visions of a polar strategy began late in World War II when Americans discovered that the Soviets were constructing strategic bases for their Tu-4 bombers (copies of the American B-29) in the northern theater. There were also indications that they were preparing to build similar bases on the Svalbard archipelago. The United States used Great Britain as its stepping-stone in strategic planning, with the Nordic region lying directly in line to the strategic heart of the Soviet Union—the shortest flight path being the Arctic route. This was before the United States had nuclear missile capability, so the Strategic Air Command (SAC) and its contingent of bombers comprised the extent of U.S. atomic strategy.[3] Since these plans involved overflight of Scandinavia, the United States wanted to station fighter-escort bases in Norway to guide the bombers from England. This would entail peacetime stationing of permanent U.S. military personnel in Norway. These plans were not successful, partially due to the extremely adverse public reaction in Norway once they were made known.[4] Being a fiercely independent people, Norwegians were adamant about not having foreign troops stationed on their soil.

Strategically, Scandinavia lay on the outer edge of the five strongpoints envisaged by U.S. containment strategist George F. Kennan.[5] Early in the Cold War, Norway presented itself to the United States as a nonaligned small state in the High North that was critical of American society in general (foreign policy in particular) and reluctant to choose sides. In fact, in a 1946 poll from a group of Atlantic states, Norway proved to be the most anti-American.[6] Nonetheless, Norway and the United States were intimately involved in Cold War security planning, each realizing the necessity of cooperation.

Cooperation on the international front became a standard platform for Norwegian politicians. However, the Norwegians were balancing between a strong need to get involved internationally on the one hand, and equally strong feelings of skepticism toward concrete international obligations on the other.[7] Immediately after the war, finding itself caught between the Soviet Union and the West, the Norwegian government decided on a "bridgebuilding" policy. Later, it opted for NATO only after a formal Nordic security organization failed. However, the United States soon learned that the Norwegians wanted to retain their unique brand of diplomacy vis-à-vis the Soviets. They decided to uphold a no-foreign-bases policy, largely in order to satisfy fears of a Soviet reaction, but also because of overwhelming public opinion against foreign incursion. Foreign Minister Halvard Lange explained to U.S. officials that it would be impossible to allow foreign troops on Norwegian soil in peacetime.

Postwar Norwegian foreign policy changed from earlier times. Most basically, foreign policy played a more central role in Norwegian politics after 1945—a common feature for most nations in the postwar world. Norwegian perspectives on the Cold War have had two different points of departure: Norway's decision to turn to the West in 1945; and the struggle in 1948-49 over participation in the Atlantic alliance. Historians have generally claimed either 1945 or 1949 to be the true turning point for Norwegian foreign policy from neutrality to alliance. Those who argue for 1945 claim that the Norwegians were already firmly in the Western camp despite the official policy of bridgebuilding between East and West; this supports what could be called a "continuity thesis."[8]   The others claim that the decision to join NATO in 1949 constituted a sharp break in policy. The key to this debate is whether one believes bridgebuilding to be a holding action until an alliance could be struck, either a Scandinavian Defense Union (SDU) or NATO, or a sincere effort at mediating between East and West.[9]

Norway strengthened its relationship to the international community since politics, economics, and power relations affected Norway to a great extent in the postwar period. The Norwegian Parliament began dealing with foreign policy questions more, as did the political parties and special interest groups. However, not all citizens in Norway had adequate knowledge of foreign policy and the international system, despite increasing interest in such matters.[10]   Norway had a strong tradition of being either half-in or half-out of international politics. Norway was a country that wanted to enjoy the benefits of membership in organizations, but only on its own terms. Norway wanted to be involved and influential in foreign affairs but did not want to be in turn influenced.[11]   Consequently, it was not accommodating in all cases. Even though the overall effect of Nordic security cooperation was that of accommodation, each of the five Nordic nations played a different role in achieving that effect.

Norway's principal statesmen during the 1950s shaped policy in decisive ways. Oscar Torp of the Norwegian social democratic party— the Labor Party—was prime minister from 1951 to 1955, and the foreign minster was Halvard M. Lange. After Torp resigned in 1955, Einar Gerhardsen returned to his prior position as prime minister (he was previously prime minister from 1945 to 1951) and served as the head of the Social Democratic party until 1965. These tough-minded politicians personified the generation that was hardened by World War II. They had resisted Nazi domination and paid with terms in German camps. They understood the inadequacies of Norway's traditional neutrality policy and noninvolvement. They realized the importance of forming security bonds with like-minded allies.[12]

As for U.S. policy and how it affected Norway, U.S. foreign policy planners tended to divide Norden into Scandinavia on the one hand and Iceland and Finland on the other. Separate policies emerged, but this division was very often strained. The basic Cold War security policy of the United States in Norden from 1947 to 1961 was contained in NSC 28/1 (September 1948), followed by NSC 121 (January 1952). This basic policy was not changed until NSC 6006 (April 1960), which was later released with amendments as NSC 6006/1.   In general, U.S. objectives were to keep the countries of Norden strong and friendly through supporting the preservation of their independence and encouraging their will and capacity to resist communism.[13] That which follows covers Norway's diplomatic history from 1947 to 1961 and its attempts to balance Norwegian and Nordic objectives with those of the United States and the Soviet Union.

THE EARLY COLD WAR, 1947-1949

In 1947 all of Europe was in a serious economic crisis. Norway's decision to participate in the Marshall Plan—whether one calls it a turning point or not—indicated a clear Western affiliation, a move away from bridgebuilding, and had the effect of extending U.S. containment to Scandinavia. Foreign policy concerns were the primary determinant in Norway's decision to accept Marshall Plan aid.[14] Additionally, Norwegian attitudes toward the Soviets became more negative in 1947 and 1948. The Norwegian government was mindful that, if it refused Marshall Plan help, it would be indicating a stand for the Soviets in the intensifying Cold War. And also, Norway desperately needed the economic help.[15]

In a 1948 report, the Norwegian Labor party laid out its postwar goals, reconstruction being number one. Yet, this reconstruction could not take place if security were threatened. Security and reconstruction were interrelated; foreign and economic policy concerns were inseparable in this sense. Party leaders realized that only a strong Norway could maintain its freedom. The Marshall Plan was one way of building up this strength. The Labor party thought that Norway could be reconstructed with Marshall Plan aid without having political strings attached to the United States.[16] At first, however, the Norwegian government was hesitant to take part, because of its bridgebuilding policy. It was afraid to get too heavily involved in the East-West conflict. Despite this official reluctance, 85 percent of Norwegians approved of the Marshall Plan initially. But by the end of the Marshall Plan in 1952, a Gallup poll taken in Norway on domestic and international issues showed that only 58 percent favored the Marshall Plan, 13 percent opposed it, and 29 percent had no opinion.[17] There was always concern that close economic cooperation with the United States would imperil Norway's preference for a planned socialist economy. The Korean War removed some of this reluctance and changed Norway's views toward U.S. help.[18]

This brings up the question of whether or not U.S. expansion into Western Europe was invited or imposed. The invitation theory holds that the Americans—unlike the Soviets, who imposed their will by force on Eastern Europe—could rely on an arsenal of diverse instruments of persuasion in dealing with the Western Europeans. Furthermore, the United States was invited to take part economically and militarily in the rebuilding of Western Europe. This invitation was carefully balanced so as not to agitate the Soviets severely. The invitation was extended, but with the expectation that no strings would be attached.[19]

Kennan was especially annoyed that the Norwegians and the other Scandinavians were so critical of U.S. policy and so "pathologically timid" in facing the Soviet threat. In a 1947 letter from the Norwegian Embassy in Washington, Ambassador Wilhelm Morgenstierne wrote about Kennan's influence on U.S. policy and how it affected Norway. This letter reported Kennan's disgust with reports that Europeans were distrustful of U.S. intentions with Marshall Plan aid. In response to those in Europe who feared that the United States wanted its European allies to be totally capitalistic, Kennan wanted it to be known that the U.S. economic system—although the best choice—would not be forced on any nation.[20]

During a conversation between U.S. diplomat W. Averell Harriman and Morgenstierne, Harriman praised Norway's role in the Marshall Plan, finding Norway to be a friendly and stable ally. However, consensus on Eastern Europe had proven more problematic in U.S. relations with the Western European nations—too much elasticity, according to Harriman.[21] Norway, like other Western European nations, had contacts with Eastern Europe, especially the Baltic states. The United States came to see this relationship as dangerous, given the position of these states behind the Iron Curtain. This was important because selling the Marshall Plan and good U.S. intentions to some reluctant Europeans was one thing; getting the expensive plan through Congress was another. To do this, the Truman administration was interested in promoting Scandinavian economic cooperation.[22] But the Marshall Plan decision for Norway, overall, must be looked upon as a clear move toward the West and away from bridgebuilding.[23]

With respect to the Soviet Union as a threat, Norwegians did not fear an all-out invasion, but they believed the Soviets would exert influence toward achieving a nonaligned Scandinavia. In the summer of 1947 Norway had to reconcile its reemphasized policy of nonalignment with participation in the Marshall Plan. It was naturally cautious. The Western initiative also served to bond the Nordic countries together. They settled long-standing disputes (e.g., over Greenland), set up permanent cultural commissions, and practiced some limited military cooperation. They also developed a joint Nordic bloc in the United Nations. Norway wanted the United Nations to be involved with the

Marshall Plan so as to dampen the plan's political impact on Eastern Europe and the Soviet Union. Norwegian Foreign Minister Halvard Lange met with Czech leader Jan Masaryk in this regard.[24]

Press reactions followed predictable lines. The Norwegian communist newspaper *Friheten* described the Marshall Plan as an attempt to turn Europe into a remote control area backed by U.S. dollars, where U.S. interests would always come first.[25] Much of the press was quick to jump to the conclusion that the United States was demanding bases in exchange for Marshall Plan help, but transcripts do not show even a clear inference to such an exchange. In fact, in a 1948 letter sent from the Norwegian Embassy in Washington, the ambassador reported that the United States had praised socialism's role in combating communism. According to this letter, Americans thought that the socialist societies in Norden believed in basic freedoms and democracy and would serve as a bulwark to communism.[26] This was unusual since most early Cold War documents pointed to a U.S. dislike of socialist tendencies.

Realizing that critical domestic issues often depend on foreign policy, Norway and the rest of Norden knew—as did many other countries—that economic rebuilding could not occur without security. However, given the limited resources available immediately after the war, security seemed economically out of reach. As a result, the Nordic countries attempted to integrate their security policies in order to ensure their region's economic development. This would prove to be a difficult undertaking, and one that could not ignore the influence of the United States.

From the U.S. perspective during this period, NSC 28/1 on Norden policy drew four specific objectives regarding U.S. interests in Scandinavia: (1) Norway, Denmark, and Sweden should be kept free from Soviet domination; (2) Norway and Denmark should be convinced to align with the Western powers; (3) Sweden should be convinced to abandon neutrality and choose Western alignment; and (4) U.S. base rights would have to be extended in Greenland and explored in Spitsbergen.[27] The most important aspect of NSC 28/1 was its conclusion, which stressed that the United States should consider increasing the security of the Scandinavian countries through their integration into, or association with, the Brussels Treaty System.[28] The United States was willing to accept a looser arrangement in terms of Scandinavian membership in order to include Sweden in the association.[29] This fit in with Norway's desire to have a Nordic security system with U.S. guarantees.

The consensus of the National Security Council was that having the Nordic region outside of the Western sphere of influence would be a loss to the United States.   A zone of neutrality was a zone of uncertainty.   Washington found Sweden's neutral position as particularly disturbing: Finland had no choice but to be neutral, but Sweden had a choice.[30] The U.S. State Department saw Scandinavian foreign policies as being tied together.   Norway's influence over Denmark and Iceland was considered most vital to the United States. The debate in the State Department centered on the nature of Nordic membership in a security alliance.[31]

Having accepted Marshall Plan aid and set on the road to economic recovery, in 1947-48 the Nordic countries decided they needed a reserve position regarding the East-West conflict.   The international situation moved Norway further toward the West, and at the same time the Swedes came upon the idea of a Scandinavian Defense Union (SDU). Even though it was obvious from the start that such a union would depend at least indirectly on the West for security (since critical weapons systems would have to come from the West), Sweden did not want this connection formalized.[32]   Because of this reluctance on Sweden's part to have any formal connection to the West, Norway had to choose between a Nordic or Atlantic alliance. It preferred a Nordic alliance with Atlantic ties. In regard to Sweden, U.S. Secretary of State George C. Marshall said that

Sweden has followed stubbornly a policy of neutrality which since the end of the war has been of more benefit to the Soviet Union than to the Western countries. Sweden is now trying to win Norway and Denmark to this policy, which is more likely to weaken the ability of all Scandinavian nations to resist aggressive Soviet expansion than to enable them to withstand it.[33]

NSC 28/1 outlined early U.S. Cold War policy toward Norden in general and, in paragraph 10b of that document, Sweden in particular

The US should endeavor by all appropriate measures to make perfectly clear to Sweden our dissatisfaction with its apparent failure to discriminate in its own mind and in its future planning between the west and the Soviet Union; to influence Sweden to abandon this attitude of subjective neutrality and look toward eventual alignment with other west powers in such form as may be found collectively acceptable; and at the same time to refrain from forcing Sweden into an attitude which would have been unnecessarily provocative toward the Soviet Union.[34]

U.S. Secretary of State Dean Acheson qualified this assessment somewhat when he said that he would "be favorably disposed" if Sweden were to join NATO as long as other members agreed and there was wide support in Sweden to do so. But Acheson was quick to add that the United States would not seek such application,[35] since he recognized a lack of popular support in Sweden to seek NATO membership, a U.S. inability to meet probable Swedish demands for concrete steps to ensure its security, and the possibility of a more aggressive Soviet policy toward Finland. He noted that this existing policy might be changed as necessary, such as if the Soviets moved against Finland. Yet, in line with NSC 28/1, Acheson remarked that "we do, however, continue to desire that Swed[en] move away from her attitude of neutrality."[36] Timing was important, and he did not want to force a Swedish decision.

In a 1948 prime minister's meeting, Sweden's officials decided that it was easier to safeguard sovereignty and freedom through cooperation with other countries or through the United Nations. Norway had to cooperate economically, politically and militarily with Denmark and Sweden, but this alone was not enough to ensure security.[37] Feeling unsettled, in late 1948 Norway wanted to secure U.S. power to protect Norway's freedom. It wanted a defensive alliance with the West so as to avoid the fate of Finland.[38]

The difference between the Norwegian and Swedish outlooks doomed the SDU, and Lange did not wish to conflict with British or American interests.[39] A neutral pact may not have been possible with pro-Western leaders like Lange, Jens Christian Hauge, Haakon Lie, and Oscar Torp. There was also flexibility on the U.S. side to fit a Nordic pact into NATO. Still, there was British and U.S. resistance to a freestanding Nordic alliance. A Nordic region outside of the superpower influence could, in the Americans' opinion, be a victory for the East and an irritant for the West. As an alternative, American officials suggested a concept of integrated cooperation (with NATO). Since Swedish resources were not enough to afford Denmark and Norway with security, the United States had to make it look as if Norden could receive U.S. help without political strings attached. U.S. officials knew it would be politically awkward to give weapons to neutrals and also to members of NATO (e.g., the Benelux countries of Belgium, the Netherlands, and Luxembourg). The Americans also felt that material given to neutrals could end up on the wrong side of a conflict.[40] Therefore, the Truman administration was willing to accept limited membership in NATO, but not neutrality.

When Norway was arguing with Sweden over the SDU, Norway began to receive less emphasis by U.S. military planners because they thought Denmark would be overrun easily by the Soviets in a war, effectively neutralizing Norway and Sweden. After the Czech coup, Finland's agreement with the Soviets, and a similar Soviet offer to Norway (all in 1948), Norway began a series of invitations to get more

U.S. defense aid through closer cooperation within the Western security system.[41] Despite its fear of continental European economic domination, Norway tried to tie together European and North Atlantic interests; but this really amounted to nothing more than wishful thinking. Sweden would not go along with such a tie-in, because of NATO.[42]

Efforts at an SDU ultimately failed in 1948. One reason was that the Truman administration did not believe a Scandinavian pact without Western attachment could be part of the Western defense. Neutrality was a dangerous concept to the U.S. government. Another reason for the SDU failure was due to problems in Norwegian-Swedish relations. Trygve Lie, the former UN general secretary, noted that the failure showed how difficult it was to work out joint programs of foreign and defense policy even in relatively homogeneous and limited areas.[43] Despite this, the papers in Oslo ran editorials about possibly resurrecting the idea of a Scandinavian alliance. The conservative paper *Aftenposten* asked, "A little more than a year ago Sweden was willing to form a Scandinavian defense union. Should it be necessary to abandon this line completely because Norway and Denmark through the Atlantic pact [i.e., NATO] have improved their political and military positions?" The Swedish Conservative party suggested that perhaps there could be Scandinavian defense cooperation in addition to the Atlantic pact

None of the Scandinavian peoples can be indifferent to the destiny of the others. We shall live together and die together. No dissatisfaction with the negotiations which did not lead to any results, or with the differences which were not ironed out, can in the long run prevent the understanding of our common destiny breaking through and finding expressions of the cooperation which is necessary to defend our freedom and peace.[44]

In addition to Nordic security cooperation, there was also the question of general European integration. How did the Norwegians envision a tie-in of the European and North Atlantic communities? Instead of joining any kind of European integration effort, Halvard Lange favored a "Scandinavian regionalism in the direction of a North Sea and a North Atlantic community working . . . closely with Great Britain and with the United States." This represented a functional rather than federal approach to integration. It is important to note that, from a Norwegian perspective, postwar North Atlantic defense cooperation was directed against the possibility of a renewed German (not Soviet) threat against Norwegian security, and toward taking Norway out of its traditional isolationism. The Soviet Union's reemergence as a major factor in Norwegian security arrangements actually contributed to the gradual eclipse of the Atlantic concept. Norway came to the rather uncomfortable realization that it lay directly between two competing superpowers.[45]

From 1946 through 1948, Norwegians thought that their bridgebuilding policy between East and West would tone down superpower tensions. With the Czechoslovakian coup in 1948 and the subsequent fate of the Czechs (who also were bridgebuilders), Norway's hopes of such neutrality faded. The Czech coup had a tremendous impact on Norway and its decision to seek guarantees from the West. Gerhardsen was well acquainted with Masaryk, the Czech leader, and was terribly devastated by his death. The Norwegians felt that their view of the Soviets had been too kind. Due to the United Nations' failure to create a collective security system, Norwegians had to take a realist view that put them in the Western camp.[46]

The SDU having failed, Norway opted for the North Atlantic Treaty in 1949, which was of great psychological value to the Norwegians. Both the United States and Norway were satisfied with the arrangement: the Americans liked it because Norway again chose the West, and the Norwegians liked it because it provided reassurance without the actual presence of U.S. troops.[47] Membership in NATO became the dominating feature of Norwegian foreign policy during the next decade. However, the United States and Norway may have perceived the role of NATO differently. These different perceptions were evident in the words of NATO Commander General Lauris Norstad and Norwegian Defense Minister Halvard Lange. In an oral interview, Norstad discussed the importance of NATO to the United States.

One thing that no scholar has picked up yet, in due time will, or I will for them when I write my book, that the great contribution of NATO was to define the nature and the extent of our interests in Europe and what we would do. And also it defined what the Soviets could do with impunity and what they couldn't do. And since wars more frequently start by mistake than any other way, this is terribly important. This is the great contribution that NATO has made. And during the confrontations and crises we sat on them pretty coolly, but we strongly and clearly indicated what we would do and what we could do under certain circumstances.[48]

Lange justified Norway's turn to NATO in 1949 by noting the differences between the Soviet Union and the great democratic powers. He noted that, through the Security Council in the United Nations, the unanimity rule made it possible to prevent the council from exerting force against a great power. For this reason, the Norwegians saw it necessary to fall back on regional agreements for collective defense. The North Atlantic Treaty was established to attain a rebalance after the

Soviet Union had tightened its grip on Eastern Europe. The result was a balance of power that gave both superpowers a sense of security. Cooperation within NATO was in accord with Norway's UN membership since Article 52 of the UN Charter provides the right to individual and collective self-defense for member states. It was this point that the Norwegians stressed to the Soviets when the latter accused Norway of upsetting the peace in Norden by joining NATO.[49]

Lange expressed his preference for the Atlantic option—as opposed to the continental European option—for geographic, economic, and security reasons. Location and communications favored the Atlantic connection, as well. Norway was economically oriented more toward the North Atlantic and world markets than toward those of continental Europe, and the country's security was almost wholly dependent on Great Britain and the United States. There was also animosity between France and Norway. (In fact, France did not want Norway to be a member of NATO.) Most importantly, Norwegians preferred functional and loosely oriented cooperation rather than supranational or federalist arrangements.[50] Prime Minister Einar Gerhardsen said in the 1949 Labor Party Congress that Norway needed Western security and material and had to choose a North Atlantic regional defense option. He supported this decision by saying that neutrality did not help Norway when faced with Hitler's invading armies. In addition, the Soviet moves in Czechoslovakia and Finland pointed Norway toward seeking effective help from Great Britain and the United States. One representative to Parliament—speaking in opposition—asked just how much security was enough. Half of the U.S. bomber force? What if the Soviet Union were to turn Finland into a base—what would happen to Norway then?[51] These questions were generally reflective of the concerns many Norwegians had at the time.

Labor party leader Haakon Lie, at the same 1949 congress, said that the United States saved Europe in 1917 and again in 1942. The North Atlantic Treaty would allow Norway to be equal partners with the other members, including the United States. Additionally, the North Atlantic Treaty would allow no vetoes, it would be part of the UN philosophy, and there would be no question of bases in Norway. However, there were those at the Congress who—representing the concerns of many Norwegians—asked whether NATO would tie Norway to pacts elsewhere, dragging Norway into a distant war.[52]

Also at the Labor Party Congress in 1949 it was decided that the United Nations alone did not provide adequate security for Norway. Halvard Lange said that NATO membership was the most important decision in Norwegian politics since 1905. He continued by pointing out that peace was necessary for a small country like Norway because it could not risk war. Peaceful thinking was strongly embued in socialism, with the number one priority being peace without conditions. The war taught Norwegians that they must actively take part in international affairs. For a while, Norway tried to stand between the two superpowers; but with the Soviet propaganda war in the United Nations, and the events in Eastern Europe (especially the fate of Masaryk and the budding Czech democracy), Norway was shown the true Soviet opinion of its bridgebuilding policy. Lange felt that UN efforts in East-West relations were at a standstill and that the main objective of the United Nations—peace—would not come to fruition until relations between the East and West had been harmonized.[53]

At the same party congress, Trygve Lie—who was serving as UN general secretary—said that, by building a regional basis for peace and security, an international basis could eventually be constructed. He outlined three fundamentals for Norwegian policy: first, never engage in aggressive politics; second, follow a Norwegian agenda and not that of the superpowers; and third, maintain a close fellowship with the United Nations. Lie felt it was natural for Norway to seek Scandinavian solutions to security problems (cooperation tied to the West) after the war. Norway wanted a freestanding Nordic union backed by realistic Western support; but Sweden was afraid to break from its traditional neutrality, thereby dooming a Nordic security organization.[54]

NATO started as a traditional military alliance but became a strong bloc under the leadership of the United States (especially after the Korean War). Twenty-five percent of Norway's defense structure was supplied by NATO nations. Tremendous NATO expenditures in Norway were justified because Norway was considered the heart of the Northern Flank of NATO. The United States realized the importance of Norway for strategic reasons; its merchant marine; its influence over Denmark's and Iceland's foreign policy; and its democratic traditions. Yet, in the larger view, Norway was still a peripheral state to the United States. From Norway's perspective, however, the United States was its most important ally.[55]

Norway distanced itself from other NATO nations on matters involving nuclear weapons and colonial politics. Norway criticized the United States in the 1950s for its inability to understand European problems and its pressure to militarize NATO further. Americans were frustrated by such criticism, especially since Norwegians continued to take U.S. supplies and aid. Also, despite its intimate security arrangements with the United States, Norway modeled itself after Great Britain in terms of domestic policies.[56]

After joining NATO, the Norwegians began to realize the impact of their membership. Finn Moe, the editor of the Labor party paper

Arbeiderbladet and chairman of the Storting (Norwegian Parliament) foreign relations committee, commented,

Although the work for integration of the NAT [North Atlantic Treaty] defense system has made great progress, many difficulties are still to be overcome. In the first place the expenses to the armed forces represent a heavy burden on the budgets of the individual countries. Secondly, it is a question how the necessary military forces should be recruited. Churchill's proposal to include German forces in the defense of Western Europe must be seen in this connection.[57]

Moe thought that NATO would bring lasting economic cooperation between the United States and Europe.

In the NATO of the 1950s there was little room for opinions other than those of the United States, Great Britain, and France. What little influence Norway and the other Nordic countries did have was restricted to matters concerning their own region. The West knew of the historic Soviet interest in the Nordic area; so, shielding these small states became a more significant issue in the 1950s.[58] The Norwegian government was also concerned about Soviet reactions regarding Norden when Norway joined NATO. It feared—as did U.S. officials—that the Soviets would want more influence in Finland.[59] Accordingly, Norway made the decision to join NATO in 1949, but did not buy into the alliance totally. Through a process of "integration and screening" toward the West, and "deterrence and reassurance" toward the East, Norway stabilized its position in Norden, between the superpowers, and on the international stage. These policies worked by defining limits of Norway's policy that appeared to remain generally Western in orientation but neutral in spirit. The objective of this policy was to enable Norway to remain outside of the conflict, retain its political maneuverability, and dedicate its resources to economic development.[60]

The Norwegian view of the United States helped to shape its foreign policy. Norwegian officials felt that Harry S Truman had some success with foreign policy but could not build a coalition on domestic issues. They tended to blame Truman for his own failures due to his inflexible all-or-nothing approach. They were worried that Truman's weakness on the domestic front and the corresponding strength of the political right could undermine pro-European foreign policy programs.[61] They also agreed with *New York Times* columnist James Reston when he said in 1949 that the United States was beginning to use a harder line and rougher talk with the Soviets—a tactic that Norwegians felt the Eastern Bloc was more proficient in using.[62]

The Norwegian government noted a chilling of the Cold War with statements made in 1949 by U.S. Secretary of State Dean Acheson.

Acheson believed that the Soviets were on the defensive because of their failure in the Berlin Blockade. He said that there was no standing still in Europe: the North Atlantic Treaty, military help programs, and the Marshall Plan were absolutely necessary. Norwegians perceived the United States as seeing no end to Soviet pressure in Europe. But Norwegians were also worried about the American ability to bear the economic burden of all three of these programs and still not sacrifice social reform at home.[63]

In keeping with its watchdog role, the Norwegian government was also concerned about how the United States was perceived in other Nordic countries. For instance, in 1949 a negative Swedish press reaction to U.S. Information Agency efforts at condemning Soviet propaganda in Europe and praising U.S. policy, the Truman Doctrine, and Marshall Plan help was a matter of some consternation to the Norwegian government.[64] This concern for the Norwegian image was not limited to within Norden as the new decade began. Norway found itself even more involved in world affairs as it defined its role within NATO, Norden, and the rest of the international system.

INTENSIFICATION OF THE COLD WAR, 1950-1952

With the internationalization of Norwegian politics in the 1950s, it became increasingly more difficult for the Norwegian government to coordinate foreign and domestic policies. This was due to Norway's complex interweaving of foreign policy through its four basic orientations; Atlantic, West European, Nordic, and global.

From Norway's Atlantic and Western European perspectives, this period was dominated by the threat posed by the Soviet Union and international communism—this perspective being heavily influenced by the United States from 1949 to 1955. The Korean War brought the East-West conflict to a head and focused it on Asia. Both blocs concentrated more heavily on military buildup. The United States was militarily, politically, and economically engaged in Asia—what with the Korean War, assistance to France in Indochina, the rebuilding of Japan, and the establishment of new alliances and agreements (e.g., Southeast Asia Treaty Organization, or SEATO). Containment doctrine reigned in Europe as military supplies were pouring in and American troops canvassed West Germany.[65] Norway's Nordic orientation placed emphasis on economic rebuilding and the integration of Norden. Security policy integration at a formal level failed, but renewed efforts continued through less formal methods. Globally, Norway was relying more and more on international organizations.

With the Korean War, the "loss of China," and the replacement of George Kennan with Paul Nitze as the director of the U.S. policy planning staff, a new form of containment emerged: military containment. NSC 68 embodied military containment and directed U.S. policy in general—thus affecting policy in Norden, although not to the same extent as elsewhere in the world. Early containment policy in Norden was not directed primarily against a military threat from the Soviet Union, but against the threat of Western communists who, in collaboration with the Kremlin, were said to be promoting revolution by exploiting economic, social, and political turmoil.[66]

After the start of the Korean War, Prime Minister Gerhardsen commented on the Soviet Union, "In order to get on speaking terms with dictatorships and in view [of the] current situation it is necessary for democracies to augment their military preparedness. The pace of developing their security system has been increased and it will now be ready two years ahead of time." The fight against communism was like the fight against Hitler in World War II, necessitating a stand together against a common enemy.[67] For Norwegians the 1950s were an era of McCarthyist extremism in the West and Stalinist extremism in the East. It was a time of polarization—East versus West bloc politics.[68]

Security policy issues that emerged during the NATO decision brought a great division within the Labor party. Communists and the left wing of the Labor party opposed NATO membership.[69] While Senator Joseph McCarthy (R-Wisconsin) led his anticommunist reign of terror in the United States, Norwegians concentrated on suspicions of governing political parties. The concepts of manipulation, conspiracy, and cooperation between elites are similar to those found in the United States during this era. However, whereas American extremists of the McCarthy genre were concerned with communist infiltration, the Norwegian extremists were concerned with radical right-wing infiltration.[70]

Arne Ording, the chief of the Norwegian Foreign Ministry's press office, wrote in his diary that the Korean War was not mainly a strategic move for the United States, but one of prestige. Also, Ording was concerned that Truman's reported plan to use the atomic bomb in Korea was inappropriate and ill conceived because, first, threats must occasionally be carried out or otherwise they lose their effectiveness; second, if military use of the bomb proved ineffective, then the United States had played its last card; and third, its use would cause a great loss of international prestige for the United States so soon after the Hiroshima and Nagasaki bombings. Ording believed that Truman was suffering from the "Munich complex" and that this was having a negative influence on his policies. He went on to write that Korea appeared to be the bridgehead for a war pitting communism versus the United States.[71]

Norwegian Labor party leader Konrad Nordahl wrote in his diary on 25 June 1950 that Soviet-backed North Korea had attacked South Korea, that the Soviets were not in the UN Security Council, and that it could be the start of a new big war.[72] Later, on 31 December 1950, Nordahl wrote that Korea could turn into a new world war. He felt the Soviets were fighting a war of nerves and were using vassal states to fight their battles. Tensions were high, and Nordahl hoped the Norwegians could keep up their nerve. As in World War II, the Norwegians had to ration again, because they could not get enough raw materials to hold normal production levels up.[73]

Throughout the West, defense was on everyone's minds. Under the impetus of the Korean War, NATO was transformed from a loosely knit, traditional alliance to an integrated defense military structure with the United States clearly perched on top. The principles of collective and balanced strength were abandoned, and weapons standardization and the buildup of military infrastructures were given more weight. Containment and encircling policies became evident with the rearmament of West Germany and with Greece's and Turkey's entry into NATO. Because there was an increasing fear that NATO military secrets would get into enemy hands with increased membership, security was tightened in all Western countries, including Norway. This effectively severed Norway's remaining ties with the Eastern Bloc.[74] Norway felt that it had to tighten security in order to avoid upsetting the United States. An article in the Soviet *Trud* in April 1950, accused Norwegian government officials of "grovelling before the dollar" and of reactionary and "wild anti-Soviet slander."[75]

Norwegians were concerned about U.S. policy in the Korean War and its implications for Nordic security, and were especially disturbed by the actions of General Douglas MacArthur and other right-wing extremists. As Ording noted in his diary in October 1950, the Norwegians believed that Truman had to journey to Wake Island to harness General MacArthur's imperialist politics in Asia. The South Korean leader Syngman Rhee found no sympathy in Norway, either—Ording calling him a "barberic [*sic*] despot." Ording noted that, despite Kennan's pleadings, Acheson supported MacArthur's move across the 38th parallel. Ording called MacArthur's offensive "idiotic," and said that after MacArthur was dismissed by Truman, "he was acting like a god upon his return to the United States." The Norwegian press official was also concerned about other dangerous elements in the United States, such as Republican presidential aspirant Robert Taft, who called for an even more aggressive stand in Korea.[76] Certainly, the newspapers in

Oslo were reflecting doubts about U.S. domestic and foreign policies. The independent paper *Verdens Gang* reported in 1951 that the conflict raging between MacArthur and Truman was important to Norway, for they were struggling over two basic views of U.S. policy: Europe first (Truman) and Asia first (MacArthur). It was also noted that the United States—seen through Norwegian eyes—was more than a country. It was like a continent with its 150 million inhabitants. This meant that public opinion could take some time to crystalize—an important point to be kept in mind when dealing with American officials.[77]

Some Norwegians reacted sharply to McCarthyism, the Korean War, and the increasing militarization of U.S. policy. As one example, the Uavhengig Norsk Gruppe—the Independent Norwegian League— underwent a drastic change in character since its founding in 1946 as a politically independent discussion group to strengthen Noway's democracy and promote social justice. Many communists entered the organization and forged a new direction of attacking Norway's NATO foreign policy and pressing for Scandinavian neutralism. At the league's meeting held 15 February 1952, its chairman said that U.S. politics were "militarized" and American politicians had only military expedients at their disposal to achieve their goals. Norway, on the other hand, had become so dependent that it had become a "vassal state" and "is a pawn in the American encircling of the U.S.S.R." The Soviet Union, it was said, was only interested in Norway because of its pro-U.S. posture. There was a question whether accepting U.S. military aid would make Norway beholden to U.S. pressure.[78]

As containment developed a more pronounced military character, Norway and the rest of the High North figured more prominently in U.S. strategic military calculations. Norway's significance to the United States increased as demands for early warning and intelligence increased. Norway appreciated more explicit guarantees from the United States in terms of defense, but remained leery, as well, of being in such an intimate relationship with a superpower.[79]   Ambassador Morgenstierne gave his opinion on the United States in a 1950 edition of the *Arbeiderbladet*. He found it hard to understand how anyone in Norway could be hard pressed to choose between the United States and the Soviet Union in terms of the superpower conflict. There could be no middle course: "As a free nation Norway has found its natural place as the ally of the United States." Since the United States was working toward a social-welfare state started by President Franklin D. Roosevelt, Norwegians need not be concerned about U.S. social conditions.[80] The communist paper in Oslo reported it was clear from the ambassador's comments that "Norway's position is no longer determined in this country, but in Washington."[81]

Other Norwegians were worried about being dragged into conflict by being so closely aligned with the United States. In his diary, Ording wondered if the Soviets understood the sometimes ambiguous U.S. intentions.[82] The Korean War had a great impact on Norway's perception of the Soviet threat and the extent to which it needed to prepare to meet that threat. As part of the accelerated defense plan justified by the North Korean invasion, a considerable amount of economic and materiel assistance began to flow to Norway through the Mutual Defense Assistance Program (MDAP), which served to further integrate Norway into NATO.[83] The Korean War dispelled many doubts Norwegians may have had concerning NATO, and led to Norway's crash rearmament. The Soviets felt that the Norwegian prime minister was duped by the Americans into a "war menace" mentality. They went so far as to call Gerhardsen a "true American lackey."[84]

After NATO came into being, Norwegian-American relations centered on U.S. military aid. The MDAP was signed into law by President Truman in October 1949 and initially provided more than $1 billion in military aid to the NATO countries. The Norwegians negotiated with the United States and signed an agreement in February 1950. As a result, Admiral Ralph E. Jennings of the U.S. Navy was assigned to Norway as the Military Assistance Advisory Group (MAAG) head. However, from the start there were difficulties over the size of the American contingent. The Norwegian government was quite sensitive to accusations that the United States had taken over little Norway. Despite efforts to downplay the arms shipments and the U.S. military staff presence, difficulties arose.[85] Norwegian Defense Ministry documents show that the U.S. entourage and supplies were on their way to Norway before the MDAP agreement was actually signed. This show of impatience may have reflected Truman's reported irritation with delays in the signing of the bilateral agreements.[86]

In reaction to criticism of Norway's receiving arms from the United States, a press release by the Norwegian Foreign Ministry of 21 April 1950 defended the MDAP. The release stated that military assistance from the United States represented a considerable contribution toward easing Norway's economic and financial problems. It went on to say that there was a necessary balance between economic recovery and the security that U.S. aid was helping to realize.[87] Oslo newspapers reported reactions to the U.S. military aid. After Norwegian Defense Minister Jens Christian Hauge spoke about Norway's base policy on 11 January 1950, the conservative paper *Aftenposten* wrote that Norwegians must now realize their obligations to defend not only Norway, but democracy as well. According to the communist paper *Friheten*, Hauge's speech confirmed that the Norwegian government was violating the basing declaration and was changing Norway into a U.S. military and political base—which would lead to a loss of independence and democracy in Norway. The same paper later reported that Norway should not want its country and people "to become guinea pigs of this desperate policy and of the war hysteria prevailing in certain US circles."[88] In the 17 February 1950 edition of *Friheten*, it was reported that Norwegians had been removed from the Hotel Terminus in Oslo to make room for U.S. military personnel. This was a very sensitive matter for the Norwegian government since there was an acute housing shortage in Oslo after World War II. However, most papers generally offered a sober appreciation of the significance of the MDAP agreements and a willingness to remind readers of their own obligations toward multilateral security.[89]

As Norway drew closer to the United States, the Norwegian Communists criticized government policy. They complained that they were not being heard in the Storting despite having received more than 100,000 votes. They also felt that information concerning defense arrangements with the United States was being withheld because such information outlined how Norway was to become a U.S. base. Accordingly, the Norwegian military would then be put under American control by new secret agreements under the North Atlantic Treaty. Norwegian Communists felt that the meeting of the Storting was now actually taking place under the shadow of the North Atlantic Treaty. The Americans gave the orders, and the Storting just endorsed their decisions. The communists concluded that the Norwegian government had adopted a policy that would lead to the regimentation of political life and the abandonment of democracy in Norway.[90]

Despite such criticism from the far left that accused the Norwegian government of involving Norway in U.S. conflicts, Lange defended the Atlantic alliance because the United Nations could accomplish very little in terms of security. From the beginning, NATO was supposed to expand into a worldwide organization based on the UN Charter. The balance between preparedness and economic health was necessary in democratic countries. Military preparedness had to be based on a solid economic and social foundation. Lange felt that the Scandinavian countries were beginning to expand their sectional cooperation into new fields—for example, trade and infrastructural needs.[91] Oscar Torp, the Storting leader of the Labor Party Parliamentary Group, supported Lange when he said in 1950 that "Norway's security must also be placed in an international perspective. It is quite clear that Norway cannot solve its security problems alone, but only in cooperation with the other democratic nations in the world. The Atlantic Pact is an instrument of peace and will not be used to support any preparations for war."[92] Norway wanted other nations to see its NATO membership as purely defensive in nature.

Plans for increased nuclearization of NATO were also accelerated by the outbreak of the Korean War. Ground defenses were built up throughout NATO, but special emphasis was given to nuclear weapons and their strategic use. As a result, discussions on base rights were renewed. From a NATO council meeting in 1952, what came to be known as the "Lisbon Force Goals" emerged. These goals were quite unrealistic in that they were economically unattainable (e.g., the maintenance of ninety-six combat divisions in Europe), which meant that reliance on nuclear force was the only natural alternative. But this was contrary to the Scandinavian preference for low-voltage politics—a policy-line preference that ran contrary to the U.S. New Look policy.[93]

As a result of increasing demands for cost effectiveness in defense, the issue of integration became important because the United States wanted Norway integrated into a greater European defense system. The problem with this plan was that the economic foreign policy elite of the Norwegian Labor party entered the 1950s with well-articulated negative preconceptions of continental Europe. Norwegian Labor party members who strongly supported an expanded role for the state in the economy—full employment and extensive welfare—were skeptical of continental Europeans who were considered "antediluvian" and socially insensitive. Foreign Minister Lange openly discussed these issues in the early 1950s.[94] Norway was distrustful of Western European integration because of an unfavorable opinion of the conservative regimes and policies on the continent. The basic viewpoints on the issue were characterized as either functionalist or federalist—Norway favoring functionalism.[95] Norway also had a sense of economic vulnerability; it did not want to be at the mercy of continental cartels. There was a fear that, since Norway was just developing in the 1950s and was at the periphery of Europe, the European cartels might interfere with the Norwegian government's control of the economy.[96]

In discussions and planning for European economic integration in the 1950s, Norway limited itself to being put on record in support of such cooperation. The overwhelming concern for Norwegians—in terms of North Atlantic cooperation—was national security, not economic integration.[97] In terms of overall Nordic support for European integration, social democratic societies were generally skeptical of such strategies. Nordic integration could be thought of as idealistic, emotional, and utilitarian-pragmatic. It was free from declared goals, idealist by virtue of its Scandinavianist movement roots (in the nineteenth century), emotional in that the Nordic peoples were inclined to cooperate because they felt strong kinship ties, and utilitarian and pragmatic in that they were close linguistically, culturally, economically, socially, and in political ideology. Norden was an example of "cobweb integration" or fine threads woven together to form a whole.[98]

The Soviet reaction to Nordic integration was that it wanted to force Denmark and Norway out of NATO. When that did not happen, it settled for the next best thing: the no-foreign-bases policy. Halvard Lange figured that Norway's basing policy would keep the Soviets from trying to establish bases in Finland, because of the serious implications for Soviet security if Norway and Denmark allowed foreign basing. This became the basis of the policy of deterrence and reassurance. But when NATO established its regional headquarters for the Northern Flank (AFNORTH) outside of Oslo in the early 1950s, base politics again emerged. The Soviets claimed this action was in violation of the base policy.[99]

Despite the derogatory use of the term *Finlandization* in the United States, a memorandum from the U.S. ambassador in Finland on 19 July 1950 stated, "It is in the interests of the United States that Finland remain neutral."[100] The Finns, he said, are bound to the Soviets by a friendship pact that in effect required Finland to resist aggression and to consult with the Soviet Union in the event Finland, or the Soviet Union across the territory of Finland, should become the object of military aggression on the part of Germany or a state allied with Germany. The ambassador wanted to make it clear that, should the Soviets take Finland, this could not happen under the rationale of protecting the Finns from American pressures, because the United States respected Finland's neutrality.[101]

Early in the Cold War era, the United States was concerned with the threat of internal communist movements in Norden. Acheson sent a telegram to the U.S. legation in Finland in which he expressed concerns over communists being included in the government (ostensibly to mollify the Soviets and pacify their need to take over the government in Finland): "Inclusion [of] and commies [in the] new Finn[ish] cabinet would be extremely unwise and would not mollify [the] Soviets but only encourage increased Sov[iet] pressure." He went on to say that inclusion of communists in the government would have a bad effect on U.S. public opinion.[102] In a 1950 despatch to Acheson, Ambassador John Moors Cabot stressed that communist propaganda seemed to be taking in some Finns, and this propaganda was not being answered appropriately by the Finnish government. A careful U.S. response was called for. Cabot felt that "we must encourage a Finnish response instead of our doing it"[103]—this adding to the evidence of U.S. policy restraint in Norden. Even though the United States was concerned with communist influence in Norden, Norwegian Communists did not hold a single seat in the Parliament in 1951, and the only official Communist newspaper had a limited readership of 15,000, compared to over 100,000 in the immediate postwar years. Heavy-handed Soviet propaganda had a backlash effect in Norway, as many people were reminded of similar tactics used by the occupying German forces in World War II.[104] The Soviet newspaper *Izvestiya* reported in December 1951 that the Nordic members, in collaboration with the United States, were trying to get Sweden to join NATO. The United States was encouraging Nordic cooperation in the direction of incorporating all Nordic countries into the North Atlantic bloc. These efforts were not directed toward peace, the paper charged, but toward U.S. imperial subjugation of Northern Europe.[105]

In a speech before the Storting on 1 December 1951, Lange noted that inter-Scandinavian cooperation would be extended in every way possible. Norway hoped that initiatives taken by Nordic interparliamentary circles would be more permanent forms of cooperation among national assemblies and would result in concrete proposals for presentation to the Storting.[106] In a conversation between U.S. Ambassador Charles Ulrick Bay and Icelandic Minister of Foreign Affairs Bjarni Bendiktsson, the minister noted his reaction to the 1951 Scandinavian foreign ministers' meeting. Bendiktsson indicated that the meeting covered a broad range of subjects, resulting principally in outlining the course which the Nordic governments might find it to their common interest to pursue.[107] Prime Minister Gerhardsen commented on Scandinavian cooperation in 1951, saying that the Nordic people had solved their defense problems in the best and most successful manner. He noted that an isolated Scandinavian defense association would have retained the same political burdens as the NATO and neutrality orientations, and the cost of defense would have been three times as much and security much less. Alluding to the interconnection of security policies in Norden, Gerhardsen went on to say that the building up of defenses in Norway and Denmark was of use to Sweden, and that Sweden's armed neutrality was of obvious advantage to Denmark and Norway.[108] In an interview with the Norwegian press in 1952, Swedish Foreign Minister Östen Undén said that the Nordic countries had chosen their lines of foreign policy: "We base our cooperation on mutual respect for each other's opinions, and I do not believe in negotiations in which one party aims at influencing or converting the other." Undén went on to say that he believed the Nordic Council could systematize Nordic cooperation, although it was not set up as a forum for security policy issues.[109]

Norway's no-bases policy came under extreme U.S. pressure in

1951-53 because the United States wanted to station fighters and have base rights in Norway. In the Norwegian Parliament in 1951, Defense Minister Jens Christian Hauge explained Norway's base policy as being conditioned on any aggression or threats of aggression. But it did allow construction of military installations to accommodate Western allied combat reinforcements and allied exercises in Norway, or short peacetime visits of allied planes and ships.[110]   The United States wanted use of Norwegian military airfields at Sola and Gardermoen. American officials presented a concrete plan in August 1951, and by October 1952 they had a guarantee to use these two fields in case of war. As a result, many American technicians and other personnel arrived to outfit the bases for wartime use.[111]   This was not done without the Soviets noticing, and they sent a note to the Norwegian government in October 1951, expressing concern about the Norwegian defense preparations. The Soviets viewed NATO as being aggressive, and of special concern to the Soviets was the status of Spitsbergen. The Norwegians by and large saw their participation in NATO as defensive, and saw the Soviet note as beginning with a false premise.[112]   The Norwegian government withstood Soviet pressure without giving in. Despite strong efforts by the Norwegians to live in harmony with their superpower neighbors, the Norwegian people were not sympathetic to communism. In an October 1952 Gallup poll taken in Norway on domestic and international issues, 7 percent favored communism as a system, 71 percent did not, and 22 percent had no opinion.[113]

Public opinion followed the generally favorable consensus in Parliament concerning NATO membership. In the same Gallup poll, 45 percent of Norwegians favored NATO, 19 percent opposed, 36 percent had no opinion.[114]   However, the broadening of NATO membership brought strains between the United States and Norway. The admission of Greece and Turkey into NATO in 1952 ran counter to Norway's belief that only Atlantic countries should be members. Lange spoke in the Storting on this subject in June 1951: Norway preferred other security arrangements, rather than Greek and Turkish membership in NATO.[115]   It preferred that Greece and Turkey be observers, rather than active members.[116]

In 1952, foreign policy was the most prominent topic of discussion in both Norway and the United States. Norwegians watched U.S. domestic politics as well. According to the U.S. Embassy, Norway reacted positively to Eisenhower's acceptance of the Republican nomination for president. However, Konrad Nordahl wrote in his diary that Norwegians and Europeans were generally disappointed because of Eisenhower's big business ties. Conservative Norwegian papers held that Eisenhower had a Democratic foreign policy and a Republican domestic policy. The communist paper *Friheten* remarked that, when generals enter politics, it is a sign of a shift to a reactionary war policy.[117] Many Norwegians sensed that the 1952 U.S. election was very important to the Free World, but they were not sure what to expect from Eisenhower's many appointments of corporate men to the cabinet. In the October 1952 Gallup poll, 40 percent of Norwegians approved of Eisenhower as a presidential candidate, and 39 percent favored Democrat Adlai Stevenson.[118]

NORWAY AND THE NEW LOOK, 1953-1961

On the day of the U.S. presidential inauguration, 20 January 1953, Nordahl wrote that the Roosevelt era had ended. Eisenhower represented the interests of big business and was more popular with the Norwegians as a general than as a Republican president.[119] Along with his conservatism came Eisenhower's emphasis on nuclear weapons for security. Opposition to nuclear weapons developed as Norwegians came to realize that the strategy of massive retaliation (part of Eisenhower's New Look) meant that atomic weapons were to be used in the Nordic defense theater in case of attack—a fact that caused Norwegians to think more about the terrors of nuclear war.[120]

In July 1953, U.S. Ambassador Bay prepared an analysis of Norwegian attitudes toward the United States. Norwegians, he reported, thought Americans were unduly emotional over communism. The Norwegians expressed confidence in Eisenhower's policies, but were still worried about isolationist elements in Congress. They also believed that the United States held onto rigid and outdated policies. Senator Joseph McCarthy's communist witch-hunts were particularly distressing to the Norwegians, as they considered this all to be part of an undemocratic movement in America. They believed that emotional anticommunist forces had exercised too great an influence over U.S. foreign policy. As an example, after Trygve Lie's resignation as secretary general of the United Nations, the Norwegian press reported that attacks against the United Nations by the American press and a U.S. congressional committee (the McCarran Committee) were reasons for Lie's departure. The Labor party paper, *Arbeiderbladet*, said that the "Commie hunt" in the United States had victimized many liberals, and this in a country with such proud traditions of liberty. In another paper, it was noted that such widespread anticommunist extremism did more damage to U.S. credibility than any "Commie spy or traitor." Norway was very concerned about its image and sensitive about its relationship to the United States. It considered itself the only clean socialist country.[121]

NATO and U.S. development of tactical nuclear weapons also unnerved the Norwegians, who feared that such weapons would be used on Norwegian soil in the event of war. Eisenhower's fiscal conservatism, however, fit into the NATO plans for building up force through use of both conventional and nuclear assets; the concept of massive retaliation would serve as a cost-saving measure. Nuclear weapons in Europe came first to England. In NSC 162/2 the new strategy took shape: in 1952 the United States changed its strategy in Europe, and in 1953 in NATO.[122] NATO plans called for the Europeans eventually to control their own nuclear weapons.[123] The Norwegians were slow and hesitant to accept the NATO nuclear strategy and were quick to abandon it. They were careful not to become overly committed. This formed a dualism in Norwegian foreign policy in response to the Eisenhower-era New Look strategy. Norway found itself trying to walk a fine line between maintaining a strong defense and staying friendly with Moscow.[124] Feeding into this dualist position, at the Labor Party Congress in 1953 the delegates expressed a fear of John Foster Dulles, his potential reactionary policies (the specter of McCarthy was pervasive for the Norwegians), and the effect that association with such policies would have on their relations to Moscow. They were especially concerned about Dulles's policy of liberation for Eastern Europe. Dulles found the previous containment doctrine futile and too defensive. He was never too clear on how his liberation plan was actually to work, except to say that the United States could arouse the Eastern Europeans into taking up arms against their Soviet masters.[125]

Once NATO's strategy became more reliant on nuclear weapons, it was clear that the United States was to retain possession of these weapons. Norway was thereby placed beneath a nuclear umbrella since it did not allow weapons on its soil. The Norwegian government was in favor of this strategy, but was also afraid of a public backlash if it were openly emphasized. By this time, the Kola Peninsula buildup by the Soviets, with a nuclear submarine base and rocket-testing facilities, brought security in the Northern Flank to the forefront of U.S. and British thinking. Norway was squeezed even harder between the two superpowers. Interestingly, Norwegian politics did not become overly concerned with these issues—with the exception of nuclear testing fallout. One reason for this was because the nuclear strategy of the superpowers seemed so far removed from everyday life. Norway was mainly concerned about balancing defense with economic security. A report to the prime minister in 1953 stressed that Norway could not continue—without serious political damage—to borrow foreign money to build its defenses. High levels of defense spending could only continue if reductions were made elsewhere. Even though Norway received matching funds from the United States for defense, it had to borrow to get the initial seed money. Denmark's policy on defense spending was seen as affecting Norway since they were both Nordic NATO members and would be expected to spend like amounts on defense. This provides more evidence of the interconnectedness of Nordic defense policies.[126]

As part of the traditional Norwegian fear of being overly committed, some in the Labor party felt that the international arrangements Norway was making could transfer power from its Parliament to international organizations. There was a populist backlash in 1953 when Labor leader Finn Moe said that he feared "an international technocracy consisting of international secretariats and international diplomatic representatives . . . [would bypass] peoples and parliaments."[127] Yet, at the Labor Party National Congress in 1953 there was almost unanimous approval of Norway's continued membership in NATO. The Liberal party, on the other hand, stressed independent Norwegian foreign policy. It held that British points of view more nearly coincided with those of Norway, and McCarthyism in the United States made that even more clear.[128] The impression was that the United States was prone to pressure exerted by right-wing extremists.

At the 1953 Labor Party Congress it was stressed that NATO was an Atlantic community of nations, not just a military pact. It was different from the Warsaw Pact in that NATO's Article 2 called for respecting an individual nation's freedom. Collective security through NATO allowed all members to pursue economic growth and to raise the standard of living for all.[129]

From 1953 to 1955 there were no new Soviet foreign policy initiatives concerning Norway or the rest of Scandinavia. This reflected the post-Stalinist leadership's pursuit of "peaceful coexistence," which brought on a modest reduction in Cold War tensions. The Soviets continued to condemn Norway for violating the peace through their military buildup. Strengthening of Nordic cooperation was seen as an attempt to bring Sweden and Finland into the Western alliance. The Soviets relinquished a base in Finland (Porkkala, near Helsinki) as an enticement for the Norwegians and Danes to act more like Sweden. They wanted to promote neutrality and a loosening of the Nordic ties.[130] Once again, Finland figured prominently in the East-West strategy.

Indeed, Finland was the focal point in the "Rockefeller Report" of 1955 on neutralism in Europe; this U.S. executive department report suggested that the United States make no attempt to formalize—overtly or covertly—defense agreements between Finland and NATO. U.S. interests would be compromised: such an attempt would bring instant disciplinary action against Finland by the Soviet Union. Likewise, public pronouncements by U.S. authorities writing off Finland as a satellite of the Soviet Union would only serve to alienate the vast majority of Finns who were Western in their basic philosophy.[131]

With Nikita Khrushchev's consolidation of power, Soviet policy after 1956 took on global dimensions. This new foreign policy offensive was combined with limited de-Stalinization, less pressure on Eastern Europe, and some concessionary moves. Despite the appearance of a softening, however, this new policy shifted between confrontation and consolidation. Norway, as a small state, felt these fluctuations in policy quite severely and began to rely more on international organizations.[132]

The 1950s brought the advent of intercontinental missile systems, putting the polar strategy in a new light. U.S. interest in the Nordic region grew as the Soviets continued to buildup the Kola Peninsula as a base of operations. The United States discovered that the Soviets were deploying new bombers on Kola—Tu-16 Badger, Mya-4 Bison, and Tu-95 Bear. As a result, the bomber gap controversy emerged in the United States in the early and mid-1950s—a gap that never really existed. A Ford Foundation commission study said that the "Gaither Report" fed popular fears. Like NSC-68 in 1950, the Gaither Report in 1957 urged a massive buildup of the U.S. military. The bomber gap controversy gave way to the missile gap controversy. In addition to the Gaither Report's influence, this may also have been a hysterical response to the Soviets testing their first ICBM (the SS-6) and the success of Sputnik, the world's first Earth satellite.[133]

At the 1955 Labor Party Congress, many delegates felt that Norway's biggest problem was the atomic bomb, that is, the need for effective international control of atomic weapons. In the eventuality of a "nuclear Ragnarok,"[134] the NATO planners in April 1955 gave consideration to civil defense against nuclear attack. The Norwegian government followed up on these plans, and its citizens began to accept nuclear weapons as part of their lives. Scenarios were played through and ambitious plans for shelters were begun—just as in the United States. After the crisis in Hungary in 1956, plans for a super shelter to protect government officials in Oslo began. In addition to civil defense, Norwegians had been monitoring radioactivity through their Forsvarets Forskningsinstitutt or FFI (Defense Research Institute) since the early 1950s. This involved a systematic measuring of radioactivity in collaboration with other Norwegian science institutes. In 1955 the alarm went off after Soviet testing in Novaja Semlja and Semiplatinsk. Public pressure mounted as the results of this testing revealed fallout in Norway. But Norway's protests were of little immediate value. Norway took the issue to the United Nations and NATO. At the 1957 party congress, Gerhardsen noted that tension between the superpowers was very high, and that there was no sign of disarmament and no clear answers to central security problems. He suggested that atomic weapons could not be controlled if they spread to smaller countries, and expressed grave concern over the effects of atomic testing.[135] In May 1957, Norway's full report of radioactivity measurements was disseminated throughout NATO. The Soviets stopped testing in 1958 partially due to these pressures. Norwegian officials saw this as an example of how Norway could rely on international organizations.

Because Norway was increasingly reliant on international organizations, it became increasingly concerned with its image in the international system. It was especially aware of the need to overhaul the relationship between the First World and the Third World. Because of the West's outdated system of relations with the Third World, and because the West's image was tarnished by its former colonialism, the Soviet system looked better in comparison.[136] With Norway's increasing Western orientation came a desire to spread its influence—especially to the Third World—in order to combat communism. On the domestic side, helping in the Third World tended to take attention away from the rapid arms buildup in NATO.[137] This was stressed by Foreign Minister Halvard Lange in 1955 at a NATO ministers meeting: we "must approach Asian and African peoples on the basis of equality and partnership and recognize their right to determine their own future if we are expected to keep them on the Western side and counter the Soviet charges against NATO as a tool of imperialism."[138]

Norway remained important to the United States based on its own strategic value, but also because of its influence on Denmark and Iceland. Iceland held America's strategic interest far out of proportion to its size. There was great U.S. sensitivity to internal politics in Iceland. A U.S. policy update in 1956 related that some NATO security information was being withheld from the Icelanders for fear that Communist members of the government would gain access to that information. It would be within the best interests of the United States if Communists were removed from the government of Iceland. Actions taken to further such aims included withholding NATO security information and asking other countries not to take economic steps that could strengthen the Icelandic government.[139]

For its small size, Iceland presented some large headaches for U.S. planners. In a National Security Council discussion on 16 May 1957,

Secretary Dulles objected to the use of the word *unacceptable* in NSC 5712 in reference to what would happen if the United States was denied basing in Iceland. Dulles felt this implied the United States would use force if the Icelanders demanded that the forces leave. Someone suggested that perhaps the Joint Chiefs of Staff "might feel that force was justified in the circumstance envisaged." Secretary of Defense Charles Wilson reported that the United States should take as many U.S. Army personnel out of Iceland as possible. Their presence was irritating to Icelanders because army personnel have "little to do but chase Icelandic women." It was decided that U.S. Army security forces could be taken out of Iceland because the president felt air force personnel could be used for security purposes.[140] Too much strong-arming in Iceland could affect Norwegian-American relations—something that Eisenhower was well aware of.

Norwegian-American relations were troubled by minor misunderstandings as well as more substantial issues involving defense. For instance, in 1956 there was an embarrassing incident involving the U.S. Embassy in Oslo and the Norwegian Left party. Apparently, the Americans had been invited to the Left Party Congress. The Norwegian Embassy in Washington, upon learning of the invitation, said that Norwegian party congresses were not open sessions. The U.S. officials had no idea that this incident would cause considerable excitement and that it would be played up in the papers in Oslo. The Polish press got the story and used it as another example of U.S. "dollar imperialism."[141]

More significantly, Prime Minister Torp wanted to talk to President Eisenhower about Norwegian concerns regarding replacement of heavy equipment in 1957-58. Torp sought assurance of U.S. help in this replacement. By that time, the U.S. government felt that Norway was spending a "fair amount" for national defense.[142] Earlier, however, U.S. officials had criticized Norway for spending too little. There was also the question of nuclear weapons. Eisenhower considered them to be cost effective, but Norway would not deal with them. Western thinking was that, due to Western nuclear superiority, the Soviet Union would use a "single massive blow" strategy against both military and civilian targets. It was not just a matter of the alliance's obtaining nuclear weapons to strike the Soviets; it was also a matter of what would happen after a "nuclear Ragnarok" had taken place.[143] Norway's concerns were evident when Morgenstierne reported in 1957 that Eisenhower and Prime Minister Harold MacMillan of Great Britain had agreed that new weapons should be put in allied hands as well—not just under U.S. control—and consideration should be given to the misuse or potential political damage to alliance partners in regard to such weapons. The ambassador observed that Dulles seemed to hold Eisenhower back and was restraining him in terms of compromise and negotiation on such issues.[144]

In Norway, debates raged over atomic weapons and Norway's tie to NATO. From the very first, it was known that NATO depended on nuclear forces. After the Lisbon Force Goals proved unattainable and NATO leaders decided that nuclear weapons would have to be part of the NATO defensive system, the debates in Norway revealed that many were skeptical of the value of nuclear weapons for Norway, while others argued that they provided an umbrella of security. In 1957 the Labor party decided that nuclear weapons were not to be stationed in Norway, and so announced this policy at the NATO ministers meeting that year. Many Norwegians feared that nuclear weapons would mean the permanent stationing of U.S. troops in Norway. However, there was some concern that, if Norway or other small allied countries zoned out nuclear weapons, the United States would abandon Europe. Norwegian military leaders wanted tactical nuclear weapons, but this proposal was met with the same opposition as their pro-basing position.[145]

In the December 1957 NATO meeting in Paris, planners—led by the United States—announced that Jupiter and Thor intermediate range ballistic missiles (IRBMs) should be placed in Europe. This was in response to the Sputnik shock and the Soviet Union's intercontinental ballistic missiles (ICBMs). The missiles were to be under the command of the Supreme Allied Commander Europe (SACEUR) and were positioned to counter Soviet forces. The Europeans thought that the United States was more likely to help them in the event of war if the Americans had control of the IRBMs.

Prior to Prime Minister Gerhardsen's no-nuclear-weapons speech at the NATO conference, and while Norway was considering the American proposal to retain nuclear stockpiles and deploy IRBMs,[146] Soviet Foreign Minister Nikolai Bulganin sent a note to Gerhardsen warning that the Norwegian people might "have to pay dearly for the bases which are built in Norway if the NATO strategists' plans are carried out." Bulganin pointed out that NATO bases in Norway and Denmark would be legitimate targets for Soviet hydrogen bombs. The Soviet view was that Norway's NATO membership—in spite of the country's no-base policy—meant it was a de facto base. The note also expressed annoyance with Norway's increasing military cooperation with the United States and West Germany.[147] Gerhardsen announced at the NATO meeting that Norway "had no plans to let atomic stockpiles be established on Norwegian territory, or to construct launching sites for IRBMs." This decision had actually been reached during the summer by the governing Labor party. At a prime minister's meeting prior to

Gerhardsen's speech, Foreign Minister Lange expressed grave doubts about the wisdom of placing such weapons in Norway, but was not sure if this position should be made known. The Norwegian government wanted NATO to delay discussion. The objective of the United States was to get tactical nuclear weapons into all NATO lands, but Norway did not want nuclear weapons. The meeting ended with the administration's deciding to take the position not to accept the nuclear-capable rockets, hoping that others would do the same in the general spirit of disarmament and that the Soviets would take this as a sign to reduce their proliferation of nuclear weapons.[148] The Norwegian government's desire was to reassure the Soviets. Bulganin expressed great satisfaction.[149]

At the NATO meeting, Foreign Minister Lange went even further, adding that Central Europe (including Germany) should be made into a nuclear-free zone—but there was no support for Lange's proposal among other members of the alliance. According to Nordahl, Gerhardsen's announcement seemed to many a signal that Norway was on the way out of NATO. Nordahl felt that Gerhardsen was, in his heart, against NATO and would like to be neutral like Sweden, but prevailing political forces did not enable Norway to have such an orientation.[150]

After Bulganin sent his threatening notes in 1957 (ostensibly to frighten Norway out of NATO), the U.S. Congress was concerned with "little Norway." On 28 March 1957 the Senate floor witnessed a show of support for Norway. Senator Henry "Scoop" Jackson (D-Washington) spoke of the Bulganin notes as "nuclear blackmail," saying,

The Kremlin is out to decimate the western alliance, if it can, by rattling its guided missiles. If the Soviet Union attempts to intimidate any of our allies, whether it be Norway, England, Turkey, or any other of the NATO nations, or any other nations joining with us in a common alliance of defense, we should make it clear that we, too, can deal decisively with atomic and hydrogen weapons in a way the Soviets will understand.[151]

Senator Hubert H. Humphrey (D-Minnesota) chimed in:

Let the Soviet Union know, once and for all, that in our minds, under the commitments we have made, any attack upon NATO or any attack upon Norway is an attack upon the United States of America; and that any derogatory comment about any ally of ours in NATO is a derogatory comment against the United States of America.[152]

These comments were well received and supported in the Senate.

By the late 1950s Norwegians believed that Cold War tensions were lessening. Khrushchev's primary objective in the Berlin Crisis (1958-59) was seen as stabilizing relations in Eastern Europe and East Germany. U.S. Vice-President Richard Nixon's visit to Moscow in 1959 was seen by Norway as intended to show the Soviets that the United States was not set on destroying the Soviet world and to convince them of the U.S. conviction not to start a war.[153] Lange, in a speech of 1 July 1959, set much the same tone when he said that "to solve conflicts through negotiation, without war, is the primary objective of the NATO cooperation." But strength would have to be maintained in order to keep the power balance.[154]

Although the Norwegians were often sympathetic to the West, they also could be critical of U.S. policy. The Norwegian government criticized Eisenhower's radio address of 16 March 1959 for airing a list of Soviet aggressive moves while offering no concrete plan against the Soviet program. It also found Secretary of State Dulles to be quite rigid in his policy deliberations, especially over Berlin.[155] Another point of friction between the United States and Norway remained over the possibility of nuclear weapons being stored in Norway. Norwegians believed that nuclear weapons in their territory infringed on their general foreign policy objectives and compromised their national integrity. How could Norway effectively work toward disarmament and détente if it took nuclear weapons into its country?[156] However, Norway could not realistically wipe its hands clean of nuclear weapons since it was a member of NATO, an organization that maintained such weapons. The Norwegian government accepted the idea of nuclear weapons within NATO, despite not wanting them on its own territory. The Norwegian government knew that, when the time came, it might have to push the button; but until that time, it would remain quiet. Gerhardsen favored strict regulation of nuclear weapons, and so assured the Soviets. In 1959 while the United States and the Soviet Union were arguing over West Germany's outfitting for nuclear weapons, Norway took a position contrary to the United States and was roundly scolded for it. Hardened by their experiences in World War II, Norwegian social democratic leaders did not like it when Germany joined NATO; so it was natural for them to be opposed to Germany's having nuclear weapons only fourteen years after the war. To U.S. officials it seemed as though the Norwegians were seeking protection under the nuclear umbrella but wanting to remain morally aloof.[157]

Norwegians expected changes in U.S. policy to occur after the death of Dulles in May 1959. It was Dulles—more than Eisenhower—who personified the nuclear terror of the massive retaliation concept. When Christian Herter was appointed and approved as his successor,

Norwegians saw evidence of bipartisan support for Eisenhower's foreign policy. The Norwegian government felt Herter would differ from Dulles in that he would not run the State Department like a one-man show. Because Herter was not Eisenhower's type and was not intimate with him, Norwegians believed that Eisenhower would take charge more of foreign policy and give U.S. policy a different tone.[158] Norwegian officials thought that the U.S. president would be more conciliatory without the bulldog Dulles at his side. Eisenhower's gestures to promote peace in 1959-60 fulfilled such expectations, although they had limited effectiveness.

After Dulles's death, the Soviets stirred controversy when Nikita Khrushchev cancelled a visit to Norden because of what he termed "hostile attitudes" among the Nordic people toward the Soviets. He especially singled out neutral Sweden, despite the fact that he usually held Sweden and Finland to be examples for Norway and Denmark to follow. The Norwegian government called Khrushchev's act a propaganda ploy designed to pull Norway and Denmark from the North Atlantic Treaty, to separate Sweden and Finland from the other three Nordic countries, and to create splits among all of the five Nordic lands. According to the Norwegian Embassy in Washington, Khrushchev did not know how Nordic countries cooperated through diversity (a key concept to Nordic success in integrating security policies). The Soviet leader was afraid of all five countries' strengthened ties to the United States and was trying to intimidate the Nordic people.[159]

The document driving U.S. policy in Norden as the new decade began was NSC 6006/1. Five specific objectives emerged from this 1960 document:

1. Finland should be kept neutral but oriented toward the West.
2. Western-oriented economies should be maintained.
3. Denmark and Norway would have to contribute equitably toward NATO defense.
4. Greenland, Iceland, and other strategic northern territories would be kept intact.
5. Sweden should be kept strong and resistant to Soviet pressure.[160]

From this document, one can see the difference in policy orientations between the Truman and Eisenhower administrations in regard to Norden. NSC 6006/1 differed from NSC 28/1 in several ways. Under Eisenhower, the United States had a more mature policy in Norden and began to realize the benefits of accepting some Nordic solutions to the security problems in that region. NSC 6006/1 stated that Scandinavia was of political interest to the United States for several reasons:

1. Scandinavian countries had world reputations as prime Western democracies.
2. There were strong cultural, sentimental, and family ties between Scandinavia and the United States.
3. Scandinavians enjoyed international prestige, making "their support of U.S. policy valuable in international organizations and for general propaganda purposes."
4. Any Soviet threat to Scandinavian security would cause apprehension among other Northern European NATO allies.

In contrast to Truman's concerns during the early Cold War period, by 1960 the communist parties in Scandinavia presented only a "nuisance" for American strategists.[161]

NSC 6006/1 stressed the importance of the northern island possessions of Denmark (Greenland; the Faeroe Islands) and Norway (Jan Mayen; with Spitsbergen being demilitarized by international treaty). The document held that the NATO defense effort in the North was hampered by Denmark's and Norway's limited military power and by certain national attitudes that restricted adequate defense measures. Neutral Sweden had by far the most effective defense forces.[162] NSC 6006/1 also stressed that the maintenance of prosperous Western-oriented economies in Denmark, Norway, and Sweden was tied to the basic U.S. policy objective of a strong, democratic, and united Western Europe.[163]

Sweden was considered in a discussion of elements of NSC 6006/1 at a 1 April 1960 National Security Council meeting. Provisions in NSC 6006/1 held that the United States would come to the defense of Sweden if attacked. The president decided to strike this from the policy document until it was revised, because it gave benefits to Sweden without any compensation to the United States. The wording was changed to read: "Encourage and assist Sweden, without prejudice to U.S. commitments to NATO, to resist Soviet bloc attack against Sweden." If the Soviets attacked only Sweden, the United States was "prepared to come to the assistance of Sweden as part of a NATO or UN response to the aggression." The footnote to this paragraph in NSC 6006/1 stipulated that it was for unilateral U.S. planning only and not for planning within NATO.[164] There were also problems with NATO coordination and the Nordic countries themselves. These plans to defend Sweden would have to be shared with all of those countries.[165]

The document also stressed that, in general, Scandinavia was an area that presented relatively few problems for the United States except for their support of Communist China's UN membership. There was a discussion in the document of how the United States would not sell modern weapons systems to nonaligned countries except Sweden, making Norden somewhat of an exception. There was also some concern over the depressed areas of Northern Scandinavia where communist tendencies prevailed and where the Soviet Union was interested in expanding economically.[166]

Iceland still figured prominently in U.S. strategic policy in the beginning of the 1960s—a policy that again stressed the influential role Norway played with Iceland. A later NSC document, NSC 6025 (December 1960), reiterated many of the same U.S. objectives in Iceland that NSC 6006/1 contained, and the later document pointed out that the negotiations in 1956 between the United States and Iceland—ostensibly concerning withdrawal of U.S. forces—had resulted instead in Iceland's permitting U.S. forces to remain under essentially the same provisions as in the original 1951 basing agreement. NSC 6025 further noted that economic security concerns seemed most pressing regarding Iceland in 1960. Fish exports accounted for 70 percent of its foreign exchange income, and U.S. forces accounted for 15 percent. A unilateral decision to extend territorial-waters boundaries in the 1950s caused rifts between Iceland and the United Kingdom, which traditionally bought most of Iceland's fish. As a result, the Soviet bloc increased its share of Iceland's exports from around 6 percent in the early 1950s to nearly 35 percent in the later 1950s. In exchange, 25 percent of Iceland's imports came from the Soviet bloc.[167] This was disturbing for the Americans because one of the fundamental objectives of U.S. policy in Norden was to reduce Soviet economic leverage.

U.S. strategists were also concerned about both Norway's and Denmark's NATO contributions. The United States saw neutralist forces in Denmark as being the cause of Denmark's opposition to maintaining adequate defense measures. In 1954 the social democrats in Denmark rode the popular protest against foreign basing and also embraced radical liberal ideals of lowering conscription periods and reducing defense expenditures.[168] In 1960, NATO Commander General Lauris Norstad told the Danish defense minister that the United States appreciated Denmark's agreeing to storage facilities for NATO forces, but he also noted Denmark's inadequate defense budget. Norstad was disappointed with Denmark's failure to meet even minimum levels of security.[169] The U.S. government preferred that Denmark spend more on defense and accept nuclear weapons as a cost-savings measure. In 1959, there was considerable discussion over a stronger defense organization as well as adoption of atomic weapons for defense. A resolution by the Moderate Liberals, the party in opposition to the government, advocated atomic missiles and NATO depots—which was most heartening to U.S. officials.[170]

The nuclear issue served as an obstacle between the United States and Norway, although not an insurmountable one. Norway was concerned because it saw U.S. nuclear strategy as perpetuating the nuclear arms race and encouraging Soviet nuclear testing, which took place near its borders. The U-2 affair of May 1960 (described below) ended the possibility of a superpower agreement to stop testing nuclear weapons—something that the Norwegians had worked hard to get. The Soviets immediately resumed nuclear testing in the North, with larger devices and more radioactive fallout. Norway's renewed protests were ignored. The issue of nuclear testing galvanized Norwegians into their antinuclear position.[171]

Norwegian-American relations were also troubled by questions of whether Norway had enough trained technical personnel to maintain sophisticated U.S. equipment. A message from the U.S. military advisory group in Norway in November 1960 discussed an article in the Oslo paper *Morgenbladet* that portrayed Norway as a problem child in NATO. The country did not have enough electronic personnel to man the communication and warning systems provided by the United States. In other words, there was too much for the Norwegians themselves to handle. The article warned that, if Norway could not demonstrate competency, then political support for continued development of the communications and early warning facilities in Norway that were required by the NATO common defense would be jeopardized.[172]

U.S.-Norwegian relations were put to the test when incidents of their alliance in the early 1960s proved to be even more dangerous than the Soviet threats against Norway in the 1950s. In May 1960 a pilot for the U.S. Central Intelligence Agency (CIA), Francis Gary Powers, was shot down in his U-2 spy plane over Sverdlovsk in the Soviet Union and was captured. Norway found itself in the middle of a potential superpower showdown. When it was discovered that Powers's flight began in Pakistan and was to terminate at the Bodø Air Station in northern Norway, the Soviets threatened to "obliterate" those bases which countries made available for aircraft that violated Soviet airspace. Norway responded with a diplomatic note that denied authorization of landing rights, and even requested that the United States not plan such flights again. Apparently, only the Norwegian military knew of the authorization. Evidence seems to point to the fact that this was not the first time these landing rights had been extended. As far as only the Norwegian military's knowing about the flights, the simple fact is that the Bodø airfield is in plain view, so that anyone could see anything unusual—especially a strange long-winged black plane with no markings. In any case, the Soviets were not impressed with Norway's profession of ignorance, and said that it did not matter whether the Norwegian government consented or not; the bottom line was that the Americans did whatever they wanted to do in NATO countries.[173]

U-2 operations in Norway had gone on for some time before the infamous Mayday in 1960. Since 1958, Americans had conducted such flights over international waters. Only a few Norwegians were informed of these extremely sensitive operations at the Bodø airfield. The Norwegian government allowed U-2 operations only under the condition that they conduct no overflights of Soviet territory (a rather ill-conceived policy, seeing as how this aircraft was designed to conduct overflight missions).

The U.S. mission planners made no mention of the U-2 aircraft in laying out the Mayday flight plan—only C-130 transports. There was also no briefing of an overflight of Soviet territory. The Norwegian government did not really know what had happened until it heard Khrushchev's accusations and Eisenhower's explanations after Powers had been shot down. The Norwegians then had two tasks: to investigate what had really happened, and to handle relations with both superpowers. Investigations were hampered by the high level of secrecy of the operation, major flaws in the Norwegian decision-making system, and delays in finding out the Norwegian military's involvement in the affair. It was later revealed that the CIA covered up the flight, masking it as a training flight that would involve only the transport aircraft. But evidence reveals that the Norwegian military authorities had enough bits of information to figure out what kind of operation was taking place, but chose not to alert anyone. The feeling was that a successful mission would bring great credit to the organization, and the risk of failure was slim. In keeping with this, some Norwegians criticized their military leaders for being too subservient to the British and Americans.[174]

Two months later the Soviets shot down another American plane: an RB-47 reconnaissance plane. This occurred off the Kola Peninsula—territorial waters under the Soviet interpretation, and international waters according to the U.S. interpretation. The Soviets claimed that Norway had authorized landing rights for the flight. This the Norwegians denied. The Soviets concluded once again that, even if the Norwegian authorities had not authorized landing rights, the United States acted as if it did not need permission anyway. These two incidents brought Soviet-Norwegian relations nearly to the breaking point—even closer than Norway's decision to join NATO.[175]

Gerhardsen was also not pleased with the United States over this incident, complaining that "they treat us like a vassal state."[176] Although the Norwegian government was upset with the United States, collaboration in terms of defense continued unabated. This incident highlights Norway's difficult position in the Cold War and the necessity of its deterrence/reassurance and integration/screening policy strategies.

The Cold War also renewed the Spitsbergen issue that had troubled Soviet-Norwegian relations since World War I. An incident in 1961 brought the issue to the forefront once more. The United States was granted permission to send a team of scientists to the island chain. Later it was discovered that the team was surveying the island for an airbase and that its mission was in fact military and not scientific. Amid strong protests that emanated from Moscow, the Norwegians ended the mission.[177]

Having looked at Norwegian diplomatic history from 1947 to 1961 in the shadow of superpower rivalry, the focus will now turn to a comparison of Truman and Eisenhower's policies in Norden, and will make this examination in the light of Norway's perspective. This will allow a glimpse of how Norwegian/Nordic policy affected the United States as the hegemonic power. Following that, a comparison can be made of U.S. and Nordic/Norwegian policy objectives: Were they compatible? And were they realized?

COMPARING TRUMAN'S AND EISENHOWER'S POLICIES TOWARD NORDEN

If the United States came to accept the Nordic region's own solution to security, did this occur under Truman or Eisenhower? By looking at four significant points of comparison based on Nordic issues, one can determine if the Truman and Eisenhower administrations defined national security interests similarly in Norden.

1. Was there danger of the communists taking over Iceland?
2. Was the United States willing to defend Norway against attack?
3. What were the prevailing U.S. attitudes toward Sweden? And, what policies were made?
4. What were the U.S. attitudes toward Finland and the concept of Finlandization?
5. What were the U.S. attitudes toward social democracy in Norden?

First, Truman and Eisenhower differed in their style of foreign policy leadership. Truman deferred to his policy experts (General George C. Marshall, George Kennan, and Dean Acheson) and largely stayed out of the way. Eisenhower had a more hands-on approach, in spite of Dulles's reputation. The Truman administration believed Iceland was vulnerable to an internal communist takeover. A document prepared by the State Department (25 November 1949) entitled "Program Designed to Decrease the Vulnerability of the Icelandic Government to Communist Seizure of Power" outlined certain steps for the United States to take in stimulating Icelandic self-help in this regard. Informal talks with the foreign minister were recommended. Other measures included stimulating a home guard; developing an official Icelandic counterintelligence organization; encouraging Scandinavian labor groups to send representatives to Iceland where they would suggest ways of combating communism in Icelandic labor groups; and securing and maintaining availability of the Keflavik airport.[178]

In the 1950s, Communists in Iceland made up 20 percent of the national vote and seats in the Icelandic Parliament. However, the Icelandic Communists, thought of themselves more as radical Icelanders than as agents of any foreign power. The State Department felt that the Social Democratic party was rather weak, which may have explained the popularity of the Communists. U.S. officials also thought that it was "our policy discreetly to encourage this opposition and to point out whenever possible the true nature of the Communist Party." Also of concern was "Icelandic parochialism and nationalism," which were considered a significant factor in Icelandic behavior and remained obstacles to closer relations between Iceland and the United States.[179]

In contrast, the Eisenhower administration believed that the Icelandic Communists were not a significant threat, and that Icelanders could effectively control their own radical elements. The administration felt that "a firm but understanding position on the part of the United States will assist Iceland in reducing communist influence within the country." But it also noted that an effort should be made within NATO to assist Iceland in countering its growing dependence on trade with the Soviets.[180]

The Eisenhower administration based its assumptions on the fact that 80 percent of the population in Iceland favored the West, and the number of hard-core Communists had dropped from 1,000 to around 500 by 1957. Iceland was the first NATO country to admit Communists to the government—a fact that initially made the United States very apprehensive and nervous, but this attitude changed over time. Communist influence decreased, lessening the fears. Ultimately, the recommendation was that the United States should take a firm but understanding position toward Iceland. The administration felt that, overall, Iceland had shown that it could control the Communists in its government, especially on security and foreign policy matters.[181]

Another difference between the two presidential administrations was over the issue of defending Norway in the event of an attack by the Soviet Union. In regard to a possible attack on Norway and Denmark, Britain's Deputy Director of Northern European Affairs Joseph C. Satterthwaite wrote in 1950 that the obligations of the NATO pact would naturally apply. Satterthwaite continued by stating that, although an attack on Norway and Denmark would not be as serious as an attack on the British Isles, their loss would imperil Britain: "We are, therefore, pretty close to being committed to protect them."[182]

In a National Security Council meeting on 29 October 1953, Eisenhower's Secretary of State John Foster Dulles expressed

some impatience with the talk about commitments. He insisted that we are not committed to the maintenance of any specified number of ground forces in Europe. We were committed to go to war there if there were an attack on a NATO country. Certainly, however, if the Soviets attack Norway, we were not committed to reply by fighting a war in Norway. We would be much more likely to retaliate somewhere else where the military advantages would be clear.[183]

The U.S. position had changed, somewhat subtly. Under the New Look, dependence on nuclear weapons figured prominently into the strategic calculus. In a 1957 telegram to the president, Dulles quoted a source (identity still classified) in Copenhagen as saying,

When in a few years' time the American continent comes within range of heavy Russian rocket attack, can we be confident that the American people will be willing to provoke wholesale death and destruction in their midst to prevent Soviet aggression in Turkey or Western Europe? Can we be sure that a wave of emotionalism such as we have recently seen here and in Germany, coupled with traditional isolationism, might not compel a future American administration to retreat from the policy of the nuclear deterrent? If, as I believe, we cannot rely indefinitely on the nuclear deterrent, then we must find some other method of preserving peace.[184]

Dulles went on to say that "we should not put all of our eggs in the general nuclear-war basket." He believed that

however confident we may be in our own minds as to our willingness to respond to an attack on Europe by starting a general nuclear war, our friends and allies will not believe that in fact we will do this. So, therefore, unless there seems to be some alternative they will turn to pacifism and neutralism.[185]

Although there is not a great deal of archival evidence concerning this issue, one can infer from these sources that it would not make sense under a New Look strategy to counter the Soviets in Norway; a global atomic war could not be risked over a such a small nation. Eisenhower and Dulles realized that the nuclear threat could not be the only method available to them, so they sought others. The New Look did not rely on atomic weapons alone, but also on negotiation, covert operations, and alliances.[186]

Officials in the Truman administration believed that Sweden should abandon its neutrality, but without antagonizing the Soviets.[187] U.S. Ambassador to Sweden H. Freeman Matthews reported in 1950 that Sweden should not be given the benefits of a NATO member without the cost and risk of membership. Waiting for Sweden to turn away from neutrality was unfair to Sweden, he felt, since it greatly exaggerated its own strength and ability to maintain neutrality. Sweden tended to underestimate the U.S.S.R., "which many Swedes still regard as that of Finn[ish] winter war."[188] Matthews was also afraid that Norway would be unrealistically dependent on Swedish defenses— defenses that were not adequate and were not guaranteed if war came. He stressed that Norway should be "encouraged to abandon any illusions in this regard and look to the West for her security."[189] In regard to the sale of radar to neutral Sweden, he felt that this would show the Danes and the Norwegians that nonmembers of NATO can also get benefits from the United States. The Swedes would concede that Norwegian and Danish membership was bringing added security, but would insist that it was also bringing war that much closer to Norden. Matthews warned that the Swedes would not miss any opportunity to convince the Danes and Norwegians to leave the pact.[190]

The Truman administration also was concerned about the Swedes' extremes in socializing their economy. In 1946 when Sweden planned to nationalize its petroleum industry, this meant that three American companies would lose their investments. The U.S. reaction was rather mild. The United States was against nationalization, but said that the decision ultimately lay with Sweden. From a political point of view, a sharp U.S. reaction would only have served to weaken the social democrats and strengthen the communists in Sweden.[191]

Both in National Security Council reports in 1948 and in a policy statement in 1949, the U.S. tone was critical of Swedish foreign policy. In terms of Sweden's domestic policy, the U.S. criticism was mild. The Truman administration could not understand how the Swedes were standing so firm domestically against the communists yet refusing to assume responsibilities in terms of the Western security system of which they were a part.[192]

Eisenhower officials realized that Sweden feared Soviet imperialism much more than communism. One of the reasons Sweden did not want to antagonize the Soviets was because of Finland. Sweden did not want the Soviet Union to move into Finland—which would place the Soviets on Sweden's border. The main problem in U.S.-Swedish relations was that the Swedes were upset with U.S. policies toward blacks. Nevertheless, the ambassador saw U.S. relations with Sweden as largely a holding operation.[193]

To Americans there was doubt whether Finland's treaty with the Soviets in 1948 was a realistic move, the best possible decision under adverse conditions, or an example of appeasement—the latter being alluded to with usage of the term *Finlandization*. Under the Truman administration, Kennan positioned himself on the Finlandization side of this argument. In a National Security Council meeting on 29 June 1950, the members discussed possible Soviet counter-moves in response to the U.S. response in Korea. Kennan said that

Finland was right in the Soviet orbit already. We would not want to intervene if the Russians took over in Finland, nor would we want to do anything to provoke Russian action in Finland or Sweden. He said we had never challenged Russia behind the lines drawn as a result of the settlements closing World War II, but that anything this side of that line engaged our interests. Finland, however, was behind that line.[194]

The Eisenhower administration seemed to show more appreciation for Finland's difficult situation. They sought to avoid any steps threatening the balance in the relationship between Finland and the Soviet Union, while endeavoring to strengthen the ability of Finland to maintain its independence.[195]

U.S. Ambassador to Finland John Hickerson said that the survival of Finland as a nation was a miracle. Despite a long history of Russian rule, the Finns have retained their national characteristics. Russian influences are lacking in Finland (even in its architectural styles). As a result of losing two wars with Russia, Finland lost 10 percent of its territory. But the entire population of the ceded areas moved, rather than live under Soviet rule. Ambassador Hickerson felt that the Soviets would use seduction rather than force against the Finns, because of their nonaggression pact. He felt that this effort would take at least two generations, and by that time the character of the Soviet Union would have changed anyway. The ambassador felt that the Finns (not unlike the Swedes) regarded the Russian people—rather than communism—as the real menace.

According to Hickerson, one of the most serious developments in Finland was the split in the Social Democratic party. Communist propaganda was active and was carried on through a Helsinki newspaper with a circulation of 50,000 and through a half-dozen smaller papers in other cities.[196]   But despite all of those activities, the Finns still remained independent and neutral. U.S. policy regarding Finland was discussed at a Northern European Chiefs of Mission Conference in 1957. The recommendation was that the United States "should avoid any action in . . . relations with Finland which would increase its difficulties in maintaining the delicate balance of Finnish-Soviet relations."[197]   Finland, in effect, served as a buffer for the rest of Norden. The Soviets had an acceptable diplomatic and strategic situation with the Finns that kept them from wanting more from Norden. A passage in NSC 5914 of 1959 (U.S. Policy toward Finland) noted that, if Finland were able to preserve its present neutral status despite heavy Soviet pressure, it could serve as an example of what the Untied States might like to see achieved by the Soviet-dominated nations of Eastern Europe. CIA Director Allen Dulles preferred to retain that passage in the policy despite some reservations by Secretary of State Christian Herter. Dulles said he would be delighted if a Finnish-type government developed in Poland or Czechoslovakia, because Finland was essentially a Western-oriented democratic country: "In effect we are saying to the USSR, you can live with a Western-oriented, democratic Finland, why not with Eastern European countries organized along the same lines?"[198]

The Nordic social democrats were instrumental in helping the Nordic countries accommodate to each other's methods in achieving the overarching goal of peaceful security. Despite this, Truman and Eisenhower held different views on the value of social democracy. Truman's domestic agenda was seen by the Norwegians as an extension of those policies initiated by the popular Franklin D. Roosevelt. The Truman administration did not worry so much about social democracy as about Norden's foreign policy concerns. The Eisenhower administration—although largely content with the Nordic Balance—was disturbed by Nordic domestic politics. There has been some evidence to indicate Eisenhower's dislike of social democracy. This attitude was alluded to in NSC 6006/1 (1960), which stated that the social democratic parties "are now evolving away from doctrinaire socialism toward a moderate welfare philosophy."[199]   Also, during a speech at a Republican National Committee breakfast in Chicago on 27 July 1960, Eisenhower more than alluded to his attitude toward social democracy.

We must have fiscal responsibility, in our determination not to establish an operative, paternalistic sort of government, where a man's initiative, the individual's initiative is almost taken away from him by force. Only in the last few weeks, I have been reading quite a thesis on the experiment of almost complete paternalism in a fairly friendly European country. This country has a tremendous record for socialistic operation, following a socialistic philosophy, and the record shows that their rate of suicide has gone up almost unbelievable and I think they were almost the lowest nation in the world for that. Now, they have more than twice our drunkenness. Lack of moderation is discernable on all sides. Therefore, with this kind of example, let's always remember Lincoln's admonition. Let's do in the Federal Government only those things that people themselves cannot do at all, or cannot so well do in their individual capacities.[200]

The reaction to the president's speech was dramatic in Scandinavia. The social democratic daily in Finland carried a front-page article about the Chicago speech on socialism. Swedish Prime Minister Tage Erlander spoke to a Nordic Council assembly and said it was a pity that Eisenhower did not come to Scandinavia to see the enthusiasm for education in the Nordic youth. Erlander felt that some Nordic citizens spoil their lives by exercising their freedom too greatly, but that it was the task of society to help them. He believed the president had been speaking of Sweden.[201] U.S. Ambassador to Norway Frances E. Willis sent a telegram to the secretary of state, noting that the reaction was mainly focused on which country the president had been referring to—some thought Sweden; some thought Scandinavia collectively; and others thought that the country did not exist at all and was made up by Eisenhower to frighten voters away from John F. Kennedy. At a 1960 Nordic Council meeting, Norwegian Prime Minister Gerhardsen noted several points in reference to Eisenhower's speech: (1) the remarks were not friendly; (2) Eisenhower spoke as a party politician and not as a president; (3) he hurt himself by speaking of matters he had no knowledge of; (4) a congressional delegation to Sweden would reveal it as a model state; (5) how could an army man from a system where the welfare measures were highly developed be so concerned with their influence on a civilian population? and (6) Eisenhower's criticism affected all other parties with similar social policies. In a January 1950 diary entry Eisenhower gave more evidence of his feelings toward socialism. He pasted in the diary an editorial and cartoon from the *New York Sun* decrying the "welfare state" and the "gravy train." Eisenhower indicated his agreement with the editorial writer who wrote about "Socialism, Communism, governmental extravagance, the encroachments of bureaucracy and that form of government paternalism which eats into the marrow of private initiative and industry."[202]

What were the implications of the differences between Eisenhower's and Truman's Nordic policies? Eisenhower worried less about an internal communist takeover in Norden than did Truman. In terms of national security, Eisenhower relied on an asymmetrical response, whereas Truman's approach was at first asymmetrical and then (after NSC 68) symmetrical.[203] The key difference may have been the way in which each administration viewed Nordic domestic and foreign policies. The Truman administration generally accepted the domestic policies of Norden—socialist though they were—and criticized its foreign policy. The Eisenhower administration came to realize the benefits of Norden's special combination of security approaches and was less critical of Norden's foreign policy; however, Eisenhower was critical of social democracy. This may be indicative of the influence that domestic U.S. politics have on foreign policy—the Democrats being more receptive to social democracy, and being under pressure to be more militant Cold Warriors than the Republicans. It can be said, then, that acceptance of the Nordic Balance came during the time of the Eisenhower administration.

A COMPARISON OF NORDIC/NORWEGIAN AND U.S. POLICY OBJECTIVES

Norway's policy objectives from 1947 to 1961 largely meshed with those of the rest of Norden. Norway wanted to secure U.S. protection, cultivate Western economic contacts, preserve Nordic ties, temper superpower penetration in the region, maintain its independence, balance social democratic domestic policy with defense, and preserve the Nordic world image. From the U.S. perspective, the Nordic countries were to be kept friendly and strong. This was accomplished in spite of some misconceptions concerning the power and influence of indigenous communist groups, and in spite of certain apprehensions regarding social democracy. Even though U.S. policies divided Norden into Scandinavia on the one hand and Iceland and Finland on the other, the U.S. objectives listed earlier tied the five nations together as one unit, one region. Finland remained neutral and oriented toward the West; the Nordic economies remained oriented toward the West; Greenland and Iceland remained U.S. bases; and Sweden did not need to be convinced to resist Soviet pressure. The only remaining objective was to have Denmark and Norway share equitably in their roles in NATO defense. Here, U.S. efforts largely failed. This points out the strength of small countries: they have more flexibility than superpowers. Norwegian objectives were realized, and so too were most of the U.S. ones. The only incompatible objective was the extent to which Norway should maintain its own defenses. Based on its careful balance of social democratic domestic policy and defense policy, along with a careful watch on its international image, Norway could not meet the expectations the Americans had of it in terms of defense spending. This problem was exacerbated by Norway's stand against nuclear weapons.

Given that there was an apparent compatibility of objectives, another interesting question is whether the United States accepted—tacitly or otherwise—the Nordic regional security system. The most fascinating aspect of U.S. policy in Norden is how the United States increasingly accepted the Nordic countries'way of handling their own regional affairs. Even though the United States did not agree with the Nordic countries all of the time, the Americans were careful never to push too hard. By 1960 the National Security Council observed, in NSC 6006/1, that "there is a high degree of cooperation among the Scandinavian countries, a good part of which extends to Iceland and Finland within the framework of the Nordic Council."[204] Continuing along these lines, the document called for encouraging "cooperation among the Scandinavians and Nordic countries (Scandinavia plus Finland and Iceland), particularly in assisting Finland to oppose Soviet pressure and maintain its Western ties." Sweden was to be provided with such equipment as was necessary for early warning and compatibility within NATO.[205] Eisenhower came to see the advantage of the Nordic Balance as a regionally based security solution that also met U.S. security needs. But Americans did not view areas such as Southeast Asia or Latin America in this way. The Nordic countries were able to convince both superpowers not to do their strong-arming in the North. Concerted Nordic positions regarding international affairs were a definite advantage to the United States. Nordic policy toward Finland seemed to be based on acceptance of the status quo in which Swedish neutrality was balanced with Finnish neutrality. A desire not to provoke a Soviet reaction on Finland undoubtedly was a factor in Sweden's neutrality and in the Nordic caution about building up the region's offensive military strength. Conversely, Soviet restraint with respect to Finland may have reflected a desire not to push Sweden into NATO or to accelerate Nordic military preparations.[206] The differences between Truman and Eisenhower on Nordic policy were driven by Truman's militarized containment (after Kennan's departure) and Eisenhower's more restrained containment, which, with some exceptions, accepted the Nordic arrangements more easily. Both administrations, however, practiced more restraint in Norden than in other regions of the world.

How did Norway view U.S. policy? Norway viewed U.S. policy in somewhat the same way it viewed Soviet policy. They were both superpowers who could unleash tremendous pressure on little Norway. The difference was that Norway was much more ideologically close to the United States and the West than to the Communist side. This points to the policy of integration and screening that Norway directed toward the West, and to the deterrence and reassurance it directed toward the East. The purpose of these policies was to leave Norway more room to maneuver politically and to stay out of superpower conflicts. The Norwegians were afraid of Soviet domination and also of McCarthyist forces in the United States and the negative impact these forces would have on Norway's freedom and image. Norway appreciated U.S. support but did not want political strings attached, trouble with the Soviets, or loss of international prestige. There were some misconceptions on both sides. The Norwegians may have worried too much about McCarthyism and right-wing extremism in the United States, whereas the Americans may have worried excessively over neutralism.

How did Norway reconcile its roles in Norden and in the East-West conflict? Norway successfully interwove Atlantic, Western European, Nordic, and global policies. It reconciled these roles through its no-basing policy and the policies of integration and screening, and deterrence and reassurance. The no-basing policy kept the Soviets satisfied that NATO and the United States would not establish forward bases close to Soviet territory. It also defined the limits of Norway's membership obligations in NATO. Integration kept Norway plugged into the West so it could enjoy the benefits of this association, but screening kept it aloof from the image problems America had. Deterrence kept Norway safe from Soviet advances, and reassurance helped Norway convince the Soviets that it was not totally in the Western camp and did not require "political adjustment." This left Norway free to integrate with the rest of Norden and take part in international organizations that helped foster Third World development. By stabilizing East-West tensions through reducing superpower insecurity and opportunism, Norway and the rest of Norden were able to concentrate on economic development and their other roles in the international system.

The Norwegian perspective showed that Norway's path through the Cold War was indeed rocky and treacherous. The key lessons to be derived from Norway's experience then are that diversity can be a strength and that successful cooperation can take place in spite of diverse policy orientations. Chapter 4 will use the historical analysis and the theoretical material provided thus far to construct a model of peaceful security based on the Nordic systems.

NOTES

1. Alvin Z. Rubinstein, *Soviet Foreign Policy since World War II: Imperial and Global*, 2nd ed. (Boston: Little, Brown, 1985), p. 122.
2. An agreement was struck in 1920 with several nations (the Soviets did not sign until 1925) that effectively neutralized the archipelago, but retained Norwegian sovereignty. The strategic location of Spitsbergen guaranteed its continuing interest to both the United States and the Soviet Union. Victor B. Moon, "Soviet-Norwegian Relations since 1945," *Western Political Quarterly* 17 (December 1964): 659.
3. Rolf Tamnes, "Handlefrihet og lojalitet. Norge og atompolitikken i 1950-årene," in Trond Bergh and Helge Ø. Pharo, eds., *Historiker og Veileder: Festskrift til Jakob Sverdrup* (Oslo: Tiden Norsk Forlag, 1989), p. 204.
4. Ibid., pp. 205-206. Post-World War II bombers had limited ranges, and bases were needed as stepping-stones to reach strategic targets. The United States wanted strategic bases in Northern Europe, especially in Norway. At the same time, the Americans were afraid that the Soviets would get these bases first.
5. According to Kennan, the five strongpoints were, in addition to the superpowers, Japan, Britain, and Central Europe including Germany.
6. Rolf Tamnes, *The United States and the Cold War in the High North* (Brookfield, VT: Dartmouth Publishing) , p. 40.
7. Geir Lundestad, "Nasjonalisme og internasjonalisme i norsk utenrikspolitikk: Et faglig-provoserende essay," *Internasjonal Politikk*, no. 1 (1985): p. 41.
8. The main point for this perspective is that the Norwegian government in exile during World War II worked closely with the Allies, so the policy after 1945 continued to reflect this close relationship with the West.
9. Due to the traditional orientation of Norwegian historical research and easy access to Norwegian sources, it was natural that Norwegian aspects of the Cold War were developed earlier than international ones. Two main schools have developed in Norway in explaining the Cold War. The early works focused primarily on the Labor party (the Norwegian Social Democratic party) and its role in postwar politics. For these historians the degree of control of the Labor party is important and they largely ignore the international preconditions for Norwegian policy. The second school, which has come into dominance recently, integrated studies of the party elite within a framework of foreign and security policy issues. This school generally broadened the focus of postwar Norwegian historiography to understand how Norway fit into the Nordic region and the rest of the international system. Helge Ø. Pharo, "The Cold War in Norwegian and International Historical Research," *Scandinavian Journal of History* 10 (1985): 165-167.
10. Knut E. Eriksen, "Norge i det vestlige samarbeid," in Trond Bergh and Helge Ø. Pharo, *Vekst og Velstand: Norsk Politisk Historie 1945-1965*

(Oslo: Universitetsforlaget, 1989), p. 169.

11. Lundestad, "Nasjonalisme og internasjonalisme i norsk utenrikspolitikk," pp. 40-41.

12. Wayne S. Cole, *Norway and the United States, 1905-1955: Two Democracies in Peace and War* (Ames: Iowa State University Press, 1989), p. 151.

13. Memorandum by the Deputy Director of the Office of the British Commonwealth and Northern European Affairs ([Joseph C.] Satterthwaite) to the Deputy Assistant Secretary of State for European Affairs ([Llewellyn] Thompson), 8 February 1950, in *Foreign Relations of the United States* [hereafter *FRUS*] *1950*, vol. 1: *National Security Affairs; Foreign Economic Policy* (Washington, DC: Government Printing Office, 1977), p. 143; "Northern European Chiefs of Mission Conference, London, 19-21 September 1957: Conclusions and Recommendations," in *Foreign Relations of the United States* [hereafter *FRUS*] *1955-1957*, vol. 4: *Western European Security and Integration* (Washington, DC: Government Printing Office, 1986), pp. 610-611.

14. It is not easy to exactly mark turning points in history. Forces that lead to dramatic events oftentimes build for a long time before these events occur. Upon close examination one can see the gradual transition; but for ease of understanding, turning points are used.

15. Olav Larssen, *Den Langsomme Revolusjonen* (Oslo: H. Aschehoug [W. Nygaard], 1973), p. 63; *Konrad Nordahl Dagbøker*, Bind 2, 1950-55 (Oslo: Tiden Norsk Forlag , 1992), p. 85. Norwegian historian Helge Ø. Pharo believes that Norway decided to go along with the Marshall Plan because Denmark needed economic help desperately, and there would be serious foreign policy consequences if Denmark accepted and Norway did not. Also, other neutral-oriented European nations seemed interested in the aid. Therefore, he contends, foreign policy concerns were the dominant determinant in Norway's decision to accept Marshall Plan aid. Trond Bergh, "Norsk økonomisk politikk," in Trond Bergh and Helge Ø. Pharo, eds., *Vekst og Velstand: Norsk Politisk Historie 1945-1965* (Oslo: Universitetsforlaget, 1989), pp. 33; and Helge Ø. Pharo, "Gjenreisining of utenrikspolitikk," in Trond Bergh and Helge Ø. Pharo, eds., *Historiker og Veileder* (Oslo: Tiden Norsk Forlag, 1989), pp. 180.

16. Many Norwegians, however, thought it was odd that the Marshall Plan—coming from a capitalist stronghold such as the United States—should help build the socially planned economy of Norway. Since the early 1980s in Norway, there has been a great deal of literature on the Marshall Plan. However, there has been a big difference among the authors in terms of explaining American political motives, European politics, and the situation in Europe after George C. Marshall's 5 June 1947 speech. Traditional accounts neglected American interest in tampering with the European political economy. These accounts focused positively on the United States, based on its role in defeating the Nazis and defending Western Europe against Soviet communism. They largely ignored U.S. economic penetration. Later, revisionist accounts held that the United States had

serious plans to change radically Europe's political economy and began to question American intentions. Norwegian historiography has focused mostly on the foreign policy implications of the Marshall Plan. *Det Norske Arbeiderparti Beretning 1948* (Oslo: Aktietrykkeriet, Norwegian Labor Party Archive, 1949), p. 17; and Helge Ø. Pharo, "Marshallplanen set fra amerikansk side. Norge i komparativt perspektiv," *Historisk Tidsskrift*, no. 2 (1989): 184.

17. It should be noted that Marshall Plan aid became increasingly military in nature as the Cold War dragged on. This may have had an impact on popular opinion. Despatch, Oslo Embassy to Department of State, "Norwegian Gallup Poll on Current Topics," 9 February 1953, Record Group 59, Box 3762, File 757.00/2-953, National Archives of the United States of America.

18. Helge Ø. Pharo, "Marshallplanen set fra amerikansk side. Norge i komparativt perspektiv," *Historisk Tidsskrift*, no. 2 (1989): 191-192, 208-209.

19. Geir Lundestad, "Empire by Invitation? The United States and Western Europe, 1945-1952," *Journal of Peace Research* 23, no. 3 (1986): 263-277; and Geir Lundestad, *The American "Empire"* (Oslo: Norwegian University Press, 1990), pp. 54-56.

20. The primary concern was for containing Soviet communism. In a meeting between U.S. Secretary of State George C. Marshall and Norwegian Ambassador Wilhelm Morgenstierne, Marshall said that there were only two courses for the United States: to accept or challenge communist aggression in all of Western Europe. He felt that the Soviets wanted peace but only if they could dictate it. Marshall felt that only after Western Europe was stabilized could there be meaningful dialogue between East and West. Letter from the Norwegian Embassy in Washington to the Foreign Ministry, 16 December 1947, no. 1217, "Unanhåndsuttalelser av George F. Kennan, State Department," in Folder 25.4/47, De Forente Stater Politikk, bind 13, 1 to 31 December 1947, Royal Norwegian Foreign Ministry, Oslo; and Letter from Norwegian Embassy in Washington to the Foreign Ministry, 6 February 1948, no. 138, "Marshall-planen uttalesen av utenriksminister Marshall", Folder 25.4/47, De Forente Stater Politikk, bind 14, 1 January 1948 to 14 February 1948, Royal Norwegian Foreign Ministry, Oslo.

21. Letter from Norwegian Embassy in Washington to the Foreign Ministry, no. 524, 24 April 1951, "Amerikansk syn på Norge samtale med Mr. Harriman," File 34.4/47, Norges politiske forhold til U.S.A., bind 2, 1 January 1950 to 31 December 1959, Royal Norwegian Foreign Ministry, Oslo.

22. Government Economic Commission, 18 November 1949, Statsministerens kontor, referat fra regjeringskonferanser, 1947-61, Norwegian National Archives, Oslo.

23. Olav Riste, *Isolasjonisme og Stormaktsgarantier: Norsk Tryggingspolitkk 1905-1990*, vol. 3 (Oslo: Institutt for Forsvarsstudier, 1991), p. 17; and Knut E. Eriksen, "Norge i det vestige samarbeid," in Trond Bergh and Helge Ø. Pharo, eds., *Vekst og Velstand: Norsk Politisk*

Historie 1945-1965 (Oslo: Universitetsforlaget, 1989), pp. 186-191. Part of the reason for Norway's reluctance was the perception of many Norwegians that Americans were extremists—either vehement anticommunists or communists. *Arbeiderbladet*, 25 April 1947, in Folder 25.4/47, De Forente Stater Politikk, bind 13, 1 to 31 December 1947, Royal Norwegian Foreign Ministry, Oslo.

24. Nils M. Udgaard, *Great Power Politics and Norwegian Foreign Policy: A Study of Norway's Foreign Relations, November 1940-February 1948* (Oslo: Universitetsforlaget, 1973), pp. 41, 208, 219, 223.

25. *Friheten*, 25 April 1947, in Folder 25.4/47, De Forente Stater Politikk, bind 13, 1 to 31 December 1947, Royal Norwegian Foreign Ministry, Oslo.

26. Letter from the Norwegian Embassy in Washington to the Foreign Ministry, 26 January 1948, no. 99, "Gjenreisingsplanen for Europa. Forsvarsminister Forrestal avgir vitreprov," and Letter from the Norwegian Embassy in Washington to the Foreign Ministry, 20 January 1948, no. 65, "Amerikansk syn på forholdet mellom vesteuropeisk sosialisme og kommunismen," in folder 25.4/47, De Forente Stater Politikk, bind 14, 1 January 1948 to 14 February 1948, Royal Norwegian Foreign Ministry, Oslo.

27. Report by the National Security Council, NSC 28/1, "The Position of the United States with Respect to Scandinavia," 3 September 1948, in *Foreign Relations of the United States* [hereafter *FRUS*] *1948*, vol. 3: *Western Europe* (Washington: Government Printing Office, 1974), pp. 232-234.

28. The Brussels Treaty (1948) brought Britain, France, and the three Benelux nations together for the purpose of self-defense.

29. Geir Lundestad, *America, Scandinavia, and the Cold War, 1945-1949* (New York: Columbia University Press, 1980), pp. 247-248.

30. Ibid., p. 252.

31. Kennan favored a graduated membership, but others did not. Ibid., pp. 253-256.

32. Riste, *Isolasjonisme og Stormaktsgarantier*, pp. 17-18. An excellent article on the Swedish point of view—based on recently opened material in Sweden—is Gerard Aalders, "The Failure of the Scandinavian Defence Union, 1948-1949," *Scandinavian Journal of History* 15, no. 2 (1990): 125-153.

33. Eriksen, "Norge i det vestlige samarbeid," pp. 205-206.

34. Telegram from the Ambassador in Sweden ([H. Freeman] Matthews) to the Secretary of State [Dean Acheson], Stockholm, 7 February 1950, in *FRUS 1950*, vol. 3: *Western Europe*, p. 15.

35. Telegram from the Secretary of State [Dean Acheson] to the Embassy in Sweden, 16 February 1950, in *FRUS 1950*, vol. 3, p. 19.

36. Denmark presented difficulties in terms of defense because of its virtually indefensible location, and it was afraid of being isolated. Ibid., p. 19.

37. Government Meeting Minutes, 14 October 1947 and 27 May

1948, Statsministerens kontor, referat fra regjeringskonferanser, 1947-61, Norwegian National Archives, Oslo.

38. Letter from Norwegian Embassy in Washington, 3 April 1948, no. 422, "De Forente Statens utenrikspolitikk. Det militære beredskap"; Letter from the Royal Danish Embassy in Washington to the Foreign Ministry, no. 12, "Det amerikanske syn paa skandinavia"; and Letter form Norwegian Embassy in Washington to the Foreign Ministry, 6 March 1948, "Statminister Gerhardsens tale"—all in Folder 25.4/47, De Forente Stater Politikk, bind 15, 15 February 1948 to 31 August 1948, Royal Norwegian Foreign Ministry, Oslo.

39. Norwegian historian Geir Lundestad believes that the United States was more flexible in regard to the SDU than popularly thought, but Lange did not desire an alliance without U.S. guarantees. Another Norwegian historian, Trond Bergh, disagrees and believes that Lange truly wanted an SDU. Lundestad also believes that an alliance-free Scandinavian pact could not rely on receiving weapons from the United States. Lange hoped to mesh the two security alternatives—Nordic and North Atlantic—and he felt that delaying the decision on the SDU would further this aim. He realized Norway needed a firm foothold in the West. Knut E. Eriksen and Helge Ø. Pharo, *Norsk Sikkerhetspolitikk som Etterkrigshistorisk Forskningsfelt*, LOS-senter notat 92/13 (Bergen, Norway: LOS-senter, 1992), p. 31; Geir Lundestad, "USA, skandinavisk forsvarsforbund og Halvard Lange: En revurdering," *Internasjonal Politikk*, no. 1 (January-March 1977): 140, 166; and conversation with Trond Bergh in Oslo, May 1992.

40. Eriksen, "Norge i det vestige samarbeid," p. 215.

41. Tamnes, *United States and Cold War*, p. 41.

42. Helge Ø. Pharo, "Norwegian Social Democrats and European Integration in the 1950s," mimeographed colloquium paper, 15-16 November 1988, p. 9.

43. Despatch, Oslo Embassy (Marselis C. Parsons) to State Department, Meeting of COMISCO, London, March 2-4, 1951, Foreign Service Posts of the Department of State, Record Group 84, Norway, Oslo Embassy, 1950-1952, Box 46, Washington National Records Center; also Statsministerens Kontor, Protokoll for Hemmelige Saker, Regjeringskonferanser, 5 November 1946 to 5 October 1948, Norwegian National Archives, Oslo.

44. Despatch, Oslo Embassy, *Aftenposten* Discusses Scandinavian Defense Cooperation, 24 March 1950, Foreign Service Posts of the Department of State, Record Group 84, Norway, Oslo Embassy, 1950-1952, Box 47, Washington National Records Center.

45. Helge Ø. Pharo, "The Third Force, Atlanticism, and Norwegian Attitudes." EUI Working Paper No. 86/255, (Florence, Italy: European University Institute, 1986), pp. 2-4.

46. Ibid., p. 660. The Czech leader's death was a case of convenient suicide for the Soviets. Masaryk was reported to have jumped to his death from the window of a tall building.

47. Tamnes, *United States and Cold War*, p. 44.

48. Lauris Norstad, oral interview conducted as part of Columbia University Oral History Project, 11 November 1976, no. OH-385, transcript pp. 48-49, Eisenhower Library. Note: he never wrote the book he spoke of in the quote.

49. Despatch, Oslo Embassy (Marselis C. Parsons) to State Department, "Lange's Speech on 'The Atlantic Democracies and the UN,' " Foreign Service Posts of the Department of State, Record Group 84, Norway, Oslo Embassy, 1950-52, Box 46, Washington National Records Center.

50. Pharo, "Norwegian Social Democrats and European Integration," p. 6.

51. *Det Norske Arbeiderparti Landsmøtet 1949 Protokoll* (Oslo: Aktietrykkeriet, Norwegian Labor Party Archives, 1950), pp. 131, 135-136, 161. From the Norwegian perspective, and despite Norway's NATO membership and close relations with the United States, Defense Minister Lange felt that the United States put too little emphasis on nonmilitary cooperation under NATO. Memo from John Foster Dulles to [Dwight D.] Eisenhower, "Visit of Foreign Minister Halvard Lange of Norway," 3 March 1953, Whitman File, International Series, Box 37, Folder Norway 3, Eisenhower Library; Report to Nelson A. Rockefeller from Robert Murphy, Deputy Under Secretary of State, "Neutralism in Europe," 19 August 1955, White House Office, NSC Staff Papers, 1948-61, Planning Coordination Group Series, Box 2, Folders 1-4 Bandung, pp. 1-3, Eisenhower Library.

52. Ibid., pp. 168, 185.

53. Ibid., pp. 117-123.

54. Ibid., pp. 125-127.

55. Eriksen, "Norge i det vestige samarbeid," pp. 221-225. In an interview in the *Manchester Guardian*, Halvard Lange said that in regard to recent agreements proposed by the United States over Iceland and Greenland, and in answer to the question of whether these agreements had found approval in Oslo, "Norway's geographical situation naturally leads us to take a lively interest in the defence of the Arctic. The treaties were concluded and the defence of Greenland and Iceland have received our entire approval." *Manchester Guardian*, "Norway Looks Westward: Nation Solidly behind Policy of Close Collaboration," 23 July 1951.

56. Eriksen, "Norge i det vestige samarbeid," pp. 221-225.

57. Despatch, "*Arbeiderbladet* Discusses Further Development of the Atlantic Pact," 4 April 1950, Foreign Service Posts of the Department of State, Record Group 84, Norway, Oslo Embassy, 1950-52, Box 47, Washington National Records Center.

58. Pharo, "Cold War in Norwegian and International Historical Research," p. 2.

59. Letter from Norwegian Embassy in Washington to the Foreign Ministry, 10 March 1949, no. 233, "State Departments reaksjon på utskiftingen i Sovjet-Samveldets Regjering", in Folder 25.4/47, De Forente Stater Politikk, bind 17, 1 February 1949 to 31 December 1949, Royal Norwegian Foreign Ministry, Oslo.

60. Eriksen and Pharo, *Norsk Sikkerhetspolitikk*, p. 35. A fuller explanation of these concepts can be found in Chapter 2.

61. Letter from Ambassador [Wilhelm] Morgenstierne to the Norwegian Foreign Ministry, 31 October 1949, "Den 81. kongress' 1ste sesjon," in Folder 25.4/47, De Forente Stater Politikk, bind 17, 1 February 1949 to 31 December 1949, Norwegian Foreign Ministry, Oslo.

62. Letter from Norwegian delegation to the United Nations, 27 October 1949, no. 89, "U.S. Politics with Communist Lands," in Folder 25.4/47, De Forente Stater Politikk, bind 17, 1 February 1949 to 31 December 1949, Royal Norwegian Foreign Ministry, Oslo.

63. Letter from Norwegian Embassy in Washington to the Foreign Ministry, 25 June 1949, no. 729, "Amerikanskutenrikspolitikk, uttalesen av utenriksminister Acheson," and Letter from Norwegian Embassy in Washington to the Foreign Ministry, 17 April 1949, no. 395, "Finansiering av amerikansk støtte til Europa," in Folder 25.4/47, De Forente Stater Politikk, bind 17, 1 February 1949 to 31 December 1949, Royal Norwegian Foreign Ministry, Oslo.

64. Memo from Norwegian Embassy in Stockholm to the Foreign Ministry, 6 July 1949, "U.S. Information Service Message Criticized in Swedish Press," in Folder 25.4/47, De Forente Stater Politikk, bind 17, 1 February 1949 to 31 December 1949, Royal Norwegian Foreign Ministry, Oslo.

65. Knut E. Eriksen and Helge Ø. Pharo, "Norsk Utenrikspolitikk 1949-61," mimeograph, p. 1, University of Oslo, 1990.

66. Tamnes, *United States and Cold War*, p. 39.

67. Telegram, Oslo Embassy to Secretary of State [Dean Acheson], 8 August 1950, Record Group 59, Box 3762, File 757.00/8-850, National Archives of the United States of America.

68. An example of this extremism came when a seventeen-year-old Norwegian boy was denied entry into the United States in New York because his father was a communist and he had been to a children's school in Czechoslovakia. When this issue was brought up in the Norwegian Parliament, members questioned whether the Norwegian police had intimate contact with the U.S. authorities. The MPs were afraid that the U.S. intelligence service had easy access to information on Norwegian internal affairs. Finn Gustavsen, *Rett På Sak* (Oslo: Pax Forlag, 1979), pp. 74-77.

69. Henry Valen, "Cleavages in the Norwegian Electorate as a Constraint on Foreign Policymaking," in Johan J. Holst, ed., *Norwegian Foreign Policy in the 1980s* (Oslo: Universitetsforlaget, 1985), pp. 26-27.

70. Pharo, "Cold War in Norwegian and International Historical Research," p. 167.

71. Arne Ording, Diary, 28 June, 10 July, 17 August, and 1 December 1950, Manuscript Collection, University of Oslo Library.

72. *Konrad Nordahl Dagbøker*, Bind 1, 1950-55 (Oslo: Tiden Norsk Forlag , 1991), p. 25.

73. Ibid., p. 49.

74. Eriksen and Pharo, "Norsk Utenrikspolitikk 1949-1961," p. 1.

75. Despatch, Oslo Embassy, Transmittal of Soviet Press Article on the Alleged Popular Opposition of the Norwegian People to Their Government's Policies," 9 May 1950, Record Group 59, Box 3762, File 757.00/5-950, National Archives of the United States of America.

76. Arne Ording, Diary, 24 October and 8-24 November 1950, 3 May 1951, Manuscript Collection, University of Oslo Library.

77. Despatch, Oslo Embassy, "Oslo Paper's Appraisal of Present U.S. Political Scene," 19 April 1951, Foreign Service Posts of the Department of State, Record Group 84, Norway, Oslo Embassy, 1950-52, Box 50, Washington National Records Center.

78. Despatch, Oslo Embassy to Department of State, "Recent Developments in the Independent Norwegian League (Uavhengig Norsk Gruppe)," 6 March 1952, Record Group 59, Box 3762, File 757.00/3-652, National Archives of the United States of America; Despatch, Oslo Embassy to Department of State, "Meeting of the Norwegian Independent League (Uavhengig Norsk Gruppe)," 10 March 1952, Record Group 59, Box 3762, File 757.00/3-1052, National Archives of the United States of America.

79. Tamnes, *United States and Cold War,* p. 63.

80. Despatch, "*Arbeiderbladet* Interviews Ambassador [Wilhelm] Morgenstierne," 3 July 1950, Foreign Service Posts of the Department of State, Record Group 84, Norway, Oslo Embassy, 1950-52, Box 47, Washington National Records Center.

81. Despatch, "*Friheten* Attacks Ambassador [Wilhelm] Morgenstierne and Atlantic Policy," 3 July 1950, Foreign Service Posts of the Department of State, Record Group 84, Norway, Oslo Embassy, 1950-52, Box 47, Washington National Records Center.

82. Arne Ording, Diary, 6 January 1950, Manuscript Collection, University of Oslo Library.

83. Tamnes, *United States and Cold War*, p. 65.

84. *Current Digest of the Soviet Press*, vol. 2, no. 39, p. 19, quoted in Moon, "Soviet-Norwegian Relations," p. 661.

85. According to a 1950 report, 35 percent of Norway's gross national product (GNP) was dedicated to foreign policy objectives. Additionally, Norway had become a more exportoriented nation with a 25-30 percent increase in exports between 1945 and 1950. Despite the dangers of the Cold War political-economic environment, the government in Norway made it clear that defense and security were number one priorities. But this could not be accomplished without consideration of the impact of this policy on the people. The Norwegian government combined an enhanced defense program with aid to all other sectors. Cole, *Norway and United States,* pp. 139-140; Statsministerens Kontor, Protokoll for Hemmelige Saker, Regjeringskonferanser, 5 November 1946 to 5 October 1948, Norwegian National Archives, Oslo; andReport, 10 December 1957, "Foreløpig analyyse av Norges politisk-økonomiske evne til å møtre forsvarets behov," pp. 1-6, Statsministerens Kontor referat fra regjeringskonferanser, 1947-61, Norwegian National Archives, Oslo.

86. Memos, 16 February 1950 and 21 January 1949, Saks nr. H-43,

ref. 71, "Melding fra ambassaden i Washington bilaterale avtale," Forsvarsdepartement H-Arkiv, 1946-52, Norwegian National Archives, Oslo.

87. Memo, Norwegian Defense Minister Jens C. Hague to Henry Villard, U.S. Chargé d'Affaires, Attached Press Release, 20 April 1950, Foreign Service Posts of the Department of State, Record Group 84, Norway, Oslo Embassy, 1950-52, Box 47, Washington National Records Center.

88. Airgram, Oslo Embassy, 12 January 1950, and Despatch, Oslo Embassy, 16 February 1950, Foreign Service Posts of the Department of State, Record Group 84, Norway, Oslo Embassy, 1950-52, Box 47, Washington National Records Center.

89. Despatch, Oslo Embassy, "Communist Cartoon Lampoons ECA and MAAG," 20 February 1950, Foreign Service Posts of the Department of State, Record Group 84, Norway, Oslo Embassy, 1950-52, Box 47, Washington National Records Center; Despatch, Oslo Embassy, "Norwegian News Coverage of MDAP Bilateral Agreements," 2 February 1950, Foreign Service Posts of the Department of State, Record Group 84, Norway, Oslo Embassy, 1950-52, Box 47, Washington National Records Center.

90. Despatch, Oslo Embassy, "Statement of Chairman of Communist Party, Emil Løvlien, on Occasion of the Opening of Storting," 26 January 1950, Record Group 59, Box 3762, File 757.00/1-2650, National Archives of the United States of America.

91. Despatch, Oslo Embassy, "Foreign Minister's Report to the Storting on the Conduct of Norwegian Foreign Affairs," 24 July 1950, Record Group 59, Box 3762, File 757.00/7-2450, National Archives of the United States of America.

92. Despatch, Oslo Embassy, "Oscar Torp Speaks on Norway' Situation in 1950," 23 March 1950, Record Group 59, Box 3762, File 757.00/3-2350, National Archives of the United States of America.

93. John Fitsmaurice, *Security and Politics in the Nordic Area* (Brookfield, VT: Gower Publishing, 1987), pp. 38-39.

94. Pharo, "Norwegian Social Democrats and European Integration," p. 4.

95. *Functionalism* and *federalism* are terms used in integration theory. Functionalism refers to a series of intermeshing agreements that form a comprehensive system. Federalism refers to a system run from a central organ that makes all important decisions.

96. Pharo, "Norwegian Social Democrats and European Integration," pp. 4-5.

97. Ibid., p. 29.

98. Nils Andrén, "Nordic Integration and Cooperation—Illusion and Reality," *Cooperation and Conflict* 19, no. 4 (1984): 252, 259; and Eriksen and Pharo, "Norsk Utenrikspolitikk," p. 10.

99. Jahn Otto Johansen, *Sovjetunionen og Norden: Konfrontasjon eller naboskap?* (Oslo: J.W. Cappelens Forlag A/S, 1986), pp. 130, 134;

Robert K. German, "Norway and the Bear: Soviet Coercive Diplomacy and Norwegian Security Policy," *International Security* 7 (Fall 1982): 62-63; and *Konrad Nordahl Dagbøker*, Bind 2, 1950-55 (Oslo: Tiden Norsk Forlag, 1992), p. 104. Nils Petter Gleditsch and Sverre Lodgaard, well respected Norwegian political analysts, hold that Norwegian base policy was illusory and had little if any deterrent effect on the Soviet Union. See Nils P. Gleditsch, and Sverre Lodgaard, *Krigsstaten Norge* (Oslo, Norway: Pax Forlag A/S, 1970); and Sverre Lodgaard and Nils P. Gleditsch, "Norway—the not so Reluctant Ally," *Cooperation and Conflict*, no. 4 (1977).

100.   Memo by the Ambassador to Finland ([John Moors] Cabot), 19 July 1950, in *FRUS 1950*, vol. 4, p. 581.

101.   Ibid., p. 582.

102.   Telegram from the Chargé in Finland ([Samuel] Chase) to the Secretary of State [Dean Acheson], 25 February 1950, in *FRUS 1950*, vol. 4, p. 578. I was somewhat surprised by the use of the term *commies* by the secretary of state.

103.   Despatch, Ambassador to Finland ([John Moors] Cabot) to the Secretary of State [Dean Acheson], 23 March 1950, in *FRUS 1950*, vol.4, p. 579.

104.   Despatch, Oslo Embassy, "The Status of Public Information on Defense in Norway," 12 July 1951, Foreign Service Posts of the Department of State, Record Group 84, Norway, Oslo Embassy, 1950-52, Box 47, Washington National Records Center. According to Konrad Nordahl, communists were strong in the northern part of Norway (Finnmark), *Konrad Nordahl Dagbøker*, Bind 1, 1950-55 (Oslo: Tiden Norsk Forlag , 1991), p. 71.

105.   Despatch from Oslo Embassy, with Enclosure, "The Peoples of the Scandinavian Countries in the Struggle for Peace" (*Izvestiya*, 28 December 1951), 21 January 1952, Foreign Service Posts of the Department of State, Record Group 84, Norway, Oslo Embassy, 1950-52, Box 46, Washington National Records Center.

106.   Telegram, Oslo Embassy to State Department, 3 December 1951, Foreign Service Posts of the Department of State, Record Group 84, Norway, Oslo Embassy, 1950-52, Box 47, Washington National Records Center. Eisenhower's popularity also came from his views toward Norway's security policy made clear while NATO commander. Arne Ording, Diary, 25 May 1951, Manuscript Collection, University of Oslo Library.

107.   Memo, Conversation between Ambassador [Charles Ulrick] Bay and Foreign Minister [Bjarni] Bendiktsson, 13 March 1951, Foreign Service Posts of the Department of State, Record Group 84, Norway, Oslo Embassy, 1950-52, Box 47, Washington National Records Center.

108.   Despatch, Oslo Embassy, "Prime Minister Gerhardsen Speaks on Scandinavian Cooperation," 4 December 1951, Foreign Service Posts of the Department of State, Record Group 84, Norway, Oslo Embassy, 1950-52, Box 50, Washington National Records Center.

109.   Despatch, Oslo Embassy, "Norwegian Press Interview   with Swedish Minister Unden,"   17 March 1952, Foreign Service Posts of the

Department of State, Record Group 84, Norway, Oslo Embassy, 1950-52, Box 50, Washington National Records Center.

110. *Det Norske Arbeiderparti Landsmøtet 1959 Protokoll* (Oslo: Aktietrykkeriet, Norwegian Labor Party Archives, 1960), p. 88; and Tamnes, "United States and Cold War,"p. 86.

111. Rolf Tamnes, "Handlefrihet og lojalitet. Norge og atompolitikken i 1950-årene," in Trond Bergh and Helge Ø. Pharo, eds., *Historiker og Veileder: Festskrift til Jakob Sverdrup* (Oslo: Tiden Norsk Forlag, 1989), pp. 206-207.

112. Despatch, Oslo Embassy, 17 October 1951, Foreign Service Posts of the Department of State, Record Group 84, Norway, Oslo Embassy, 1950-52, Box 47, Washington National Records Center.

113. Despatch, Oslo Embassy to Department of State, "Norwegian Gallup Poll on Current Topics," 9 February 1953, Record Group 59, Box 3762, File 757.00/2-953, National Archives of the United States of America.

114. Ibid.

115. Telegram, Oslo Embassy to Secretary of State, 25 June 1951, Record Group 59, Box 3762, File 757.00/6-2551, National Archivesof the United States of America.

116. Conference Report, 28 October 1951, Statsministerens Kontor, Referat Fra Regjeringskonferanser, 1947-61, Norwegian National Archives, Oslo. Germany's admission to NATO in 1955, so soon after World War II, was also particularly distressing to Norwegians. Cole, *Norway and United States,* pp. 152-155.

117. Despatch, Oslo Embassy, "Eisenhower's January 7 Statement," 16 January 1952, Foreign Service Posts of the Department of State, Record Group 84, Norway, Oslo Embassy, 1950-52, Box 50, Washington National Records Center.

118. Despatch, Oslo Embassy to Department of State, "Norwegian Gallup Poll on Current Topics," 9 February 1953, Record Group 59, Box 3762, File 757.00/2-953, National Archives of the United States of America.

119. Eisenhower appointed many more businessmen to high positions than did his predecessor—76 percent for Ike and 43 percent for Truman. Norwegians were surprised when they learned that Ike would name a Democrat as labor secretary (Martin P. Durkin). Thomas G. Paterson, J. Garry Clifford, and Kenneth J. Hagan, *American Foreign Policy: A History since 1900,* 3rd ed. (Lexington, MA: D.C. Heath, 1988), p. 482; Cole, *Norway and United States,* p. 152; Despatch, "Public Comment on General Eisenhower's Visit to Oslo," 19 January 1951, Foreign Service Posts of the Department of State, Record Group 84, Norway, Oslo Embassy, 1950-52, Box 47, Washington National Records Center; and *Konrad Nordahl Dagbøker,* Bind 1, 1950-55 (Oslo: Tiden Norsk Forlag , 1991), pp. 177, 186-187, 195.

120. Tamnes, "Handlefrihet og lojalitet," p. 203.

121. Despatch, Oslo Embassy to State Department, "Press Reaction to

Resignation of Trygve Lie," 1 December 1952, and Telegram, from Ambassador [Charles Ulrick] Bay to the Secretary of State [Dean Acheson], 17 November 1952, Foreign Service Posts of the Department of State, Record Group 84, Norway, Oslo Embassy, 1950-52, Box 46, Washington National Records Center; *Det Norske Arbeiderparti Landsmøtet 1953 Protokoll* (Oslo: Aktietrykkeriet, Norwegian Labor Party Archives, 1954), pp. 168-169.

122. There were two phases: first, to install tactical nuclear weapons to supplant conventional weapons (detailed in MC 48, December 1954); and second, to plan how nuclear weapons were to be used in Europe (contained in MC 14/2 and the "New Weapons Concept" for 1958-63, MC 70).

123. But by 1960 it became clear that massive retaliation was dying as a concept. John F. Kennedy called for a new flexible response that was reliant on conventional weaponry—not unlike the early NATO plans.

124. The following points summarize this dualist position: (1) Norway expected NATO aircraft to be outfitted with nuclear weapons, (2) Norway held that, while certain situations would require Norwegian handling of nuclear weapons, NATO would handle centralized control; and (3) Norway was ambivalent about the use of nuclear weapons and did not want them on its soil. Tamnes, "Handlefrihet og lojalitet," pp. 216-219.

125. *Det Norske Arbeiderparti Landsmøtet 1953 Protokoll* (Oslo: Aktietrykkeriet, Norwegian Labor Party Archives, 1954), p. 163; and Paterson, et al., *American Foreign Policy,* p. 481.

126. Notat, 5 October 1953, "Forsvarsutgiftene for perioden 1. juli 1954 til 30. juni 1957," Statsministerens Kontor, Referat Fra Regjeringskonferanser, 1947-61, Norwegian National Archives, Oslo.

127. Pharo, "Third Force, Atlanticism, and Norwegian Attitudes," pp. 11-12.

128. In 1949, by contrast, there had been many who held grave doubts. Despatch, Oslo Embassy to Department of State, "34th National Congress of the Norwegian Labor Party," 24 April 1953, Record Group 59, Box 3762, File 757.00/4-2453, National Archives of the United States of America; and Despatch, Oslo Embassy to Department of State, "Liberal Party Attempt to Inject Foreign Policy Issues into Election Campaign," 29 September 1953, Record Group 59, Box 3762, file 757.00/9-2953, National Archives of the United States of America.

129. In the 1955 Labor Party Congress, delegates pointed out that, if the Soviet Union had demobilized its armies like the West and had not interdicted in Czechoslovakia, then there would have been no need for NATO. *Det Norske Arbeiderparti Landsmøtet 1953 Protokoll* (Oslo: Aktietrykkeriet, 1954), pp. 173, 175; *Det Norske Arbeiderparti Landsmøtet 1955 Protokoll* (Oslo: Aktietrykkeriet, Norwegian Labor Party Archives, 1956), p. 52.

130. Tom M. Hetland, *Atomrasling og Avspenning: Sovjet og Norsk Tryggingspolitikk, 1953-1958,* FHFS notat 5 (Oslo: Forsvarshistorisk Forskningssenter, 1984), pp. 1-37.

131. Report to Nelson A. Rockefeller from Robert Murphy, Deputy

under Secretary of State, "Neutralism In Europe," 19 August 1955, White House Office, NSC Staff Papers, 1948-61, Planning Coordination Group Series, Box 2, Folders 1-4 Bandung, pp. 1-3, Eisenhower Library.

132.   Nordahl represented some of the Norwegian fears during this period when he wrote that in 1956 the Cold War had returned in full force, led by the Russians again. Stalinism was again in bloom. *Konrad Nordahl Dagbøker*, Bind 2, 1950-55 (Oslo: Tiden Norsk Forlag , 1992), p. 85.

133.   Ibid., pp. 208-209. In an interview with the Norwegian ambassador in Paris, Eisenhower's press secretary James Hagerty said that the Sputnik hysteria caused the United States to step up its technical research. The Norwegian ambassador wrote he did not agree that the Soviets would outdistance everyone in technology or that they were totally unchangeable in their foreign policy goals. Letter from Norwegian Embassy in Paris to the Foreign Ministry, 25 November 1957, no. 739, "Samtale med Eisenhowers pressecretær, James C. Hagerty," in Folder 25.4/47, De Forente Stater Politikk, bind 39, 11 October 1957 to 31 December 1957, Royal Norwegian Foreign Ministry, Oslo; and Paterson et al, *American Foreign Policy,* p. 494.

134.   Ragnarok, in Norse mythology, denotes the end of time when the Frost Giants rise up from the Earth and fight the Norse gods and fallen Viking warriors from Valhalla.

135.   *Det Norske Arbeiderparti Landsmøtet 1957 Protokoll* (Oslo: Aktietrykkeriet, Norwegian Labor Party Archives, 1958), pp. 50-58, 138.

136.   *Det Norske Arbeiderparti Landsmøtet 1959 Protokoll* (Oslo: Aktietrykkeriet, Norwegian Labor Party Archives, 1960), p. 80.

137.   Pharo, "Cold War in Norwegian and International Historical Research," p. 178.

138.   *FRUS 1955-1957*, vol. 4, pt. 1, p. 38.

139.   Memo, Discussion at the 420th Meeting of the National Security Council, 1 October 1959, Whitman File, NSC Series, Box 11, pp. 4-5, 7-8, Eisenhower Library.

140.   Memo, Discussion at the 323rd Meeting of the National Security Council, 16 May 1957, Whitman File, NSC Series, Box 9, p. 7, Eisenhower Library.

141.   Memo from Foreign Ministry, 1 June 1956, and Memo from Norwegian Delegation in Warsaw to the Foreign Ministry, no. 362, 4 June 1956, File 34.4/47, Norges politiske forhold til U.S.A., bind 2, 1 January 1950 to 31 December 1959, Royal Norwegian Foreign Ministry, Oslo.

142.   Memo, [Henry] Saltzman to DDE [Dwight D. Eisenhower], "Private Conversation with Norwegian Prime Minister, Mr. Oscar Torp", 24 November 1954, Whitman File, Dulles-Herter Series, Box 3, Folder November 1954, Eisenhower Library.

143.   Tamnes, "Handlefrihet og lojalitet," pp. 210-211.

144.   Prior to the 1957 NATO conference, British Foreign Minister Selwyn Lloyd told the Norwegian ambassador in London that Eisenhower would be cooperative on the issue of nuclear weapons being put in NATO countries. Letter from the Norwegian Embassy in London to the Foreign

Ministry, 1 November 1957, no. 1010, "Samtale med utenriksminister Selwyn Lloyd," in Folder 25.4/47, De Forente Stater Politikk, bind 39, 11 October 1957 to 31 December 1957, Royal Norwegian Foreign Ministry, Oslo; Letter from Norwegian Embassy in Washington to the Foreign Ministry, 29 October 1957, no. 1037, "Møte mellom Eisenhower and MacMillan," in Folder 25.4/47, De Forente Stater Politikk, bind 39, 11 October 1957 to 31 December 1957, Royal Norwegian Foreign Ministry, Oslo. In a meeting with Khrushchev, the Norwegian ambassador in Warsaw, and Adlai Stevenson, Khrushchev called Dulles "Eisenhower's Sputnik" with only mild protest from Stevenson. Memo from Norwegian Embassy in Warsaw to the Foreign Ministry, no. 362, 12 August 1958, File 34.4/47, Norges politiske forhold til U.S.A., bind 2, 1 January 1950 to 31 December 1959, Royal Norwegian Foreign Ministry, Oslo.

145. Riste, *Isolasjonisme og Stormaktsgarantiar,* pp. 35-37; Clive Archer, "The North as a Multidimensional Strategic Arena," in *Annals of the American Academy of Political and Social Science* 512 (November 1990), 24; Johan J. Holst, "Ensidge bindinger i norsk sikkerhetspolitikk," and "Norsk nedrustningspolitikk i en opprustet verden," in Johan J. Holst and Daniel Heradstveit, eds., *Norsk Utenrikspolitikk* (Oslo: TANO, 1985); *Aftenposten* 5 (May 1958), pp. 1, 7; and Lundestad, "Nasjonalisme og internasjonalisme i norsk utenrikspolitikk," pp. 41-46. Traditionally, Norway has had an aversion to supranational organizations—especially economic ones. For example, voters refused to approve Norwegian membership in the European Economic Community (EEC) in 1972. However, Norway is a member of the more loose-knit European Free Trade Association (EFTA). Also important were Norway's anti-European (continental) sentiments. Norway's Atlantic ties were strong, as seen in 1963 when they were asked which particular ally they favored or did not: the United States got a 66 percent favorable rating, Great Britain got 67 percent, and France and Germany received only 22 percent combined.

146. That is, Nike and Honest John missiles that were dual capable: they could carry both conventional and nuclear payloads.

147. Torleiv Harstad, "Fra Paris til Boris Gleb," hovedoppfag (thesis), University of Oslo, 1989, pp. 10-11, 195; and Holst, *Norwegian Foreign Policy in the 1980s,* p. 87.

148. Conference Memo no. 93, 10 December 1957, Statsministerens Kontor, Referat Fra Regjeringskonferanser, 1947-61, Norwegian National Archives, Oslo.

149. Johansen, *Sovjetunionen og Norden,* pp. 130, 134; German, "Norway and the Bear," pp. 62-63; and *Konrad Nordahl Dagbøker,* bind 2, 1950-55 (Oslo: Tiden Norsk Forlag , 1992), p. 104.

150. *Konrad Nordahl Dagbøker,* bind 2, 1950-55 (Oslo: Tiden Norsk Forlag , 1992), p. 148. An example of U.S. sensitivity about neutralism occurred at a 1957 NATO meeting when Eisenhower accused Norwegian Prime Minister Einar Gerhardsen of sounding neutralist. This was in reference to Gerhardsen's announcement that Norway would not deploy middle-distance rockets. Memo from Norwegian Ambassador Paul Koht to

the Norwegian Foreign Ministry, 27 March 1958, no. 346, "Overlevering av akkreditere," File 34.4/47, Norges politiske forhold til U.S.A., bind 2, 1 January 1950 to 31 December 1959, Royal Norwegian Foreign Ministry, Oslo.

151.   *Congressional Record*, 85th Congress, 1st Session, vol. 103, pt. 4, 28 March 1957, pp. 4627-4630.

152.   Ibid.

153.   Letter from Norwegian Embassy in Moscow to the Foreign Ministry, 4 August 1959, no. 441, "Nixon's Visit," in Folder 25.4/47, De Forente Stater Politikk, bind 43, 1 May 1959 to 10 August 1959, Royal Norwegian Foreign Ministry, Oslo.

154.   Transcript of speech by Norway's Defense Minister Halvard Lange, 1 July 1959, White House Office, Office of the Staff Secretary: Records of Paul T. Carroll, Andrew J. Goodpaster, L. Arthur Minnich, and Christopher H. Russell, 1952-61, International Series, Box 11, p. 7, Eisenhower Library.

155.   Letter from Norwegian Embassy in Washington to the Foreign Ministry, 18 March 1959, no. 311, "President Eisenhowers Radiotale 16 March 1959," and Letter from Norwegian Embassy in London to the Foreign Ministry, 2 April 1959, "Dulles, Tyskland," in Folder 25.4/47, De Forente Stater Politikk, bind 42, 1 January 1959 to 30 January 1959, Royal Norwegian Foreign Ministry, Oslo.

156.   *Det Norske Arbeiderparti Beretning 1959-1960* (Oslo: Aktietrykkeriet, Norwegian Labor Party Archives, 1961), pp. 89-91.

157.   Tamnes, "Handlefrihet og lojalitet," pp. 222-224.

158.   Letter from Norwegian Embassy in Washington to the Foreign Ministry, 23 April 1959, no. 443, "Utenriksministerskiftet," in Folder 25.4/47, De Forente Stater Politikk, bind 42, 1 January 1959 to 30 January 1959, Royal Norwegian Foreign Ministry, Oslo.

159.   Letter from the Norwegian Embassy in Washington to the Foreign Ministry, 28 July 1959, no. 820, "Amerikansk presse om utsettlesen av Khrusjovs besøk," in Folder 25.4/47, De Forente Stater Politikk, bind 43, 1 May 1959 to 10 August 1959, Norwegian Foreign Ministry, Oslo; and *Konrad Nordahl Dagbøker*, bind 2, 1950-55 (Oslo: Tiden Norsk Forlag , 1992), p. 190; *Konrad Nordahl Dagbøker*, bind 2, 1950-55 (Oslo: Tiden Norsk Forlag , 1992), p. 216.

160.   NSC 6006/1, U.S. Policy toward Scandinavia (Denmark, Norway, and Sweden), 6 April 1960, p. 7, White House Office, Office of the Special Assistant for National Security Affairs, NSC Series, Briefing Notes Subseries, Box 16, Eisenhower Library.

161.   Ibid., p. 1.

162.   Ibid., pp. 3-4.

163.   Memo, Briefing Notes for the NSC Meeting 1 April 1960, pp. 1-2, Whitman File, NSC Series, Box 12, Eisenhower Library; NSC 6006/1, U.S. Policy toward Scandinavia (Denmark, Norway, and Sweden), 6 April 1960, p. 7, White House Office, Office of the Special Assistant for National Security Affairs, NSC Series, Briefing Notes Subseries, Box 16, Eisenhower

Library.

164.   Memo, "U.S. Policy toward Scandinavia" (Denmark, Norway, and Sweden), 10 November 1960, attached p. 8 of NSC 6006/1, White House Office, Office of the Special Assistant for National Security Affairs, NSC Series, Policy Papers Subseries, Box 28, Eisenhower Library.

165.   Memo, Discussion at 439th Meeting of the National Security Council, 1 April 1960, Whitman File, NSC Series, Box 12, p. 2, Eisenhower Library.

166.   Memo, Briefing Notes for the NSC Meeting 1 April 1960, Whitman File, NSC Series, Box 12, pp. 1-2, Eisenhower Library. Since the Russians liberated northern Norway from the Nazis, they have had a more favorable rating among Norwegians in the north.

167.   NSC 6025, U.S. Policy toward Iceland, 29 December 1960, pp. 1-7, White House Office, Office of the Special Assistant for National Security Affairs, NSC Series, Policy Papers Subseries, Box 29, Eisenhower Library.

168.   Nordic nations required young males to serve in the armed forces. The length of this required service was an extremely sensitive issue. Report to Nelson A. Rockefeller from Robert Murphy, Deputy Under Secretary of State, "Neutralism in Europe," 19 August 1955, White House Office, NSC Staff Papers, 1948-61, Planning Coordination Group Series, Box 2, Folders 1-4 Bandung, pp. 1-9, Eisenhower Library.

169.   Letter from Lauris Norstad to Denmark Defense Minister Poul Hansen, 23 January 1960, Lauris Norstad Papers, 1930-87, Country Series, Box 47, Folder 3 Denmark, Eisenhower Library.

170.   Letter from USAF Brigadier General Ross Chief, MAAG Denmark, to Lauris Norstad, 13 May 1959, Lauris Norstad Papers, 1930-87, Country Series, Box 47, Folder 4 Denmark, Eisenhower Library.

171.   In the late 1950s and early 1960s, Norwegian national security research focused on base politics and atomic diplomacy. Some analysts held that base politics was illusory and did not have a deterrent effect against the Soviet Union. Critics of Norway's policies also point out that in 1960 and 1961 Norway compromised its position when, despite its antinuclear testing activities, it did not counter the positioning of nuclear weapons elsewhere in NATO. The atmospheric tests finally stopped in 1963, after the Cuban Missile Crisis, with the signing of the Limited Test Ban Treaty (actually driving the tests underground, not eliminating them). Tamnes, "Handlefrihet og lojalitet," pp. 212-215; and Eriksen and Pharo, *Norsk Sikkerhetspolitikk* , pp. 36-42.

172.   Message from MOD Norway to SACEUR, 17 November 1960, FDX 1249, "Manning of Communications and Early Warning Facilities in Norway," Lauris Norstad Papers, Box 49, Folder 1 Norway, Eisenhower Library.

173.   Johansen, *Sovietunionen og Norden,* pp. 131-132; German, "Norway and the Bear," pp. 64-65; and *Det Norske Arbeiderparti Beretning 1959-1960* (Oslo: Aktietrykkeriet, Norwegian Labor Party Archives, 1961), pp. 87-88.

174.   One can never rule out the impact of bureaucratic foul-ups in foreign policy crises. Tamnes, *United States and Cold War*, pp. 176-181.

175.   Johansen, *Sovietunionen og Norden,* pp. 132-133; Moon, "Soviet-Norwegian Relations," pp. 665-666.

176.   Jens Haugland, *Dagbok Frå Kongens Råd* (Oslo: Det Norske Samlaget, 1986), p. 111.

177.   Ibid., p. 664.

178.   Progress Report, "Program Designed to Decrease the Vulnerability of the Icelandic Government to Communist Seizure of Power," 25 November 1949, prepared by the Department of State in compliance with NSC 40/1 [NSC 40/1, The Position of the United States with Respect to United States and North Atlantic Security Interest in Iceland], approved 5 August 1949, in *FRUS 1950*, vol. 3, pp. 1457-1467. In terms of U.S. objectives in Norden and the use of its labor sector, former U.S. Secretary of Labor David Morse was elected to head the International Labor Organization headquartered in Switzerland. This would serve to solidify U.S. control of international labor organizations and keep NATO strong. Labor shortages were hurting U.S. attempts to build up economic strength to resist communism in Europe. David Morse Papers, NATO Secret Folder, Seeley G. Mudd Manuscript Library, Princeton University.

179.   Policy Statement Prepared in the Department of State, 15 May 1950, in *FRUS 1950*, vol. 3, pp. 1457-1467.

180.   "Northern European Chiefs of Mission Conference, London, 19-21 September 1957: Conclusions and Recommendations,"in *FRUS 1955-1957*, vol. 4, p. 637.

181.   Ibid., pp. 620-621.

182.   Memorandum by the Deputy Director of the Office of the British Commonwealth and Northern European Affairs (Satterthwaite) to the Deputy Assistant Secretary of State for European Affairs (Thompson), 8 February 1950, in *FRUS 1950*, vol. 1, p. 144.

183.   Memorandum of Discussion at the 168th Meeting of the National Security Council, Thursday, 29 October 1953, in *Foreign Relations of the United States* [hereafter *FRUS*] *1952-1954*, vol. 2: *The United Nations; The Western Hemisphere* (Washington, D.C.: Government Printing Office, 1979), p. 570.

184.   Telegram from [John Foster] Dulles to [Dwight D.] Eisenhower, 7 May 1958, p. 1, Whitman File, Dulles-Herter Series, Box 8, Eisenhower Library.

185.   Ibid., p. 2.

186.   Ibid.

187.   Telegram from the Ambassador in Sweden ([H. Freeman] Matthews) to the Secretary of State, Stockholm, 7 February 1950, in *FRUS 1950*, vol. 3, p. 15.

188.   Telegram from the Ambassador in Sweden (Matthews) to the Secretary of State, Stockholm, 21 February 1950, in *FRUS 1950*, vol. 3, p. 24.

189.   Ibid.

190.   Ibid.
191.   Lundestad, *America, Scandinavia, and Cold War,* pp. 121-122. This appears to be in stark contrast to most other cases in U.S. foreign economic relations when U.S. assets have been threatened with nationalization (e.g., Cuba, Mexico).
192.   Ibid., p. 129.
193.   "Northern European Chiefs of Mission Conference, London, 19-21 September 1957: Conclusions and Recommendations," in *FRUS 1955-1957,* vol. 4, pp. 624-625.
194.   Kennan later changed his mind on Finland. Memorandum of National Security Council Consultant's Meeting, Thursday, 29 June 1950, in *FRUS 1950,* vol. 1, p. 329.
195.   "Northern European Chiefs of Mission Conference, London, 19-21 September 1957: Conclusions and Recommendations," in *FRUS 1955-1957,* vol. 4, pp. 610-611.
196.   Ibid., pp. 619-620.
197.   Ibid., p. 637.
198.   Memo, Discussion at the 420th Meeting of the National Security Council, 1 October 1959, Whitman File, NSC Series, Box 11, pp. 7-8, Eisenhower Library.
199.   NSC 6006/1, U.S. Policy toward Scandinavia (Denmark, Norway, and Sweden), 6 April 1960, p. 1, White House Office, Office of the Special Assistant for National Security Affairs, NSC Series, Briefing Notes Subseries, Box 16, Eisenhower Library.
200.   "The Transcript of the Remarks by President [Dwight D.] Eisenhower at Republican National Committee Breakfast, Morrison Hotel, Chicago, Illinois, July 27, 1960," p. 3. Whitman File, Speech Series, Box 35, Eisenhower Library. This was briefly mentioned in Eric S. Einhorn and John Logue, *Modern Welfare States: Politics and Policies in Social Democratic Scandinavia* (New York: Praeger, 1989), pp. 266, 278n.
201.   Telegram, [Llewellyn] Thompson in Oslo to the Secretary of State, 29 July 1960, White House Office, Office of the Staff Secretary, International Series, Box 13, Eisenhower Library.
202.   Telegram, [Frances E.] Willis to the Secretary of State, "President Eisenhower's Remarks on the Welfare State," 4 August 1960, White House Office, Office of the Staff Secretary, International Series, Box 11, Eisenhower Library; and Fred I. Greenstein, *The Hidden-hand Presidency: Eisenhower as Leader* (New York: Basic Books, 1982), pp. 49-50.
203.   In terms of a security strategy, "asymmetrical" means concentrating on strongpoints whereas "symmetrical" refers to setting up a perimeter.
204.   NSC 6006/1, U.S. Policy toward Scandinavia (Denmark, Norway, and Sweden), 6 April 1960, p. 6, White House Office, Office of the Special Assistant for National Security Affairs, NSC Series, Briefing Notes Subseries, Box 16, Eisenhower Library.

205. Ibid., pp. 8-9.
206. Ibid., p. 3.

4

A Model of Peaceful Security

Nonviolence and cowardice go ill together. I can imagine a fully armed man to be at heart a coward. Possession of arms implies an element of fear, if not cowardice. But true nonviolence is an impossibility without the possession of unadulterated fearlessness.

—Mohandas K. Gandhi, 1939

We have inherited a large house, a great world house in which we have to live together—black and white, Easterner and Westerner, Gentile and Jew, Catholic and Protestant, Moslem and Hindu—a family unduly separated in ideas, culture, and interest, who, because we can never again live apart, must learn somehow to live with each other in peace.

—Martin Luther King, Jr., 1967

Having looked at the historical context, the focus will now turn to Norden's special role in superpower politics—balanced between ideological alignment with the West on the one side and the geopolitical reality of its Soviet neighbor on the other—through use of a regional integration framework.[1] This chapter will address the question of how regional cooperation in Norden helped keep the peace in the North in spite of systemic bipolarity that ordinarily focused superpower tensions and fought battles on the periphery. What made this situation different? Norden's regional integration system, the Nordic Nexus, and regional security system, the Nordic Balance, will then be combined to form a "peaceful security" system model. This system model will then be analyzed and tested for possible applications.[2]

A testable model may be developed by combining the Nordic Nexus and the Nordic Balance. But how did the Nordic Balance and Nordic Nexus work? A note of clarification must be made at this point. One might well ask how the Nordic Balance can be separated from the reliance, at least in part, on the U.S. nuclear umbrella for its security. Early thinking in Norway, for example, supports this contention. But later, as antinuclear protesting became stronger in the late 1950s and early 1960s, this reliance lessened. The Nordic people then began to see nuclear weapons for what they really were: psychological terror weapons. So, they set out to stabilize superpower interests and maintain peace and security in their region. Nuclear weapons eventually became less of a factor. It follows, then, that the Nordic Balance did not totally rely on the system of nuclear deterrence, because it was assumed the weapons were too terrible ever to be used. It was more important to maintain low tension levels and avoid volatile ideological clashes. Despite the militarization of the Nordic region and despite the oil and gas competition between the Soviets and the Norwegians, the Nordic area remained free from major Cold War incidents and has remained relatively stable and peaceful. The following reasons seem probable:

1. Absence of internal conflict in the region.
2. Presence of strong neutral nations as semi-independent buffer states (Sweden and Finland).
3. Conditional NATO membership (Denmark and Norway) that ameliorated tensions with the Soviets yet promoted security domestically and reduced strains between the United States and the Soviet Union.[3]

The Nordic Balance existed on two levels. One was static and was established by alliances and agreements and set policies. The other was dynamic: the latitude and flexibility of informal arrangements that allowed each member of the Nordic region to adapt to changes in the other members. The Nordic region successfully created functional links that kept peace in the region and allowed for the development of all members in an egalitarian manner—the Nordic Nexus.[4]

There is a widespread view that integration on the regional level is more likely to succeed than international integration; regional integration is meant to be an alternative to fragmentation or universalism. Sometimes these regional solutions are seen as stepping-stones to a later world union. It follows then that regional organizations must be the basic element in any multiple-level broader union, sharing the responsibilities and handling issues of sufficient regional, but not worldwide, consensus.[5] In terms of the two basic incentives for political integration presented in Chapter 1, the Nordic countries gained and retained cohesiveness because they shared common values and, to a lesser degree, a procedural consensus. But they also remained cohesive because of the presence of a threat: the Soviet Union; the United States, to a lesser degree; and the demands of both superpowers during the Cold War. The Nordic community integrated from the ground up, establishing informal ties that were then taken for granted in the overall spirit of cooperation. This went along with the Nordic preference for "low-voltage" politics. The Nordic countries remained low key in order to avoid conflict with one another and with the rest of the world. So, given the success of Norden in terms of peace and development, perhaps a less self-conscious approach to integration—coupled with low-voltage politics—is the best course to take for other regions as well.[6]

Having discovered what characterized Norden's system of security, a significant model can now be developed. The Nordic Nexus provided a solid base on which the Nordic Balance was to be built, allowing for peaceful solutions to international problems. This was done while maintaining territorial integrity, largely avoiding the stationing of foreign troops, and providing a thriving economic base that produced some of the highest standards of living in the world. Nonviolent means were used to assure freedom, security, prosperity, and peace. In looking at the Nordic example, one could also point out cultural affinity as the basis for integration. However, this should not be thought of as a model for strictly homogeneous societies. On the contrary, as humans advance culturally and socially they will be able to develop closer ties between what appear now to be adversarial societies. Affinity can be nurtured just as war can be cultivated.[7] The Nordic experience demonstrates that much can be accomplished through intergovernmental cooperation. The lesson is really relevant for developing nations whose leaders do not want to relinquish power to higher central authority and whose people do not want to submerge their identity in a larger whole. This, of course, presents a severe challenge to nationalism as it is now understood.[8]

An analogy would be helpful in illustrating how the Nordic Balance and Nexus worked. The Nordic regional system—and the concept of cooperation through diversity, as well—can best be envisioned by imagining a hand. Each finger has the capability to move independently of the others, adjusting its movement forward and backward, up and down. Yet each of the five fingers is attached to the palm, which simultaneously allows for this articulation and provides the security of a base. Sometimes the fingers move individually and sometimes together—each responding differently to stimuli that they encounter in the environment, yet each remaining attached to the palm. Were it not for the palm, the fingers would fling off into five different directions, and nothing would be accomplished. Were it not for the ability of the fingers to exercise flexibility, the hand would be stiff and useless. One finger or thumb alone cannot do the whole job. Even though the thumb is powerful, it needs the other fingers to grasp something and to create something. Likewise, the delicate nature of the small finger alone is weak, but it adds subtlety to the overall effect when used together with the others.

The Nordic system acted like a hand. As do the five fingers, each nation retained its ability to move and adjust to world pressures, yet also remained attached to the palm—the overriding regional objective of maintaining peace. Flexibility and a firm hold of the overriding objective helped maintain peace for Norden during the Cold War years. Although some contend that security arrangements in Norden were not the "product of deliberate design but rather the aggregated result of incremental decisions and adjustment," this does not discount the idea that they can be used to form a model deliberately constructed in some other region.[9] It is vitally important to find out what elements made up the Nordic Balance, regardless of whether or not the originators had the Nordic Balance in mind at the outset. One must also not forget the clandestine nature of these security arrangements. If everyone had known how the Nordic countries worked together on security issues, the Nordic Balance would not have worked. As stated in a 1959 Norwegian Embassy letter, Norden "cooperated through diversity."[10] This phrase best represents the reason for Norden's success in navigating through the Cold War, and may be the most important lesson to be learned from the entire period. Although a seemingly homogeneous region, Norden was in actuality quite diverse. Nordic security orientations certainly reflected this diversity. Yet, it was this diversity that strengthened the region's security and reduced superpower tensions that would have hindered economic development or would even have led to war. Diversity can be a strength; and in the world today—with ethnic conflict raging—cooperation through diversity seems worth studying and emulating in order to stop the violence.

Nordic cooperation can be examined through the overarching concept of peaceful security. This study has shown the Nordic Nexus to be Norden's regional integration system and the Nordic Balance to be its regional security system. Together these two concepts form the model

Figure 9
Peaceful Security Model

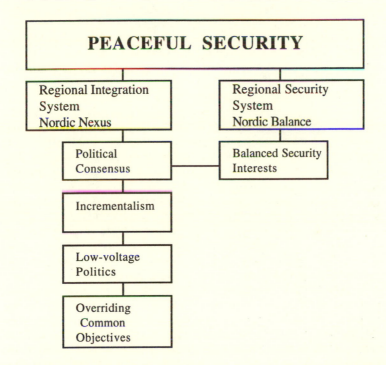

of peaceful security—a model for security, peace, freedom, and prosperity. Since the key to the Nordic countries' success was their cooperation through diversity, differences were turned into strengths and elements of cooperation, rather than into points of conflict among the regional members.

Figure 9 depicts the model of peaceful security, combining the concepts of Nordic Nexus (the regional integration system) and Nordic Balance (the Nordic regional security system). Any region that would like to consider such a strategy should first begin with identifying overriding common objectives. These objectives make up the base of the model. Next, a preference for low-level politics and incrementalist approaches in seeking cooperation seems appropriate. For if a regional group does not have clear objectives and a rational, cool-headed, incremental approach, then it will not build political consensus or be able to balance sensitive security interests. A regional group must have a regional integration strategy in order to have a regional security strategy. The political and socioeconomic levels of cooperation are fundamental to successful military cooperation. On top of Figure 9 stands "peaceful security," made up of the foregoing concepts. Once one has achieved peaceful security, one has successfully combined prosperity with security, solving the age-old dilemma.

Admittedly, in terms of the underlying concept of peaceful security in this study, and in terms of the applicability of the Nordic Balance and Nordic Nexus models to other regions of the world, much is yet to be done. However, given the success of the Nordic Balance and Nexus system, and given the many regions of the world that could use some different ideas on building peace, security, freedom, and prosperity, it would be unwise not to fully explore the possibility of adapting the Nordic system elsewhere—especially in the former Eastern bloc and the Third World.

Regional integration in the Third World has often failed in the past because of a lack of democratic and cooperative traditions (e.g., OPEC, the Andean Pact, the Cartagena Group, etc.) and because of superpower penetration. So, just how useful can this Norden-based peaceful security model be for further research? One way to find out is to look for successful examples of military-security cooperation in the Third World. One such example may be the Association of Southeast Asian Nations (ASEAN). In 1967 the five founding members of ASEAN (Thailand, Malaysia, Singapore, Indonesia, and the Philippines) agreed in the Bangkok Declaration to promote economic growth and regional peace.[11] The ASEAN group believed the key to success for regional integration in the Third World was not in the *form* but in the dynamic *function* that underlies the regional group, that is, its a search for autonomy and the exclusion of external powers. An earlier attempt at subregional cooperation had taken place in 1961 with the formation of the Association of Southeast Asia (ASA) by Malaya, the Philippines, and Thailand. However, ASA was ended by a territorial dispute between the Philippines and Malaya. The ASEAN states shared a common vulnerability to internal dangers aggravated by external forces taking advantage of a region ridden with conflict.[12]

Bent on ensuring individual security, ASEAN wanted to reduce the external threats and prevent unnecessary diversion of its development resources. Thus, member states saw the relationship between security and development. In their regional cooperation, the ASEAN states did not want to lose their national identities. The concept of national resilience emerged as a way of promoting self-sufficiency and resourcefulness in achieving political stability, economic development,

Figure 10
ASEAN

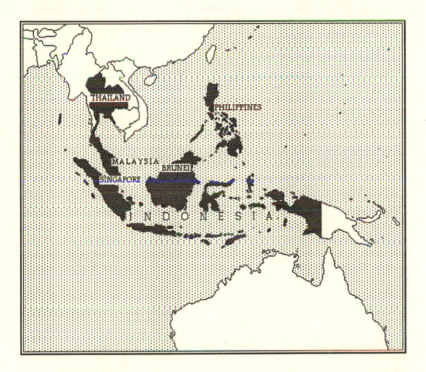

and security within the region and in each country. It was vital to uphold the political identity and integrity of each member state, irrespective of stature.[13]

ASEAN, as shown in Figure 10, was formed as the member nations sensed that the United States would scale back its commitment in Vietnam and its overall presence in Southeast Asia. The organization was slow to evolve, beginning with economic agreements and gradually expanding to political agendas. ASEAN security cooperation has been viewed as the "hidden dimension" and was stressed less than economic and political cooperation. During the Bangkok meeting that led to the birth of ASEAN, security was uppermost in the minds of the delegates, but not conspicuously addressed. However, there was a threefold security consensus: (1) to pursue socioeconomic development, thus reducing the threat of outside influence in the region; (2) to reduce and limit the influence of external powers; and (3) to limit competition among members. Despite this consensus on security goals, there was no consensus on policy. The ASEAN states realized that, in Third World regional integration, countries must overcome their tendency to favor immediate gains over long-term ones. They must also find consensus among various national interests. Cooperation based on abstract ideals that do not merge with national interests will not work. ASEAN promoted cooperation based on the convergence of national interests, but allowed differences in terms of pursuing national policies as long as they did not conflict with regional goals. The ASEAN nations shared some geopolitical, historical, and cultural factors that brought them together (although in a weaker bond than the Nordic ties). The plan was to promote peace and stability through economic development.[14]

Two basic forms of regional military security have been identified in the Third World: regional autonomous, and hegemonic. ASEAN regional security demonstrated a third way. Regional autonomous (e.g., the Arab League) and hegemonic (e.g., SEATO) alliances have not proven to be a viable basis for regional military-security cooperation in the Third World. Autonomous arrangements tend to fail because of technical, logistical, and doctrinal reasons, and because of hierarchies of interest, conflicting priorities, and competition for leadership and influence within the alliance. Hegemonic groups serve the interests of the major power and were not appropriate deterrents against internally generated threats to Third World client states that had roots in the socioeconomic imbalances and political cultures of their societies.[15]

ASEAN presented itself as a third option: a subregional and microregional group. Security measures are taken up on a bilateral and multilateral basis among the membership of the region. ASEAN was characterized by a marked preference for narrow geographic scope as well as a more specific security agenda, aimed at developing a political and military approach against a particular conflict in their geostrategic neighborhood, rather than espousing general ideological objectives and the principle of regional autonomy. There was no formal approach to collective security within ASEAN's regional framework. Bilateral security linkages formed through cooperation, causing an overlapping and interlocking network of regional security.[16]

The ASEAN states maintained a careful balance between their quest for regional autonomy and their dependent security arrangements with the great powers. Like the Nordic Balance, ASEAN's balance worked by reducing superpower insecurity and opportunism. Both systems addressed external threats in a similar way. ASEAN saw Communist China as its largest threat. Norden saw the Soviet Union as its largest threat. These threats played a role in holding both ASEAN and Norden together. Both systems relied on U.S. military guarantees. In Norden, Norway, Denmark, and Iceland were NATO members with close U.S. ties. In ASEAN, Thailand, the Philippines, and Singapore relied heavily on the United States for security. Another interesting similarity between Norden and ASEAN was that the nonaligned countries in ASEAN (Indonesia and Malaysia) provided a basis for decoupling the region from superpower rivalry, much as did Sweden's and Finland's neutrality in Norden. ASEAN techniques were not unlike the Nordic concepts of "deterrence and reassurance" and "integration and screening." Like the Nordic Balance and the Nordic Nexus, the structure of ASEAN military-security cooperation placed less emphasis on institutional and formal mechanisms.

Although it may only be coincidental that both Norden and the original ASEAN had five members, what is not coincidental is that Asian planners had the Nordic countries in mind when originating ASEAN. The first suggestion of a regional organization in Southeast Asia came from Prime Minister Tunku Abdul Rahman of Malaya in February 1958. A favorite integration example of his was the Nordic Council, which he referred to as a "model for Southeast Asia." Having borrowed some ideas from Norden, Tunku saw the advantage of reaching some sort of regional consensus based on rebuilding the regional economy to bolster security. Just as Nordic governments came to realize that economic stability would lessen the threat from Soviet incursion, ASEAN countries saw economic stability as a way of resisting Communist Chinese infiltration.[17] Both regions faced tremendous economic challenges after World War II, and both saw a connection between economic strength and the ability to remain secure from outside threats. Regional planners in ASEAN and the Nordic governments all realized that survival depended on being united in purpose and economically strong.

For the purpose of our model building, it is important to note also the differences between Norden and ASEAN. First, the Nordic countries did not have to place much emphasis on settling interregional conflict (that had been settled more than 150 years ago). ASEAN, even on the eve of its formation, was characterized by suspicion and animosity among its members. Second, the ASEAN system of security did not have to remain hidden as did the Nordic Balance system. Although ASEAN downplayed the security element in its organization, it was still more open than the Nordic Balance. Third, ASEAN was much more culturally diverse than Norden. There was no strong indigenous tradition of thinking that conceived of the region as a political, economic, or cultural entity—historical tensions and conflict among ASEAN countries hindered such thinking. Even the common experience of colonialism tended to exacerbate feelings of separateness, rather than unite the ASEAN countries.

To compare and contrast in brief, ASEAN relied more on the threat motivation for integration, whereas Norden relied on both threat and a general procedural consensus.   They both shared a goal of limiting superpower influence in their regions, the idea being that limiting such penetration promoted peace.   Overall, the comparison of Norden and ASEAN has revealed both interesting similarities and notable differences.   The importance here is that a Nordic-inspired system can work in the Third World.[18]

One must, however, proceed with caution in building models because the diversity of the Third World precludes the application of blanket theories.   In the past, the developed world has presented magic models to the underdeveloped world that have had negligible or even disastrous results.   Any model that hopes to be effective in the Third World must consider the impact of colonialism and the nation-building process.   Nation-building is especially important.   The developed world is impatient with underdeveloped nations and it tends to forget that most Third World countries have only been independent since World War II.   Regional integration in the Third World should (1) provide benefits for each member; (2) not threaten current beneficial relationships; (3) not restrain nation-building; and (4) not threaten the base of support for existing national political elites.[19]

One might also ask how a model based on the Cold War international system can still be viable for use today.   Although it has been said that the bipolarized Cold War international system is gone, there are remnants of this past system and there are other threats that equal the Cold War danger (e.g., the fragmentation and ethnic conflict in the former Soviet empire, and global environmental devastation).[20]   By using the principles of peaceful security, countries could learn to cooperate through diversity, integrate from the ground up, and each use their own approaches to solve environmental problems collectively, for example.   The conference in Rio de Janeiro in 1992 was one example of this type of transnational awareness.   Small agreements will need to come first, to be followed by more sweeping ones.

Showing that the Nordic and ASEAN systems of cooperation and security were similar and seem to have worked may prove to be encouraging for the development of these cooperative techniques elsewhere in the world.   Given the trouble that the EC nations have had in instituting their top-down form of integration, it would seem impossible for Third World regions to emulate that type of regional cooperation.   The bottom-up, loosely configured Nordic example (with plentiful contacts and few commitments) may be more appropriate, as demonstrated in ASEAN. Although the preceding is only a rough outline, further exploration of these concepts may lead other regions of the world toward developing their own approaches in the quest for world peace and prosperity.

NOTES

1. See Louis J. Cantori and Steven L. Spiegel, eds., *The International Politics of Regions: A Comparative Approach* (Englewood Cliffs, NJ: Prentice-Hall, 1970), p. ix; and Peter Berton, "International Subsystems— A Submacro Approach to International Studies," *International Studies Quarterly* 13 (December 1969): 329-332.

2. The term *Nordic Balance* expressed a notion that the stability of the Northern European area reduced superpower insecurity and opportunism. What did the binational and interdisciplinary approaches add? From the Norwegian perspective, the 1950s era took on a different look. There were many nuances that a strictly American perspective would have missed. One of the most important insights gained from this study's binational perspective was how U.S. domestic politics affected America's international image. Yet another interesting finding was that foreign archives research helps the researcher piece together a clearer picture. A case in point was the Nordic Balance. There was very little direct evidence in either archive when taken alone, but together there was enough to support some conclusions about this very important security system. A researcher relying on strictly English language sources would have missed recent documents coming from the Nordic countries that point to the existence of a Nordic Balance. The interdisciplinary approach illuminated the historical evidence and allowed for the construction of a potentially helpful model based on international relations theory. Without a theoretical foundation, this study would just be a nice set of interesting historical findings. Simply stating that Norden was a region that cooperated in certain ways and did not in others does not help find solutions to today's pressing problems. Finding out just how this cooperation or integration emerged and functioned, and tying the historical analysis to the theoretical framework, moves the study toward the direction of problem solving.

3. Paul M. Cole and Douglas M. Hart, eds., *Northern Europe: Security Issues for the 1990s* (Boulder, CO: Westview Press, 1986), pp. 1-2

4. Norden demonstrated, organizationally, the positive effects of what political scientist Joseph Nye calls a "micro-regional organization."

5. Bruce M. Russett, *International Regions and the International System: A Study in Political Ecology* (Westport, CT: Greenwood Press, 1975), p. 12.

6. Peace researcher Johan Galtung identified five conditions for peaceful cooperation among nations: (1) cooperation must be symmetric or egalitarian; (2) nations should be relatively similar in structure; (3)

cooperation must be functional; (4) cooperation must lead to supranational institution-building; and (5) cooperation should be dispersed over as many forms, channels, and frameworks as possible. Johan Galtung, "Analysis and Recommendation," in Johan Galtung and Sverre Lodgaard, eds., *Cooperation in Europe* (Oslo, Norway: Universitetsforlaget, 1970), pp. 1-14.

7. Successful cosociational democracies like Switzerland (containing three distinct ethnic groups) provide evidence against the absolute necessity of homogeneity to foster cooperation.

8. Stanley V. Anderson, *The Nordic Council: A Study of Scandinavian Regionalism* (Seattle: University of Washington Press, 1967), pp. 143, 147-148. In Africa, for instance, southern African nations have grouped together in cooperative efforts (e.g., Southern African Development Coordination Conference, or SADCC) and have sought guidance from other nations—particularly the Scandinavians.

9. Johan J. Holst, "Nordic Security: Past Mirrors and Future Faces," *Annals of the American Academy of Political and Social Science* 512 (1990): 8.

10. Letter from the Norwegian Embassy in Washington to the Foreign Ministry, 28 July 1959, no. 820, "Amerikansk presse om utsettlesen av Khrusjovs besøk," in Folder 25.4/47, De Forente Stater Politikk, bind 43, 1 May 1959 to 10 August 1959, Norwegian Foreign Ministry, Oslo.

11. Brunei joined ASEAN in 1984.

12. Michael Leifer, *ASEAN and the Security of South-east Asia* (New York: Routledge, 1989), pp. 1-3.

13. Ibid., pp. 4, 14. National resilience was first promoted by President Suharto of Indonesia.

14. Thomas P. Thornton, "Regional Organizations in Conflict Management," *Annals of the American Academy of Political and Social Science* 518 (November 1991): 135-136; Mark G. Rolls, "ASEAN: Where from and Where to?" *Contemporary Southeast Asia* 13 (December 1991): 324-325.

15. Amitav Acharya, "Regional Military-security Cooperation in the Third World: A Conceptual Analysis of the Relevance and Limitations of ASEAN (Association of Southeast Asian Nations)," *Journal of Peace Research* 29 (1992): 7-18.

16. Acharya, Military-security Cooperation," p. 10; and Leszek Buszynski, "Southeast Asia in the Post-Cold War Era," *Asian Survey* 32 (September 1992): 842-843.

17. Arnfinn Jørgensen-Dahl, *Regional Organization and Order in South-east Asia* (London: Macmillan Press, 1982), pp. 14, 19, 70.

18. Buszynski, "Southeast Asia in Post-Cold War," p. 831; and Jørgensen-Dahl, *Regional Organization*, pp. 70, 73. Regional peace and security is not only the absence of war; the goal should be to create a nonviolent region where multiculturalism can blossom and all groups can share equitably in economic development. Even though there have been human rights violations in ASEAN and ethnic troubles in Norden, we should not discount their methods of cooperation. Plato said that humans cannot

live without authority or freedom, the trouble was finding the right mixture. Perhaps we still have a long way to go before we will know the right mixture. However, sociologist Orlando Patterson may have provided some clues while identifying what he calls "three notes in the chord of freedom." According to Patterson, for freedom to work ideally, the three notes—individual freedom, community freedom, and sovereign freedom—should be played together. Address by Orlando Patterson on 8 October 1993, Pacific Lutheran University.

19. See Brian Job, ed., *The Insecurity Dilemma: National Security of Third World States* (Boulder, CO: Lynne Rienner Publishers, 1992); Rama S. Melkote, ed., *Regional Organisations: A Third World Perspective* (New Delhi, India: Sterling Publishers, 1990); and World Bank, *The Long-term Perspective Study of Sub-Saharan Africa*, Background Papers, Vols. 1, 4 (Washington, DC: World Bank, 1990).

20. As historian Paul Kennedy notes in his new book, there are new nonmilitary threats to national and international security that deserve great attention. Paul Kennedy, *Preparing for the Twenty-first Century* (New York: Random House, 1993), p. 14.

Selected Bibliography

ARTICLES, BOOKS, AND REPORTS

Aalders, Gerard. "The Failure of the Scandinavian Defence Union, 1948-1949." *Scandinavian Journal of History* 15, no. 2 (1990): 125-153.

Acharya, Amitav. "Regional Military-security Cooperation in the Third World: A Conceptual Analysis of the Relevance and Limitations of ASEAN (Association of Southeast Asian Nations)." *Journal of Peace Research* 29 (1992): 7-18.

Agrell, Wilhelm. *Alliansfrihet och Atombomber*. Stockholm, Sweden: Liber Förlag, 1985.

————. "Farväl till Svensk Neutralitet," in Wilhelm Agrell, Jörgen Bengtson, Per Olov Enquist, Per Gahrton, Per Jensen, Karl Erik Lagerlöf, Håkon Larsson, Gudrun Schyman, Ronny Svensson, Gunilla Thorgren, Marta Ulvskog, Sören Wibe, and Michael Williams, eds., *EG/EU: Till Vilket Pris?* Stockholm, Sweden: LTs Förlag, 1992, pp. 12-20.

Ambrose, Stephen E. *Rise to Globalism: American Foreign Policy, 1938-1970*. Baltimore: Penguin Books, 1971.

Andemicael, Berhanykun, ed. *Regionalism and the United Nations*. New York: Oceana Publications, 1979.

Anderson, Stanley V. *The Nordic Council: A Study of Scandinavian Regionalism*. Seattle: University of Washington Press, 1967.

Andrén, Nils. *Government and Politics in the Nordic Countries*. Stockholm: Almqvist and Wiksell, 1964.

————. "Nordic Integration and Cooperation—Illusion and Reality." *Cooperation and Conflict* 19, no. 4 (1984): 251-262.

————. "Prospects for the Nordic Security Pattern." *Cooperation and*

Conflict 13, no. 4 (1978): 181-192.

Annals of the American Academy of Political and Social Science 512 (November 1990). Special issue entitled: The Nordic Region: Changing Perspectives in International Relations.

Archer, Clive. "The North as a Multidimentional Strategic Arena." Annals of the American Academy of Political and Social Science 512 (November 1990): 22-32.

——. Organizing Western Europe. New York: Edward Arnold, 1990.

Axelrod, Robert. The Evolution of Cooperation. New York: Basic Books, 1990.

Banks, Michael. "Systems Analysis and the Study of Regions." International Studies Quarterly 13 (December 1969): 335-360.

Bennett, A. LeRoy. International Organizations: Principles and Issues, 5th Edition. Englewood Cliffs, NJ: Prentice-Hall, 1991.

Bergh, Trond. "Norsk økonomisk politikk," in Trond Bergh and Helge Ø. Pharo, eds., Vekst og Velstand: Norsk Politisk Historie 1945-1965. Oslo: Universitetsforlaget, 1989, pp. 11-98.

Bergh, Trond, and Helge Ø. Pharo, eds. Historiker og Veileder: Festskrift til Jakob Sverdrup. Oslo: Tiden Norsk Forlag, 1989.

Berner, Ørjan. Soviet Policies toward the Nordic Countries. New York: University Press of America, 1986.

Berton, Peter. "International Subsystems—A Submacro Approach to International Studies," International Studies Quarterly 13 (December 1969): 329-334.

Beukel, Erik. "Norges basepolitik—nogle overvejelser i Arbejderpartiets ledelse." Internasjonal Politikk, no. 3 (1977): 483-493.

Bitzinger, Richard A. Denmark, Norway, and NATO: Constraints and Challenges. Rand Note N-3001-RC. Santa Monica, CA: Rand Corporation, November 1989.

Bomsdorf, Falk. Sicherheit im Norden Europas: Die Sicherheitspolitik der Fünf Nordischen Staaten und die Nordeuropapolitik der Sowjetunion. Baden-Baden, Germany: Nomos Verlagsgesellschaft, 1989.

Bonsdorff, Goran von. "Regional Cooperation of the Nordic Countries." Cooperation and Conflict 1 (1965): 32-38.

Brøndsted, Johannes. The Vikings. New York: Penguin Books, 1975.

Brundtland, Arne Olav. "Den klassiske, de omsnudde og den fremtidige Nordiske Balanse," in Ole Nørrgaard and Per Carlsen, eds., Sovjetunionen, Østeuropa og dansk sikkerhedspolitik. Esbjerg, Denmark: Sydjysk Universitetsforlag, 1981, pp. 83-99.

——. "The Nordic Balance." Cooperation and Conflict, no. 2 (1966): 30-63.

——. "The Nordic Balance and Its Possible Relevance for Europe," in Daniel Frei, ed., Sicherheit durch Gleichgewicht? Zürich, Switzerland: Schulthess Polygraphischer Verlag, 1982, pp. 119-138.

——. "Nordisk Balanse før og nå." Internasjonal Politikk, no. 4 (1966): 491-541.

——. "Nordisk Balanse på nytt." Internasjonal Politikk (July-September

1976):   599-639.

————. "Norwegian Foreign Policy: Cooperation in Three Overlapping Circles." *Cooperation and Conflict* 12, no. 3 (1968): 169-183.

Buszynski, Leszek. "Southeast Asia in the Post-Cold War Era." *Asian Survey* 32 (September 1992): 830-847.

Cantori, Louis J., and Steven L. Spiegel, eds. *The International Politics of Regions: A Comparative Approach.* Englewood Cliffs, NJ: Prentice-Hall, 1970.

Castles, Francis G. "Scandinavia: The Politics of Stability," in Roy C. Macridis, ed., *Modern Political Systems: Europe,* 5th Edition. Englewood Cliffs, NJ: Prentice-Hall, 1983, pp. 387-434.

————. *The Social Democratic Image of Society: A Study of the Achievements and Origins of Scandinavian Social Democracy in Comparative Perspective.* Boston: Routledge & Kegan Paul, 1978.

Cervenka, Zdenek. "Scandinavia: A Friend Indeed for Africa?" *Africa Reports* 20 (May/June 1974): 39-42.

Clancy, Tom. *Red Storm Rising.* New York: Berkeley Books, 1986.

Cole, Paul M., and Douglas M. Hart, eds. *Northern Europe: Security Issues for the 1990s.* Boulder, CO: Westview Press, 1986.

Cole, Wayne S. *Norway and the United States, 1905-1955:   Two Democracies in Peace and War.* Ames: Iowa State University Press, 1989.

Committee for Economic Development. *Economic Aspects of North Atlantic Security.* New York: Research and Policy Committee of the Committee for Economic Development, 1951.

Dædalus 113 (Spring 1984). Special issue "Nordic Voices."

Dædalus 113 (Winter 1984). Special issue "The Nordic Enigma."

Dalsjø, Robert. "Tungt vågande kritik? En granskning av kritik mot teorin om Nordisk Balans." *Militærhistorisk Tidskrift* (Svensk 1987): 131-184.

Davidson, Nicol. "Interegional Co-ordination within the United Nations: Role of the Commonwealth," in Berkhanykum Andemicael, ed., *Regionalism and the United Nations.* New York: Oceana Publications, 1979, pp. 95-144.

Derry, T. K. *A History of Modern Norway, 1814-1972.* Oxford, England: Clarendon Press, 1973.

————. *A History of Scandinavia: Norway, Sweden, Denmark, Finland, and Iceland.* Minneapolis: University of Minnesota Press, 1979.

Deutsch, Karl W., Sidney A. Burrell, Robert A. Kann, Maurice Lee, Jr., Martin Lindgren, Francis L. Loewenheim, and Richard W. Van Wagenen. *Political Community and the North Atlantic Area: International Organization in the Light of Historical Experience.* Publication of the Center for Research on World Political Institutions at Princeton University. Princeton, NJ: Princeton University Press, 1957.

Devlin, Dale. "Soviet-Norwegian Relations. Norwegian Reactions to Soviet Pressures." M.A. thesis, Naval Postgraduate School, 1979.

Dickerman, C. Robert. "Transgovernmental Challenge and Response in Scandinavia and North America." *International Organization* 30 (Spring 1976): 213-240.

Diehl, Paul F., ed. *The Politics of International Organizations: Patterns and Insights.* Chicago: Dorsey Press, 1989.

Diplomatic History 14 (Fall 1990).

Dougherty, James E., and Robert L. Pfaltzgraff, Jr., eds. *Contending Theories of International Relations: A Comprehensive Survey,* 2nd Edition. New York: Harper & Row Publishers, 1981.

East, Maurice A. "Coordinating Foreign Policy: The Changing Role of the Norwegian Foreign Ministry." *Cooperation and Conflict* 19 (1984): 121-134.

―――. "Size and Foreign Policy Behavior: A Test of Two Models." *World Politics* 25 (1973): 550-566.

Egeland, Jan. *Impotent Superpower—Potent Small State: Potentials and Limitations of Human Rights Objectives in the Foreign Policies of the United States and Norway.* Oslo: Universitetsforlaget, 1988.

Einhorn, Eric S., and John Logue. *Modern Welfare States: Politics and Policies in Social Democratic Scandinavia.* New York: Praeger, 1989.

Eriksen, Knut E. "Norge i det vestige samarbeid," in Trond Bergh, and Helge Ø. Pharo, eds., *Vekst og Velstand: Norsk Politisk Historie 1945-1965.* Oslo: Universitetsforlaget, 1989, pp 167-282.

―――. "Svalbardspørsmålet fra krig til kald krig," in Trond Bergh and Helge Ø. Pharo, eds., *Historiker og Veileder: Fetskrift til Jakob Sverdrup.* Oslo: Tiden Norsk Forlag, 1989, pp. 112-161.

Eriksen, Knut E., and Helge Ø. Pharo. *Norsk Sikkerhetspolitikk som Etterkrigshistorisk Forskningsfelt,* LOS-senter notat 92/13. Bergen, Norway: LOS-senter, 1992.

―――. "Norsk Utenrikspolitikk 1949-61." Mimeograph, University of Oslo, 1990.

Etzold, Thomas H., and John L. Gaddis, eds. *Containment: Documents on American Policy and Strategy, 1945-1950.* New York: Columbia University Press, 1978.

European Free Trade Association. *Building EFTA: A Free Trade Area in Europe.* Geneva, Switzerland: EFTA Secretariat, 1966.

Fitsmaurice, John. *Security and Politics in the Nordic Area.* Brookfield, VT: Gower Publishing, 1987.

Flynn, Gregory, and Hans Rattinger, eds. *The Public and Atlantic Defense.* Totowa, NJ: Rowman & Allanheld, 1985.

Førland, Tor Egil. "Cold Economic Warfare: The Creation and Prime of CoCom, 1948-1954." Ph.D. dissertation, University of Oslo, 1991.

Gaddis, John L. *The Long Peace: Inquiries into the History of the Cold War.* New York: Oxford University Press, 1987.

―――. "New Conceptual Approaches to the Study of American Foreign Relations: Interdisciplinary Perspectives." *Diplomatic History* 14 (Summer 1990): 405-424.

———. *Russia, the Soviet Union, and the United States: An Interpretive History*, 2nd Edition. New York: McGraw-Hill, 1990.

———. *Strategies of Containment: A Critical Appraisal of Postwar American National Security Policy*. New York: Oxford University Press, 1982.

Galtung, Johan. "Small Group Theory and the Theory of International Relations: A Study in Isomorphism," in Morton A. Kaplan, ed., *New Approaches to International Relations*. New York: St. Martin's Press, 1968, pp. 292-295.

Galtung, Johan, and Sverre Lodgaard, eds. *Co-operation in Europe*. Oslo: Universitetsforlaget, 1970.

Garg, Jaynti Prasad. *Regionalism in International Politics*. Delhi, India: P. Jain, 1970.

Garthoff, Raymond L. *Détente and Confrontation: American-Soviet Relations from Nixon to Reagan*. Washington, DC: Brookings Institution, 1985.

German, Robert K. "Norway and the Bear: Soviet Coercive Diplomacy and Norwegian Security Policy." *International Security* 7 (Fall 1982): 55-82.

Gilpin, Robert. *The Political Economy of International Relations*. Princeton, NJ: Princeton University Press, 1987.

Gislason, Gylfi. "In Defense of Small Nations." *Dædalus* 113 (Winter 1984): 199-211.

Gleditsch, Nils P. and Sverre Lodgaard. *Krigsstaten Norge*. Oslo, Norway: Pax Forlag A/S, 1970.

Greenstein, Fred I. "Eisenhower as an Activist President: A New Look at the Evidence." *Political Science Quarterly* 94 (Winter 1979/1980): 575-599.

———. *The Hidden-hand Presidency: Eisenhower as Leader*. New York: Basic Books, 1982.

Groennings, Sven. *Scandinavia in Social Science Literature: An English Language Bibliography*. Bloomington: Indiana University Press, 1970.

Gustavsen, Finn. *Rett På Sak*. Oslo: Pax Forlag, 1979.

Haas, Ernst. "Turbulent Fields and the Theory of Regional Integration." *International Organization* 30 (Spring 1976): 183-210.

Haas, Peter M. "Introduction: Epistemic Communities and International Policy Coordination." *International Organization* 46 (Winter 1992): 1-35

Hagen, Anders. *Norway*. New York: Frederick A. Praeger, Publishers, 1967.

Halicz, Emanuel. *Russian Policy towards the Scandinavian Countries in 1856-1864*. Copenhagen, Denmark: Copenhagen University, 1985.

Hanhimäki, Jussi. "Containment, Coexistence and Neutrality: The Return of the Porkkala Naval Base as an Issue in Soviet-American Relations, 1955-1956." *Scandinavian Journal of History* 18 (1993): 217-228.

Harstad, Torleiv. "Fra Paris til Boris Gleb." Hovedoppfag (Thesis),

University of Oslo, 1989.

Haskel, Barbara G. *The Scandinavian Option: Oportunities and Opportunity Costs in Postwar Scandinavian Foreign Policies.* Oslo: Universtitetsforlaget, 1977.

Haugland, Jens. *Dagbok Frå Kongens Råd.* Oslo: Det Norske Samlaget, 1986.

Heisler, Martin O. "Introduction." *Annals of the American Academy of Political and Social Science* 512 (November 1990): 17.

Heradstveit, Daniel, and G. Matthew Bonham. "Decision-making in the Face of Uncertainty: Attributions of Norwegian and American Officials." *Journal of Peace Research* 23, no. 4 (1986): 339-356.

Hetland, Tom M. *Atomrasling og Avspenning: Sovjet og Norsk Tryggingspolitikk, 1953-1958.* FHFS notat 5. Oslo: Forsvarshistorisk Forskningssenter, 1984.

———. *Då Moskva sa nei til Norden: Sovjets syn på Norden og NATO 1948-1952.* FHFS notat 4. Oslo: Forsvarshistorisk Forskningssenter, 1984.

Hinshaw, Randall. *The European Community and American Trade: A Study in Atlantic Economics and Policy.* New York: Frederick A. Praeger, Publishers, 1964.

Holmsen, Andreas. *Norges Historie: Fra de eldste tider til 1660.* Oslo: Universitetsforlaget, 1964.

Holst, Johan J., ed. *Five Roads to Nordic Security.* Oslo: Universitetsforlaget, 1973.

———. "Nordic Security: Past Mirrors and Future Faces." *Annals of the American Academy of Political and Social Science* 512 (1990): 8-15.

———. "Norsk sikkerhetspolitikk i strategisk perspektive." *Internasjonal Politikk,* no. 5 (1966): 500-521.

———. *Norway and NATO in the 1980's.* NUPI notat nr. 301B. Oslo: Norsk Utenrikspolitisk Institutt, May 1984.

———. "Norway's Search for a Nordpolitik." *Foreign Affairs* 60 (Fall 1981): 63-86.

———, ed. *Norwegian Foreign Policy in the 1980s.* Norwegian Foreign Policy Studies No. 51. Oslo: Universitetsforlaget, 1985.

———. *Norwegian Security Policy for the 1980's.* NUPI rapport nr. 76. Oslo: Norsk Utenrikspolitisk Institutt, December 1982.

———. "The Pattern of Nordic Security." *Dædalus* 113 (1984): 195-226.

Holst, Johan J., and Daniel Heradstveit, eds. *Norsk Utenrikspolitikk.* Oslo: TANO, 1985.

Holsti, Ole R. "Models of International Relations and Foreign Policy." *Diplomatic History* 13 (Fall 1989): 15-43.

Huitfeldt, Tønne. *NATO's Northern Security.* Conflict Studies No. 191. London: Institute for the Study of Conflict, 1987.

Hunt, Michael H. "Internationalizing U.S. Diplomatic History: A Practical Agenda." *Diplomatic History* 15 (Winter 1991): 1-12.

Immerman, Richard H. "Confessions of an Eisenhower Revisionist: An Agonizing Reappraisal." *Diplomatic History* 14 (Summer 1990):

319-342.

———, ed. *John Foster Dulles and the Diplomacy of the Cold War.* Princeton, NJ: Princeton University Press, 1990.

Jensen, Magnus. *Norges Historie: Fra 1905 til våre dager.* Oslo: Universitetsforlaget, 1965.

Jervis, Robert. "Systems Theories and Diplomatic History," in Paul G. Lauren, ed., *Diplomacy: New Approaches in History, Theory, and Policy.* New York: Free Press, 1979, pp. 212-244.

Job, Brian, ed. *The Insecurity Dilemma: National Security of Third World States.* Boulder, CO: Lynne Rienner Publishers, 1992.

Joenniemi, Pertti. *Nordic Security.* Current Research on Peace and Violence, No. 1-2/1986. Tampere, Finland: Tampere Peace Research Institute, 1986.

Johansen, Jahn O. *Sovjetunionen og Norden: Konfrontasjon eller naboskap?* Oslo: J.W. Cappelens Forlag A/S, 1986.

Jørgensen-Dahl, Arnfinn. *Regional Organization and Order in South-East Asia.* London: Macmillan Press, 1982.

Kaiser, Karl. "The Interaction of Regional Subsystems: Some Preliminary Notes on Recurrent Patterns and the Role of Superpowers." *World Politics* 21 (October 1968): 84-107.

Kaplan, Lawrence S., and Robert W. Colawson, eds. *NATO after Thirty Years.* Wilmington, DE: Scholarly Resources, 1981.

Kaplan, Morton A., ed. *New Approaches to International Relations.* New York: St. Martin's Press, 1968.

Katzenstein, Peter J. *Small States in World Markets: Industrial Policy in Europe.* Ithaca, NY: Cornell University Press, 1985.

Kaufman, Burton I. *Trade and Aid: Eisenhower's Foreign Economic Policy, 1953-1961.* Baltimore: Johns Hopkins University Press, 1982.

Kegley, Charles W., and Eugene R. Wittkopf. *World Politics: Trend and Transformation.* New York: St. Martin's Press, 1993.

Kelman, Steven. *Regulating America, Regulating Sweden.* Cambridge, MA: MIT Press, 1981.

Kempton, Murray. "The Underestimation of Dwight D. Eisenhower." *Esquire* 68 (September 1967): 108-156.

Kennan, George F. *American Diplomacy, 1900-1950.* New York: Mentor Books, 1951.

———. *The Cloud of Danger: Current Realities of American Foreign Policy.* New York: Little, Brown, 1977.

———. *The Nuclear Delusion: Soviet-American Relations in the Atomic Age,* Revised Edition. New York: Pantheon Books, 1983. (Earlier Published 1976).

———. *Realities of American Foreign Policy.* Princeton, NJ: Princeton University Press, 1954.

———. (Mr. X). "The Sources of Soviet Conduct." *Foreign Affairs* 25 (July 1947): 566-582.

Kennedy, Paul. *Preparing for the Twenty-first Century.* New York: Random House, 1993.

Keohane, Robert O., and Joseph S. Nye. *Power and Interdependence: World Politics in Transition.* Boston: Little, Brown, 1977.

Király, Béla K., ed. *War and Society in East Central Europe: The Crucial Decade: East Central European Society and National Defense, 1859-1870,* Vol. 14. New York: Columbia University Press, 1984.

Kirby, D. G. *Finland in the Twentieth Century.* Minneapolis: University of Minnesota Press, 1979.

Knudsen, Baard B. "The Paramount Importance of Cultural Sources: American Foreign Policy and Comparative Foreign Policy Research Considered." *Cooperation and Conflict* 22 (1987): 81-113.

Knudsen, Olav F., and Arild Underdal. "Patterns of Norwegian Foreign Policy Behavior: An Exploratory Analysis." *Cooperation and Conflict* 20 (1985): 229-251.

Konrad Nordahl Dagbøker, Bind 1, 1950-55. Oslo: Tiden Norsk Forlag, 1991.

Konrad Nordahl Dagbøker, Bind 2, 1956-75. Oslo: Tiden Norsk Forlag, 1992.

Kuhn, Thomas S. *The Structure of Scientific Revolutions,* 2nd Edition. Chicago: The University of Chicago Press, 1970.

Laquer, Walter. "A Postscript on Finlandization." *Commentary* 95 (June 1993): 53.

Larssen, Olav. *Den Langsomme Revolusjonen.* Oslo: H. Aschehoug (W. Nygaard), 1973.

Leffler, Melvyn. "National Security." *Journal of American History* 77 (June 1990): 143-145.

———. *A Preponderance of Power: National Security, the Truman Administration, and the Cold War.* Stanford, CA: Stanford University Press, 1992.

Leifer, Michael. *ASEAN and the Security of South-East Asia.* New York: Routledge, 1989.

Lie, Haakon. *Slik Jeg Ser Det.* Oslo: Tiden Norsk Forlag, 1975.

Lindberg, Steve. "The Illusory Nordic Balance: Threat Scenarios in Nordic Security Planning." *Cooperation and Conflict* 26 (1981): 57-70.

Lindblom, Charles E. *The Policy-making Process,* 2nd Edition. Englewood Cliffs, NJ: Prentice-Hall, 1980.

Lindgren, Raymond E. *Norway-Sweden: Union, Disunion, and Scandinavian Integration.* Princeton, NJ: Princeton University Press, 1959.

Lodgaard, Sverre, and Gleditsch, Nils P. "Norway—The Not So Reluctant Ally." *Cooperation and Conflict,* no. 4 (1977): 400-411.

Lukacs, John. "Finland Vindicated." *Foreign Affairs* 71 (Summer 1992): 50-63.

Lund, John R. "Don't Rock the Boat: Reinforcing Norway in Crisis and War." Ph.D. dissertation, Rand Graduate School, 1987.

Lundestad, Geir. *The American "Empire."* Oslo: Norwegian University Press, 1990.

———. *America, Scandinavia, and the Cold War, 1945-1949.* New York:

Columbia University Press, 1980.

——. "Empire by Invitation? The United States and Western Europe, 1945-1952." *Journal of Peace Research* 23, no. 3 (1986): 263-277.

——. "The Evolution of Norwegian Security Policy: Alliance with the West and Reassurance in the East." *Scandinavian Journal of History* 17, no. 3 (1992): 227-256.

——. "Makt og avmakt, retorikk og realitet i amerikansk utenrikspolitikk fra 1945 til i dag." *Internasjonal Politikk*, no. 4 (1987): 9-26.

——. "Nasjonalisme og internasjonalisme i norsk utenrikspolitikk: Et faglig-provoserende essay." *Internasjonal Politikk*, no. 1 (1985): 39-54.

——. "USA, skandinavisk forsvarsforbund og Halvard Lange: En revurdering." *Internasjonal Politikk*, no. 1 (January-March 1977): 139-173.

Lyng, John. *Vaktskifte: Erindringer, 1953-1965.* Oslo: J. W. Cappelens Forlag, 1973.

Manchester Guardian, "Norway Looks Westward: Nation Solidly behind Policy of Close Collaboration," 23 July 1951.

Matláry, Janne Haaland. "Beyond Intergovernmentalism: The Quest for a Comprehensive Framework for the Study of Integration." *Cooperation and Conflict* 28, no. 2 (1993): 181-208.

McFate, Patricia Bliss. "To See Everything in Another Light." *Dædalus* 113 (Winter 1984): 29-60.

McWhinnie, A. J. "Sweden's Fear is Spies." *London Daily Herald,* 11 September 1952.

Mead, W. R. "Norden: Destiny and Fortune." *Dædalus* 113 (Winter 1984): 1-28.

Melkote, Rama S., ed. *Regional Organisations: A Third World Perspective.* New Delhi, India: Sterling Publishers, 1990.

Milner, Helen. "International Theories of Cooperation Among Nations: Strengths and Weaknesses." *World Politics* 44 (April 1992): 466-96.

Moon, Victor B. "Soviet-Norwegian Relations since 1945." *Western Political Quarterly* 17 (December 1964): 659-677.

Neumann, Iver B. "Russlands regionale rolle i Nord-Europa." *Internasjonal Politikk* 50 (1992): 123-136.

Nordstrom, Byron J. *Dictionary of Scandinavian History.* Westport, CT: Greenwood Press, 1986.

Noreen, Erik. "The Nordic Balance: A Security Policy Concept in Theory and Practice." *Cooperation and Conflict* 28 (1983): 43-56.

Nye, Joseph S., Jr., ed. *International Regionalism.* Boston: Little, Brown, 1968.

——. *Peace in Parts: Integration and Conflict in Regional Organization.* Boston: Little, Brown, 1971.

Parsons, Talcott. "Social Systems," in *International Encyclopedia of Social Sciences,* Volume 15. New York: Macmillan, 1968, pp. 458-472.

Paterson, Thomas G., ed. *Major Problems in American Foreign Policy,*

Volume 2: *Since 1914*, 2nd Edition. Lexington, MA: D.C. Heath, 1984.

Paterson, Thomas G., J. Garry Clifford, and Kenneth J. Hagan. *American Foreign Policy: A History since 1900*, 3rd Edition. Lexington, MA: D. C. Heath, 1988.

Pharo, Helge Ø. "Bridgebuilding and Reconstruction: Norway Faces the Marshall Plan." *Scandinavian Journal of History* 1 (1976): 125-153.

——. "The Cold War in Norwegian and International Historical Research." *Scandinavian Journal of History* 10 (1985): 163-189.

——. "Gjenreisning og utenrikspolitikk," in Trond Bergh, and Helge Ø. Pharo, eds., *Historiker og Veileder: Festskrift til Jakob Sverdrup*. Oslo: Tiden Norsk Forlag, 1989, pp. 164-201.

——. "Marshallplanen set fra amerikansk side. Norge i komparativt perspektiv." *Historisk Tidsskrift*, no. 2 (1989): 184-209.

——. "Norge, EF og europeisk samarbeid." *Internasjonal Politikk*, no. 6 (1988): 41-67.

——. "Norge og Europeisk Integrasjon som Etterkrigshistorisk Forskningsfelt." Mimeograph, University of Oslo, 1990.

——. "Norwegian Social Democrats and European Integration in the 1950s." Mimeograph, Colloquium paper, 15-16 November 1988.

——. "Scandinavia and the Cold War: An Overview." Mimeographed manuscript, University of Oslo, 1991.

——. "The Third Force, Atlanticism, and Norwegian Attitudes." EUI Working Paper, No. 86/255. Florence, Italy: European University Institute, 1986.

Rana, A. P. "Integrative Possibilities of Regional World Order in the Third World: The Theoretical Landscape," in Rama S. Melkote, ed., *Regional Organisations: A Third World Perspective*. New Delhi, India: Sterling Publishers, 1990, pp. 6-27.

Rapoport, Anatol. "General Systems Theory," in *International Encyclopedia of Social Sciences*, Volume 15. New York: Macmillan, 1968, pp. 452-458.

Ries, Tomas. "Amerikanska säkerhetspolitiska intressen i Norden." *Internasjonal Politikk*, no. 4 (1987): 89-110.

Riggs, Robert E., and I. Jostein Mykletun. *Beyond Functionalism: Attitudes toward International Organization in Norway and the United States*. Minneapolis: University of Minnesota Press, 1985.

Riste, Olav. *Isolasjonisme og Stormaktsgarantier: Norsk Tryggingspolitkk 1905-1990*, Volume 3. Oslo: Institutt for Forsvarsstudier, 1991.

——, ed. *Western Security: The Formative Years*. Oslo: Universitetsforlaget, 1985.

Rock, Stephen R. *Why Peace Breaks Out: Great Power Rapprochement in Historical Perspective*. Chapel Hill: University of North Carolina Press, 1989.

Rokkan, Stein, and Angus Campbell. "Norway and the United States of America." *International Social Science Journal* 12 (1960): 69-99.

Rolls, Mark G. "ASEAN: Where from and Where to?" *Contemporary Southeast Asia* 13 (December 1991): 324-325.

Rosenau, James N. "Global Changes and Theoretical Challenges: Toward a Postinternational Politics for the 1990s," in Ernst-Otto Czempiel and James N. Rosenau, eds. *Global Changes and Theoretical Challenges: Approaches to World Politics for the 1990s.* Lexington, MA: D.C. Heath, 1989, pp. 1-20.

Rubinstein, Alvin Z. *Soviet Foreign Policy since World War II: Imperial and Global,* 2nd Edition. Boston: Little, Brown, 1985.

Russett, Bruce M. *International Regions and the International System: A Study in Political Ecology.* Westport, CT: Greenwood Press, 1975.

Ryan, Stephen. *Ethnic Conflict and International Relations.* Brookfield, VT: Dartmouth Publishing, 1990.

Sather, Leland B. *Norway.* World Bibliographic Series, Volume 67. Denver, CO: Clio Press, 1986.

Schiller, Bernt. "At Gunpoint: A Critical Perspective on the Attempts of the Nordic Governments to Achieve Unity after the Second World War." *Scandinavian Journal of History* 9 (1984): 221-238.

Schlesinger, Arthur M., Jr. *The Cycles of American History.* Boston: Houghton Mifflin, 1986.

———. "The Eisenhower Presidency: A Reassessment." *Look,* 14 May 1979, pp. 40-48.

———. "The Ike Age Revisited." *Reviews in American History* 11 (March 1983): 1-11.

Scott, Andrew M. *The Functioning of the International Political System.* New York: Macmillan, 1967.

Solem, Erik. *The Nordic Council and Scandinavian Integration.* New York: Praeger, 1977.

Sternsher, Bernard. "Two Views of Eisenhower: Robert A. Divine and Piers Brendon." *Psychohistory Review* 17 (Winter 1989): 215-235.

Stråth, Bo. "The Illusory Nordic Alternative to Europe." *Cooperation and Conflict* 15 (1980): 103-114.

Sundelius, Bengt, ed. *Foreign Policies of Northern Europe.* Boulder, CO: Westview Press, 1982.

Tamnes, Rolf. "Handlefrihet og lojalitet. Norge og atompolitikken i 1950-årene," in Trond Bergh and Helge Ø. Pharo, eds., *Historiker og Veileder: Festskrift til Jakob Sverdrup.* Oslo: Tiden Norsk Forlag, 1989, pp. 203-236.

———. "Norway's Struggle for the Northern Flank, 1950-1952," in Olav Riste, ed., *Western Security: The Formative Years.* Oslo: Universitetsforlaget, 1985, pp. 215-243.

———. *The United States and the Cold War in the High North.* Brookfield, VT: Dartmouth Publishing, 1991.

Taylor, Phillip. *Nonstate Actors in International Politics: From Transregional to Substate Organizations.* Boulder, CO: Westview Press, 1984.

Taylor, William J., Jr., and Paul M. Cole, eds. *Nordic Defense:*

Comparative Decision Making. Lexington, MA: D.C. Heath, 1985.

Thomas, Tony. "The Nordic Alternative: A Survey of Finland, Norway, and Sweden." *Economist*, 21 November 1987, pp. 1-22.

Thornton, Thomas P. "Regional Organizations in Conflict Management." *Annals of the American Academy of Political and Social Science* 518 (November 1991): 135-136.

Tønnesson, Stein. "History and National Identity in Scandinavia: The Contemporary Debate." Mimeographed manuscript, University of Oslo, 1991.

Udgaard, Nils Morten. *Great Power Politics and Norwegian Foreign Policy: A Study of Norway's Foreign Relations, November 1940-February 1948*. Oslo: Universitetsforlaget, 1973.

Ulam, Adam B. *Dangerous Relations: The Soviet Union in World Politics, 1970-1982*. New York: Oxford University Press, 1983.

Valen, Henry. "Cleavages in the Norwegian Electorate as a Constraint on Foreign Policy-making," in Johan J. Holst, ed., *Norwegian Foreign Policy in the 1980s*. Oslo: Universitetsforlaget, 1985, pp. 26-53.

Villaume, Poul. "Danmarks Stilling i den Atlantiske Alliances Politiske og Militære Strategi 1949-54." M.A. thesis, University of Oslo, 1986.

Vraalsen, Tom E. "The United States and Europe, Norway's Delicate Balance." *Scandinavian Review* 74 (Summer 1986): 39-44.

Wæver, Ole. "The Language of Foreign Policy." *Journal of Peace Research* 27, no. 3 (1990): 335-343.

Wahlbåck, Kristen. *Den svenska neutralitetens røtter*, Series No. 3. Stockholm, Sweden: UD informerar, 1984.

———. *Sverige, Norden och stormakterna*, Series No. 4. Stockholm, Sweden: Kungele Krigsvetenskapsakademiens Handlingar och Tidskrift, 1978.

Wendt, Frantz. "Sikkerheds og forsvarspolitiske spørgsmål i Nordisk råd," in Sven Henningsen, ed., *Nær og Fjern: Samspillet mellom Indre og Ydre Politik*. Copenhagen, Denmark: Forlaget Politiske Studier, 1980, pp. 115-153.

Young, Oran R. "Political Discontinuities in the International System." *World Politics* 20 (July 1968): 369-392.

MANUSCRIPT COLLECTIONS AND ORAL HISTORIES

Dillon, C. Douglas. Oral interview. Dwight D. Eisenhower Library, Abilene, KS.

Dulles, John Foster. Papers. Dwight D. Eisenhower Library, Abilene, KS.

Eisenhower, Dwight D. Papers. Dwight D. Eisenhower Library, Abilene, KS.

Hickerson, John D. Oral interview. Seeley G. Mudd Manuscript Library, Princeton University.

Morse, David. Papers. Seeley G. Mudd Manuscript Library, Princeton University.

Norstad, Lauris. Oral interview. Dwight D. Eisenhower Library, Abilene, KS.

Norstad, Lauris. Papers. Dwight D. Eisenhower Library, Abilene, KS.

Ording, Arne. Diary. Manuscript Collection, University of Oslo Library.

Stevenson, Adlai E. Papers. Seeley G. Mudd Manuscript Library, Princeton University.

UNPUBLISHED GOVERNMENT DOCUMENTS

Aho, Esko. Speech, 4 May 1992. "Finlands säkerhet och närområdena: En granskning av förändringarna." Transcript provided by Finnish Embassy in Oslo, Norway.

De Forente Stater Politikk, bind 13, 17, 39, 42, 43, 1 December 1947 to 10 August 1959. Royal Norwegian Foreign Ministry, Oslo.

Eisenhower, Dwight D. Records as President, White House Central Files. Dwight D. Eisenhower Library, Abilene, KS.

Foreign Service Posts of the Department of State, Record Group 84, Washington National Records Center, Suitland, MD.

Forsvarsdepartement H-Arkiv, 1946-52, Norwegian National Archives, Oslo.

National Archives of the United States of America, Washington, DC. Record Group 59, General Records of the Department of State, Decimal Files; and Records of the Policy Planning Staff.

Norges politiske forhold til U.S.A., bind 2, 1 January 1950 to 31 December 1959. Royal Norwegian Foreign Ministry, Oslo.

Statsministerens kontor, protokoll for hemmelige saker, regjeringskonferanser, 5 November 1946 to 5 October 1948. Norwegian National Archives, Oslo.

Statsministerens kontor, referat fra regjeringskonferanser, 1947-61, Norwegian National Archives, Oslo.

White House Office, NSC Staff Papers, 1948-61. Dwight D. Eisenhower Library, Abilene, KS.

White House Office, Office of the Special Assistant for National Security Affairs, NSC Series, Policy Paper Subseries, Briefing Notes Subseries. Dwight D. Eisenhower Library, Abilene, KS.

White House Office, Office of the Staff Secretary: Records of Paul T. Carroll, Andrew J. Goodpaster, L. Arthur Minnich, and Christopher H. Russell, 1952-61, International Series. Dwight D. Eisenhower Library, Abilene, KS.

Whitman File, Administration Series, Dulles-Herter Series, International Series, NSC Series, Speech Series. Dwight D. Eisenhower Library, Abilene, KS.

PUBLISHED GOVERNMENT DOCUMENTS

Congressional Record, 1947-61.

Det Norske Arbeiderparti Beretning 1948-1960. Oslo: Aktietrykkeriet, 1949-1961, Norwegian Labor Party Archives, Oslo.

Det Norske Arbeiderparti Landsmøtet 1949-1959 Protokoll. Oslo: Aktietrykkeriet, Norwegian Labor Party Archives, 1950-60.

Etzold, Thomas H., and John L. Gaddis, eds. *Containment: Documents on American Policy and Strategy, 1945-1950*. New York: Columbia University Press, 1978.

Foreign Relations of the United States (FRUS), 1948-1957. Washington, DC: Government Printing Office, 1975-86.

World Bank. *The Long-term Perspective Study of Sub-Saharan Africa*, Background Papers, Volumes 1-4. Washington, DC: World Bank, 1990.

CONVERSATIONS, INTERVIEWS, ADDRESSES, AND LETTERS

Berdal, Mats. Oxford University.

Bergh, Trond. Norwegian Labor Party Archives and Library, Oslo.

Cole, Wayne S. University of Maryland.

Fagertun, Fredrik. University of Tromso, Norway.

Gleditsch, Nils Petter. Peace Research Institute, Oslo.

Lundestad, Geir. Norwegian Nobel Institute, Oslo.

Patterson, Orlando. Address on 8 October 1993 at Pacific Lutheran University, Tacoma, WA.

Pharo, Helge Ø. University of Oslo.

Riste, Olav. Institute for Defense Studies, Oslo.

Tamnes, Rolf. Institute for Defense Studies, Oslo.

Index

About the Author

BRUCE OLAV SOLHEIM is Instructor of History at Green River Community College in Auburn, Washington.